THE
PITTSBURGH
COCAINE SEVEN

THE PITTSBURGH COCAINE SEVEN

How a Ragtag Group of Fans

Took the Fall

for Major League Baseball

AARON SKIRBOLL

CHICAGO
REVIEW
PRESS

The Library of Congress has cataloged the hardcover edition as follows:
Skirboll, Aaron.
    The Pittsburgh cocaine seven : how a ragtag group of fans took the fall
for major league baseball / Aaron Skirboll. — 1st ed.
        p. cm.
    Includes bibliographical references and index.
    ISBN 978-1-56976-288-2 (hardcover)
        1. Baseball—Corrupt practices—United States. 2. Baseball—
Pennsylvania—Pittsburgh. 3. Pittsburgh Pirates (Baseball team).
4. Baseball players—Drug use—United States. 5. Doping in sports—
United States. I. Title.
    GV863.A1S436 2010
    796.357′640974886—dc22

                                                        2010004179

Interior design: Monica Baziuk

Copyright © 2010 by Aaron Skirboll
All rights reserved
First edition
Published by Chicago Review Press, Incorporated
814 North Franklin Street
Chicago, Illinois 60610
ISBN 978-1-61373-675-3
Printed in the United States of America

For my wife, Jamie.

BASEBALL HAS FALLEN. . . .
BARKED CHINS AND BROKEN FINGERS
MAY BE EASILY MENDED,
BUT A DISFIGURED REPUTATION
MAY NEVER BE ENTIRELY REPAIRED.

—HENRY CHADWICK
(1824—1908),
SPORTSWRITER AND HISTORIAN

Contents

PART IV **AFTERMATH**

Tough Talk

T HE WORDS rang clear. "Somebody has to say 'enough is enough' against drugs. Baseball's going to accomplish this," the commissioner claimed. "We're going to remove drugs and be an example."

It sounded like the head of baseball was finally getting tough about drug use in his sport. But this declaration came not from the ninth and current commissioner Bud Selig, talking about the sensational steroid scandals that have rocked the last decade, but rather from baseball's sixth commissioner, Peter Ueberroth, during a commencement address at Loyola Marymount University in Los Angeles. The year was 1985, and Ueberroth was talking about cocaine.

A federal investigation into possible drug trafficking involving major league ballplayers was coming to a close in Pittsburgh, and Ueberroth was steadying himself for the storm to come. Nobody knew exactly what would be revealed as a result of the investigation, but it was speculated to be big. Some of baseball's brightest stars had been seen in recent months coming to and going from Pittsburgh, only this time they weren't in uniform, and they weren't headed to the stadium. Instead, they were wearing thousand-dollar suits and speaking in front of a grand jury at the U.S. District Courthouse on Grant Street. Indictments were expected back any day.

Commissioner Ueberroth went even further, declaring that random drug urinalysis tests would be administered to all baseball personnel. Owners, batboys, secretaries, and all minor league players would be tested. There was only one exception—the major league ballplayers themselves. They would be excluded for now, because mandatory drug testing for them would have to be agreed upon by the players union. Ueberroth was hoping to persuade the players to test voluntarily.

The interim Major League Baseball Players Association executive director at the time, Donald Fehr, dismissed Ueberroth's act as nothing more than grandstanding. And with everyone awaiting word from Pittsburgh, Fehr's position certainly had merit. The commissioner surely couldn't feign ignorance; he had to get in front of the potential scandal, which he attempted to do with his purposeful statement.

Finally, on May 30 and 31, 1985, the investigation's targets were revealed when seven indictments came back from the grand jury. Major League Baseball officials could breathe a sigh of relief. The authorities were going after not the players but the dealers, a ragtag group of seven local men. The Pittsburgh cocaine seven consisted of a pair of heating repairmen, an accountant, a bartender, a caterer, a land surveyor, and an out-of-work photographer. Collectively they could be seen as nothing more than an assortment of sports groupies.

In September 1985, under the spotlight of the national media, the first of a series of trials that became known as the Pittsburgh drug trials began. In the history of baseball scandals, these trials represent the bridge between the 1919 Black Sox scandal and the steroid era that came to national attention in the 1990s. At the center of the proceedings was *United States v. Curtis Strong*, the biggest drug trial in major league baseball history.

Whispers about cocaine use within the league went back almost five years. However, as happened in Kansas City in 1983, when four players were arrested on cocaine-related charges, guilty pleas or plea bargains always served to shield the athletes' involvement from the public eye. The Pittsburgh drug trials blew a hole through such secrecy. Covered by a blanket of immunity, seven active and former major league players came before the court to admit their transgressions through testimony more detailed and sordid than anyone could have imagined.

The Pittsburgh Pirates were inextricably involved in the scandal. The sensational trials were the culmination of a story that began in 1979, the year the Pirates sat on top of the baseball world and lifted the whole city along with them. Pittsburgh was known as the city of champions. Six years later, the Pirates had become the laughingstock of the league and nearly left town after being sold to new ownership. The team's home, Three Rivers Stadium, became known as the National League drugstore. And once again, the city was taken along for the ride.

The Pirates' story can be seen as a microcosm of what was occurring on a much broader scale throughout the league. Contrary to Commissioner Ueberroth's grand statements, Major League Baseball did not set an example for eliminating drug use in sports. The players' testimonies of widespread cocaine and amphetamine use before, during, and after games should have been the catalyst to usher in major policy changes. The trials offered a brief moment when the issue was out in the open. Drug testing was talked about relentlessly, and coming out of the events in Pittsburgh most baseball observers considered it a foregone conclusion that a testing program would be implemented. Cocaine should have saved the league from steroids. Instead, league officials dropped the ball, sweeping the problem under the rug and leaving the door ajar for future scandals.

Nearly twenty years passed before the league addressed the issue of drugs in baseball, when a new era of steroid use created robotic home run machines disguised as flesh and blood. Along the way some of the game's most cherished records were broken. As a result, skewed and meaningless statistics have shaken a sport in which numbers are the backbone of the game.

In 2006 Bud Selig, pushed by the controversy surrounding Mark Fainaru-Wada and Lance Williams's groundbreaking book *Game of Shadows: Barry Bonds, BALCO, and the Steroids Scandal that Rocked Professional Sports*, as well as government interest, enlisted former U.S. senator George J. Mitchell to investigate the use of illegal, performance-enhancing drugs (PEDs) within the major leagues. A year later, presented with the results of the four-hundred-plus-page report, Selig stood up and, like Ueberroth, talked tough: "Our fans deserve a game that is played on a level playing field—where all who compete do so fairly," he said. "So long as there may be potential cheaters, we will always have to monitor our programs and constantly update them to catch those who think they can get away with breaking baseball's rules. In the name of integrity, that's exactly what I intend to do.... Major League Baseball remains committed to this cause and to the effort to eliminate the use of performance-enhancing substances from the game."

But another commissioner of baseball had already stood tall, nearly two decades earlier. Peter Ueberroth took his stand on the soapbox just prior to leaving his post for good in 1988. The commissioner spoke of baseball's drug policy, calling it "the best program of any sport, amateur or professional, anywhere in the world." "I wouldn't change it a bit," he said. "I never said the situation would be perfect.... I have said the era of scandals in baseball is over." Obviously, he was wrong.

The steroid era makes fans yearn for the golden age of baseball. Traditionally defined as the years between the 1920s and the 1960s, the "golden age" was revised in the seventh edition of *Total Baseball: The Official Encyclopedia of Major League Baseball* by John Thorn, who writes that "a golden age may be defined flexibly, it seems, so as to coincide with the period of one's youth." This means that "golden age" could conceivably describe every era of baseball. This description defies logic yet seems to hold true. The Pittsburgh Pirates were my hometown team when I was growing up in the 1980s. I came along too late to enjoy the Family, as the 1979 team that took the pennant was known, although right fielder Dave Parker's legendary arm and throws were common topics of discussion on the sandlot, and team captain Willie Stargell's whirling windmill batting stance was mimicked in batters' boxes all over town. I watched many years of baseball after these greats were gone from the Pirates that could be described as anything but golden; yet this was, and still is, my team.

And just like today, drugs were at the center of the game.

PART I

1979—CITY OF CHAMPIONS

1

The Parrot

WHEN I PUT ON MY UNIFORM, I FEEL LIKE I AM THE
PROUDEST MAN ON EARTH.
  —ROBERTO CLEMENTE

IT WAS just an innocent tryout. Certainly no lives would be altered. Granted, the tryout was for a major league baseball team, but it was not for an actual jersey and a number but rather for the position of mascot. The guys would give it a shot, have a couple of laughs, and leave it at that. At least that's what they thought.

It was a miserable cold and rainy February afternoon. At a bare minimum, they figured, they would be afforded a behind-the-scenes look at Three Rivers Stadium, and to these die-hard Pittsburgh guys, this was no small thing. Three Rivers was where their heroes came to ply their trade. The Pittsburgh Pirates were four-time world champions, with the last one secured in 1971. They had won the National League East in 1972, 1974, and 1975, and were firmly established as one of the class teams in major league baseball. Mazeroski, Clemente, Stargell: these weren't just names to these young men, these were legends of the sport and revered figures in the history of their hometown team. That's all these guys were thinking about when they showed up at the stadium.

Twenty-seven-year-old Dale Shiffman and twenty-five-year-old Kevin Koch (pronounced *coke*) were best friends. Both grew up and went to high school in Baldwin, Pennsylvania, a working-class suburb about ten miles south of Pittsburgh. After graduation they entered the military, where they served in the army. Shiffman served a tour in Vietnam, but the war ended just after Koch finished boot camp. In 1979 both were still bouncing around the South Hills suburbs and spending a good deal of time together as teammates on a local softball team named the High Rollers. They played in a highly competitive citywide league. It wasn't what they had envisioned while growing up. Koch, with his cannon of a right arm, had been scouted by both the Reds and the Pirates while he was in high school. The Pirates put him in uniform once in 1975 and had him pitch batting practice to the team in order to take a better look at him. However, three years in the military made it tough for him to reach his goal of playing in the majors.

By 1979 it was clear the softball league was as far as Koch's talents could take him. He and his pal Shiffman played as much as they could, often three or four times a week, practically year round, with Shiffman sometimes playing on as many as five teams in a given summer. They even took road trips from time to time, with teammates piling into one another's cars and heading to out-of-town tournaments. Shiffman was the pitcher, while Koch roamed the outfield.

The advertisements that played on the radio that winter for the Pittsburgh Pirates mascot auditions were vague. The candidate had to be at least five feet eight inches tall; other than that, however, no official requirements were given. As new Pirates director of promotions Steve Schanwald less than succinctly put it, "It has to be someone who... well, the way I'd put it, who's slightly insane. That's the guy we're looking for—the guy or gal."

Kevin Koch never heard the ads, but one of his friends, Yamie Liebro, did, and he had instantly thought of Koch. Liebro felt his funny, baseball-loving pal would be perfect for the position, so much so that he called the Pirates front office and announced, "I've got your guy." He then phoned Koch to fill him in on the good news: Liebro had signed Koch up for the upcoming Pirate Parrot auditions. Koch's initial reaction: "C'mon?"

Koch had recently finished welding school at Dean Tech on Liberty Avenue and was set to begin his first job in the coming weeks. Nonetheless, on Friday, February 23, the day of the tryout, Koch thought, "Why not?" If only as a practical joke, he would do it. Shiffman and Liebro would be tagging along to the audition, and the three friends had a long history of turning anything they did into a good time, Koch reasoned. Plus, it was being held at the stadium.

Sports were all people were talking about in Pittsburgh at the time. The city and its teams were quickly climbing to the top of the sports world. The Steelers had just secured their third Super Bowl title in five years, and the Pirates, coming off consecutive second-place finishes, felt they were well poised to join the Steelers on top. Dominance in sports was something the city had never known before, and to its credit Pittsburgh wore this championship glow well. The steelworkers and other blue-collar employees around the region relished it. Up and down the muddy rivers leading into the Steel City, small coal towns were decked out in black and gold.

Koch held no illusions of actually winning the audition. When the trio arrived at the stadium, they were greeted by what one local paper described as "several dozen unemployed actors, frustrated entertainers, singers-in-the-shower, publicity seekers, and almost certifiably crazy baseball fans." Nearly one hundred of them were ushered into the visiting team's clubhouse to show team officials what they would do to fire up a crowd of baseball fans.

Liebro decided that with so many other Parrot hopefuls on hand, Koch needed to do something to set himself apart from the crowd. When the time came for Koch's five-minute audition, Liebro went into a song and dance portraying himself as Koch's agent. Shiffman, a freelance photographer, happened to have his camera on hand and was thrust into the role of parrot-chasing paparazzo, furtively snapping shots of the amused Koch. The judges, a three-person team of Schanwald, his secretary, Ellen Campbell, and Olin DePolo, the Pirates' director of sales and marketing, then asked a few questions of the candidate. Koch, who was a top-notch dancer, then danced along to a short disco song. The judges were impressed. But at the end of the day, Koch may have been more surprised than anyone when he was told he was one of ten finalists and asked to return on March 12. Koch, who had been treating the whole thing as a joke, was beginning to get a little worried.

At the second tryout Koch again wowed the judges, not only with his dancing skills but also with his keen sports knowledge and sense of humor, particularly his impressions of local celebrities. When the second audition was complete, he was told the Pirates would give him a call when they had reached a decision.

A few days passed before the telephone rang. When Koch was informed that he had won the job of first-ever Pirate Parrot, he was far from elated. He knew his hometown well, and while the tryouts had provided laughs and been a good time for him and his buddies, he was also well aware that steel-tough Pittsburghers had a long history of not taking well to frilly mascots and cheerleaders. None of Pittsburgh's professional sports teams employed them at the time. But that was exactly what Koch now was—a mascot. His reward was a pair of bright green tights and an oversized cotton bird's head, not to mention a salary of twenty-five dollars per game.

=====

ONCE KOCH shook off the initial shock, he decided to make the most of his new job. It was no use second-guessing things now. Not that there was time for it anyway. Almost immediately after accepting, Koch received a call from Pirates' owner Dan Galbreath telling him to pack a bag—he was going to spring training. The club wanted him to get his feet wet in an exhibition game before his big debut and the regular season.

Koch would be the first to admit that he had spent his fair share of time picturing himself as a Pirate when he was a youngster and probably even a tad too much as an adult. But as he flew to Bradenton, Florida, on Galbreath's private Learjet, he realized this was something else entirely. What was this kid off the streets of Pittsburgh doing sitting shotgun in the personal jet of the owner of the Pirates? Things got even more surreal for Koch when he arrived at

McKechnie Field and suited up. Before he had a chance to catch his breath, he found himself standing in the outfield, face-to-face with the two biggest Bucs of them all: team captain Willie Stargell and right fielder Dave Parker.

"Man, I'm really nervous," Koch told the pair as he stared into the stands. "This is crazy—I wasn't expecting this."

Parker and Stargell laughed at the excited new Pirate and told him, "Wait until opening day," when the attendance would be close to fifty thousand and ten times the tiny crowd on hand in Bradenton. Koch snapped out of it. He wasn't ready to think about any of that. He was going to enjoy the moment. "I felt like I had died and gone to heaven," he recalled. The scene on McKechnie Field resembled a painting that had come to life. Players were languidly stretching and tossing warm-up balls on plush, verdant grass amid swaying palm trees, floating seagulls, and a cloudless blue sky. And there in the middle of it was Koch, shooting the shit in the outfield with Stargell and Parker. He hardly dared to think it, but had he actually gained entrance into this circle? This was the team he had always loved and cheered for but as an outsider looking in. Now he was a *part* of it.

2

The Pirates

IT IS SUPPOSED TO BE FUN. THE MAN SAYS "PLAY
BALL," NOT "WORK BALL." YOU ONLY HAVE A FEW
YEARS TO PLAY THIS GAME, AND YOU CAN'T PLAY
IT IF YOU'RE ALL TIED UP IN KNOTS.
    —WILLIE STARGELL

A S THE 1979 season got under way, Kevin Koch concentrated on controlling his nerves and working out a routine. He had to walk a fine line, however, ensuring this routine was well-choreographed but did not become stale. The key was to keep things fresh. His antics were entirely up to him; the Pirates management gave him no instructions. The young welder was essentially being asked to put on a nightly improv show.

Koch hit it off right away with a lot of the players. He had his own quarters in which to change and shower, but he spent a lot of time in the clubhouse with the guys, who accepted the new addition to the team. "They looked at me, and if I was going to be there," says Koch, "then I was a part of their deal." Koch saw a close, tight-knit team that was all business on the field but a loose group of practical jokers off it.

The Pirates took a cue from the city in which they played. From the nineteenth century with iron, brass, tin, and glass, through World War II and into the early seventies with steel and coal, Pittsburgh was a city known for its production. Industry thrived, and as a result the city was at one time so enveloped in dirt and black clouds from the mills that the sun was obscured, forcing drivers to turn on their car headlights upon approaching the downtown area each morning. Pittsburgh Steelers patriarch Art Rooney, who lived his entire eighty-seven years in Pittsburgh, once said, "In the old days the lights never went out. We'd leave for school in the morning with clean clothes and get there covered with soot." The people of the city grew up with a hardened exterior and a fierce work ethic. The professional sports teams of the area followed suit. "We're a blue-collar team in a blue-collar town… a dirty-shirt ball club," manager Chuck Tanner said of his Pirates. Steelers quarterback Terry Bradshaw echoed Tanner's sentiments when he called Pittsburgh "a shot and a beer town" and Pittsburghers "good, honest working people" who "lead a tough life" and "like a team with a tough defense, because that's where character shows."

Despite playing in a town once described as "hell with the lid taken off," players from around the country came to Pittsburgh and adopted the city as their own. Willie Stargell, who grew up in the East Bay of Northern California, moved to Pittsburgh permanently in 1969. "I like the warmth of the place," Stargell said. The citizens of Pittsburgh like to think of their city as one big small town where everyone knows and talks with one another. Pirates pitcher Jim Rooker, from Oregon, eventually made the city his permanent home and opened up his own restaurant, Rook's, in the area. Rooker sums up the city's attraction plainly: "It may not be the prettiest city, but it's a city you grow to love because of the people."

Native son Chuck Tanner, from nearby New Castle, was brought in to manage the club in 1977. Tanner came to the team via a rare trade involving a manager. The trade partner was the Oakland A's and their unorthodox owner, Charlie Finley. Anything was possible with Finley. This was, after all, the same man who once named a live mule after himself—Charlie O—and debuted the animal as the team's new mascot. He even took it along to cocktail parties with him. Finley also introduced ball girls to the league, paid his players

$300 apiece to grow mustaches as part of a "Mustache Day" promotion, and unsuccessfully attempted to replace the game's white baseballs with orange ones. Trading a manager was considered a mild move for Charlie Finley. The A's received catcher Manny Sanguillen and $100,000 cash in the exchange.

Tanner was a fatherly and down-to-earth manager. His philosophy toward his craft was simple: get the players to relax and enjoy the game, and the physical talents that allowed the young athletes to reach the majors and the pinnacle of their sport in the first place would shine. In other words, let them play and have just as much fun as they did growing up. As he told the *New Yorker* in 1979, he saw too many of his new recruits "look around and suddenly baseball becomes a job for them." He felt the true work of the manager was "to reach the kid who's sitting over in the corner of the dugout and get him to play with the same attitude he had back in American Legion ball."

Off the field or in the clubhouse, Tanner was known as someone who liked to keep one eye open and one eye closed with respect to his club. He tried to not even mention the word "curfew." Outsiders couldn't understand his hands-off approach. His explanation: "Paul Waner used to wander into the lobby at 1:00 A.M., and Babe Ruth always managed to find a little spot to have some fun, and I think if somebody had slapped a curfew on them, there might be two empty spaces in the Hall of Fame today.... You have to handle people like they are men. You try and be nice."

The team's expectations for the 1979 season were the same as every year; it was looking for a championship. Tanner told the baseball world, "We can win it.... This is the most relaxed team in baseball, not worried about yesterday or tomorrow, just right now."

The Pirates always seemed to be in the hunt. But, as *Sports Illustrated* predicted in its special baseball issue as the season opened, the team would need to overcome "age, injury, and giveaway defense" to get past the Philadelphia Phillies, who were on the verge of their fourth consecutive National League East title. Epitomizing the age factor was eighteen-year veteran Willie Stargell. While it was possible that young slugger Dave Parker could repeat his MVP award–winning 1978 season, expectations were not as high for the thirty-eight-year-old Stargell. Counted out following his injury-prone 1977 campaign, Stargell surprised everyone with a stellar twenty-eight home run, ninety-seven RBI season in 1978 to pick up the National League Comeback Player of the Year award. Still, it was unclear how long the first baseman could continue to carry the team. Such uncertainty assuredly came from outside the Steel City, however; for inside the Pirates clubhouse, if it was Tanner who directed the ship, it was Stargell who was the unquestioned leader of the team.

Stargell was a man of prodigious power, known for his signature windmill twirling of the bat as he awaited the pitch from inside the batter's box, his very own stepless swagger. His towering upper-deck shots in stadiums around the league were the stuff of legend. In 1978 he hit a ball so far into the seats at Montreal's Olympic Stadium the Expos had the seat where it landed painted gold to commemorate the monster 535-foot shot. He was also the first man to hit a ball out of Dodger Stadium, which he did twice (a feat achieved since only by Mike Piazza and Mark McGwire, one time apiece). Dodger pitching great Don Sutton once said of Stargell, "He didn't just hit pitchers, he took away their dignity." Stargell had more home runs from 1970 to 1979 than any other player in the major leagues.

Along with Stargell the 1979 Pirates had right fielder Dave Parker, who was reaching his peak and coming into his own as a player. Parker was a rare talent and no slouch in the power department himself; he once literally knocked the cover off a ball with a strapping base hit to right field that ruptured the seams.

But even with these two sluggers in the middle of the lineup, this wasn't the same "lumber company" of power hitters the city had grown to know in the mid-1970s, when players like Richie Zisk, Al Oliver, and Richie Hebner joined Stargell to hit blast after blast, up and down the lineup, to lead the league in home runs. This new Chuck Tanner–led squad became a more balanced team, with speedy center fielder Omar Moreno providing the spark at the top of a lineup that lived up to its new moniker of Lumber and Lightning, which appeared across the Three Rivers Stadium scoreboard during the home team's rallies. It was a team just as likely to win a game with the hit-and-run and the bunt as with the long ball.

The pitching staff was without a clear-cut ace but had a number of reliable, high-caliber slingers, namely John Candelaria, Bert Blyleven, Bruce Kison, Jim Bibby, and the rubber-armed, submarine-throwing Kent Tekulve. At a time when pitchers looked at the mound as *their* mound and the game as *their* nine innings, nobody embodied this stance better than the right-hander Blyleven. Said Stargell, "I'll go out to talk to him during a game, and he'll say, 'Get off my damn mound.' *His* damn mound." Talk of pitch counts or left-handed, one-batter relief specialists was unheard of in the 1970s. When a pitcher took the mound to start a game, he had every intention of being around when it was finished. A coach like Tanner, who liked to go with his gut and let the moment dictate his strategy, was not always a starting pitcher's best friend. Relievers, on the other hand, loved him, as he always found a way to keep everyone on the staff involved. One of Tanner's more unconventional moves came during a game against the San Francisco Giants. With two outs and a man aboard in the ninth he put his closer, Tekulve, into left field and brought in Grant Jackson to pitch to a single batter. If Jackson was unsuccessful in getting the out, then Tanner would still have the luxury of putting Tekulve back on the mound. Jackson ended up getting the out, even if it was a fly out to left field and the awaiting Tekulve.

Despite its better efforts, the team came out of the gate slow to start the 1979 season, and after one month of baseball had been played, the Pirates found themselves at 7–12 and in the division cellar. That's when general manager (GM) Harding "Pete" Peterson decided to make a move by swapping shortstops with the New York Mets. The trade was roundly criticized, as longtime Pirate Frank Tavares was sent packing for the light-hitting Tim Foli and minor league pitcher Greg Field. By June 28 the Pirates were in third place, trailing not just the Phillies but the surprising Montreal Expos by six and a half games. Once again, Peterson struck a deal. This time, he raided his minor league cupboard, sending three prospects to the San Francisco Giants in exchange for veteran third baseman and two-time batting champion Bill Madlock.

Peterson's trades put the finishing touches on the team. Catcher Ed Ott called Madlock the "missing piece of the puzzle," while Tim Foli surprised everyone and found a home in the number two spot in the batting order, where his strengths were utilized in getting the fleet-footed Moreno into scoring position for the middle-of-the-lineup boys Parker, Stargell, and Madlock.

Before long, the club began to play winning ball once again and was slowly starting to turn into a family. Stargell, known as Pops to the team, had even devised his own signature sign of approval for his disciples. For every positive contribution made in a game, he would award his teammates a gold star, which would be stitched into their Cuban-style pillbox caps. Whether earned for a decisive hit or a game-changing defensive play, "Stargell's stars" were considered a badge of honor for the players, who wore them proudly. "You not only wanted to win, you wanted a 'Stargell star,'" pitcher Bert Blyleven said. As the year rolled along, some of the player's caps would become littered with them.

With their bumblebee black-and-gold uniforms, studded earrings (the Pirates were the first players allowed to wear them), and carefree, laid-back attitudes, the Pirates were a spirited bunch, and their clubhouse was the envy of the league. While some teams, such as the Red Sox, did their best to rid their organizations of free spirits and outlandish characters, the Pirates welcomed individuality. In contrast with a place like Los Angeles, where the Dodgers ran what was called a white-collar clubhouse, Pittsburgh, *Sports Illustrated* reported, "traditionally has the loudest, trashiest-mouthed, loosest, most uproarious dressing room in baseball."

Legendary baseball writer Roger Angell, writing in the *New Yorker* in 1979, credited Chuck Tanner for creating the carnivalesque clubhouse atmosphere. Angell described "knots of people shouting at one another in apparent rage and then collapsing in laughter, somebody sleeping and somebody else preparing to wake up the sleeper in a singularly frightful or comical fashion." Angell was impressed by the cacophony of various cultures eating, drinking, joking, and playing games together while a mix of music, from rock to salsa, constantly blasted in the background.

For over twenty years, since the days of broadcasting icon Bob Prince, the Pirates' players had been pegged with nicknames that rolled off the tongue: Caveman, Hitman, Crazy Horse, the Hammer, Pops, Cobra, Mad Dog, Scrap Iron, Candyman, and Rooster were the latest edition of Bucs to fill out Tanner's lineup card every night. While other teams shied away from the racial issues of the day, the Pirates welcomed the differences on their twenty-five-man roster, which included eleven black and four Hispanic players. Second baseman Phil Garner insisted there were no factions among races on the team. He credited Willie Stargell with being the glue that held everyone together, noting that he was respected by blacks and whites alike. Once again it came back to Stargell, whose enthusiasm for the game carried over and was just as obvious in his love of his teammates.

One day during the middle of the season, Stargell was sitting in the dugout getting ready for a game when he heard a song come across the PA. His foot started tapping, and right away he knew it. The song "We Are Family" by the disco band Sister Sledge encapsulated all the feelings inside of him.

All of the people around us they say
Can they be that close?
Just let me state for the record
We're giving love in a family dose.
We are family.

Upon hearing the song, Stargell walked directly up to the press box and told the announcer that from that day forward, he wanted the song to be the club's new theme song. This was a captain's decision—nobody else was consulted—and sure enough his teammates fell in line and stood behind the selection. "We Are Family" became much more than a song for the team—it became their motto.

The fellowship felt among the players at the time is evident in a 1979 *Sports Illustrated* interview with Willie Stargell, who said, "We got Pancho Villa out there. That's [Enrique] Romo. And [Phil] Garner and Parker.... You hear music from the hills of West Virginia or, maybe, Panama, rhythm and blues, oldies but goodies.... We got everything going in our clubhouse. We win together, lose together." Stargell described the various dugout "neighborhoods," including "the ghetto, where I sit; Park Avenue; Spanish Harlem; and... the low-rent district. Kent Tekulve sits there."

Fitting the team's character, the sluggish start didn't temper the squad's enthusiasm. According to pitcher Jim Rooker, Stargell would constantly remind the team that "the cream always rises to the top." The captain instilled a "never say die, never panic" attitude within the team. It wasn't merely a charade put on by the veteran, either. He, like his manager, Tanner, simply believed it all came down to talent. Stargell was wise enough to know talent when he saw it, and he knew this group of twenty-five guys had it. With Stargell leading the way, the Pirates got on a roll and won 86 of their last 133 ball games. Their fearless leader's "go down swinging" attitude was apparent in the fact that twenty-five of those wins came in the team's last at-bat.

By September the Pirates were still battling the Expos in a tense pennant race that had the two clubs changing the top spot almost daily. The winner of the National League East pennant would be decided the last week of the season, with the Bucs taking three of four games from the Expos and then splitting the last four games to take the division by two games. In a heroic season-long performance, Willie Stargell showed the naysayers he wasn't ready for the pasture just yet, hitting thirty-two home runs and picking up his first-ever league MVP award (sharing it with Keith Hernandez).

===

"NICE GOING, Dude Parrot," outfielder Mike Easler said to Kevin Koch as he slapped Koch five in the champagne-soaked Pirates clubhouse on the final day of the regular season. The congratulations were flowing as easily as the booze. Koch was sweating and shirtless, just another one of the guys as he talked with pitcher Bruce Kison. Chuck Tanner called winning the division pennant the greatest day of his life.

No doubt about it, the Bucs had enjoyed a great season, but on October 2 it was time to get back to work, and the task ahead was certainly daunting—a best-of-five series against the vaunted Big Red Machine of Cincinnati in the National League Championship Series.

The neatly trimmed and businesslike Reds were the antithesis of the loose Pirates and made a poetic adversary for the Buccos. The teams had squared off on three previous postseason occasions during the 1970s, with the Reds taking each of the match-ups. This time the Pirates eked out consecutive extra-inning wins to set the stage for a momentous game three at Three Rivers Stadium. Win, and the Pirates would be World Series–bound.

Pitcher Bert Blyleven, who was perhaps the only member of the squad to have had problems with Tanner during the season, was tapped to start. Blyleven had become sick and tired of Tanner wearing a path to the mound during his starts, as well as what he perceived as premature hooks, and he vented these frustrations publicly. Still, with a chance to get to the Series, Tanner didn't hesitate to call on the nine-year veteran.

The Pirates wasted little time securing a lead, pushing across runs in each of the first three innings to go ahead 4–0. Stargell and Madlock put things to rest in the bottom of the fourth with their matching solo shots that put the score at 6–0. The hometown crowd could smell victory and demanded curtain calls following each home run. The *New York Times*'s Joseph Durso described the spectacle: "The festive mood reached a peak when a cluster of players' wives climbed onto the dugout roof-extension in the seventh inning and danced in unison." The rest of the 42,240 fans in attendance could read the women's lips as they sang out, what else, but "we are fam-a-lee!" Approximately forty more women joined the wives, hopping onto the platform behind home plate and onto the Pirates' dugout roof. The crowd was officially in a frenzy. Never mind that there were still two innings left to play; Blyleven was rolling, and the Pirates were well on their way. By the eighth inning chants of "We want Baltimore!" had begun. With two outs in the bottom of the ninth, the Reds center fielder, Cesar Geronimo, stood at the plate with two strikes. The *Pittsburgh Post-Gazette* set the scene: "An explosion was imminent. Even the ball girls dashed for the safety of the dugouts. Clearly, no prisoners would be taken." At 6:49 P.M. Geronimo was caught standing still on Blyleven's called third strike, and thousands leaped from their seats and onto the playing field at Three Rivers Stadium. Pirates 7, Reds 1. Seconds later a group of teenagers could be seen digging up the rubber from the pitchers mound. The Pirates were the National League champions. The moment was not lost on Dave Parker as he came running in from right field at game's end, screaming for reporters and anyone else to hear, "It's my first World Series, baby, first one! The sweet taste of victory.... Ever since the first time I picked up a ball and a bat as a baby, I dreamed about it. Now I'm here. This is better than everything else I've ever done."

Stargell finished the game with two hits in four plate appearances and three RBIs, on his way to collecting the NLCS MVP award to go along with his regular season hardware. Blyleven was sterling, striking out nine batters and going the distance in the Series clincher. Perhaps even more satisfying for the pitcher was that his manager didn't make a single visit to the mound during the contest. Asked why afterward, Tanner answered plainly, "Bert told me to stay in the dugout."

Next up, American League champions the Baltimore Orioles and a rematch of the seven-game 1971 Series. "The Series will be like this," Stargell said, referring to the just-completed Reds match-up. "We'll be out there playing good, country baseball. Nothing fancy. If we keep that up, we'll give Baltimore a good Series."

═══

OCTOBER 17, 1979. The Pirates were trailing 1–0 with one out and a man aboard in the sixth inning of the final game of the World Series. Up to the plate came the aging number eight. He had been given directives from his field manager: "Pops, you've got to do it for us," Tanner told him. Eight years prior, Stargell had scored the winning run in the seventh game of the World Series against this very team, but his heroics then were soon forgotten, for the 1971 season was Clemente's time. Now the stage was Stargell's. The lefty dug in. Around and around his bat twirled, a big looping windmill, as he awaited the pitch.

Game seven. A season full of emotion was coming down to one game. President Jimmy Carter was in attendance at Baltimore's Memorial Stadium. Enjoying first-row box seats along the third base line, Carter, along with House Speaker Tip O'Neill, watched and smiled, putting the world's problems aside to take in some good old-fashioned baseball. The taut series between Pittsburgh and Baltimore would finally be decided. "World Series Is Fun Again" had been the headline of the *New York Times* sports page prior to the first game of the series. It had not disappointed, and as columnist Dave Anderson forecasted, the series was being played the way baseball was intended—"for fun, not finances." Battling back from a seemingly insurmountable 3–1 deficit had certainly been a team effort for the Pirates. Collectively the team hit .323 for the series, second highest in Series history at the time. The pitching staff and bullpen had come through in the clutch, limiting the O's to only two runs in the final twenty-seven innings of World Series play. In all, twenty-four men out of twenty-five eligible players made an appearance and a contribution in the series. But in the end there wasn't a person in attendance who didn't know how, or by whom, this game would be decided.

Orioles 1, Pirates 0. Stargell at the dish. Players on the Buccos bench felt the urgency as their season drew to a close. They needed their leader to pick them up. "Come on Pops, get us going!" they shouted. Stargell couldn't hear a thing. He was zeroing in on pitcher Scott McGregor. Despite getting a pair of hits already off McGregor, Stargell was unhappy with the way he had struck the ball. This time, when the captain swung his big brown bat, he got good wood on the ball and sent the McGregor pitch through the outstretched arms of outfielder Ken Singleton, over the fence, and into the Pirates bullpen in right-center for a home run. The two-run blast gave the Pirates a 2–1 lead. They added two more runs in the ninth to make the final score 4–1.

Inside the clubhouse, after President Carter, who assisted with the presentation of the championship trophy, had come and gone, Willie Stargell sat at his locker with his customary postgame bottle of wine. For the series he pulled out a 1977 Mondavi Chardonnay. A tear was in his eye. He had hit .400 for the series with three home runs. He had also stepped up when it counted the most, highlighted by his four hits in the game-seven clincher. And while there was a bevy of deserving candidates for MVP—Garner hit .500, Parker .345, Tekulve pitched in five of the seven games with the fifth one marking his 101st trip to the mound for the season—in the end, the new car and the trophy fell once again to Stargell, who summed up the season while taking umbrage at a Baltimore reporter who a day earlier had mocked the team's familial references. "And now I'd like to talk about a columnist here who wrote that we weren't a family. That man didn't live with us all year," Stargell said. He later added, "There has been a closeness on this team that there are no words I can think to describe. We scratched and clawed our way to this day.... We are a family, and that's not being sassy or fancy. It typified this ball club."

Kevin Koch did not have to don the Parrot suit for the final two Series road games, but he was in Baltimore for the final out. Team owner Dan Galbreath had flown Pirates employees, secretaries and all, into Baltimore to be part of the action. Back in Pittsburgh Koch's best friend, Dale Shiffman, sat on a barstool, just another guy in a sea of black and gold along the three rivers. Shiffman sang and cheered and bounced from party to party. He epitomized the pride the Steel City was beaming with. Fans danced in the streets. Throughout the ninety different ethnic neighborhoods that made up the big small town of Pittsburgh, fans bragged and shouted from the rooftops. By 3:39 A.M. thousands more made their way to the airport to greet their heroes at the United Airlines tarmac.

The morning box score: twenty-thousand fans reveling in the streets around the University of Pittsburgh, five thousand celebrating in downtown's tiny Market Square, 120 arrests throughout the city, ten dog bites from the police K9 patrol, and countless streams of toilet paper and much debris left behind.

Shortly thereafter, in the first month of the New Year, 1980, the Pittsburgh Steelers added their fourth Super Bowl ring in six years. There was no doubt about it; Pittsburgh had become the city of champions, on top of the world and the envy of a sports-crazed nation.

==

KEVIN KOCH's first season as the Pirate Parrot came to a close. It was deemed a success by all involved. "He absolutely met our expectations and provided the entertainment value we were seeking," says Steve Schanwald, then director of Pirates promotions. In a matter of months Koch had become, in the words of the *Pittsburgh Post-Gazette*, "a genuine local celebrity." From smashing enemy batting helmets to run-ins with the umpires, his unpredictable antics were becoming legendary. During one between-innings exploit, Koch, driving a miniature replica Corvette, led a parade of mopeds around the stadium. The mascot made a spur-of-the-moment route change and led the merry band through the center-field gates and out of the stadium. With no lights on his tiny vehicle, Koch crossed the Sixth Street Bridge, "shaking his Parrot head and screaming at people." He was finally stopped by city cops outside a disco. "They asked for the Parrot's autograph and gave us an escort back to the stadium," groundskeeper Carmine DiNardo told *USA Today*. "Seventy-nine was a blast. It seemed like it was never going to end."

It wasn't all fun and games, however, as the mascot position proved to be demanding. In the course of each game Koch lost about six pounds from his six-foot, 175-pound frame. During one particularly hot and humid August doubleheader the temperature reportedly reached 135 degrees inside the Parrot suit. He lost a total of thirteen pounds that day and passed out twice. He suffered countless bumps and bruises throughout a season spent scaling seats, fences, and dugouts. Nonetheless, if Koch kept it up, the sky would be the limit. "If Kevin continues to work as hard as he's working now, he could make $30,000 to $40,000 next year," Pirates vice president Jack Schrom said. Not a bad raise from the twenty-five dollars per game he received during his debut season. His mascot brethren, particularly the San Diego Chicken, who had gone on strike in a pay dispute, were only helping the Parrot's case. The Chicken and the Padres ended up settling for $100,000 per year.

While everyone else in the Steel City was celebrating the Series win, it was right back to work for the Parrot. The Pirates had scheduled an appearance for the mascot on the very next day. Koch was quickly learning there was much money to be made as the Parrot. From appearances at shopping malls to advertising engagements, promotional events featuring the mascot had been lined up around the clock by team officials. He was even booked at weddings and bar mitzvahs for the hardest-core Buccos fans. Koch would have plenty to keep him busy until the new season came back around. His coworker Carmine DiNardo described Koch at that time as "young, single, and taking on the world."

3

The Loner Meets the Star

HE WAS A NATURAL ATHLETE. HE WAS ALSO ONE OF
THE STRONGEST MEN I'D EVER MET. HE COULD TEAR
TELEPHONE BOOKS IN HALF ALL DAY LONG. HE NEVER
USED A KNIFE TO CUT AN APPLE; HE SIMPLY SPLIT IT
IN TWO WITH HIS FINGERS. AND HE WAS FAST. DAVE
COULD OUTRUN ANYONE ON OUR TEAM. . . . THE LORD
HAD GIVEN FREELY TO DAVE.
    —WILLIE STARGELL ON DAVE PARKER

SHELBY GREER had just boarded his United Airlines flight
from Pittsburgh to Denver and noticed something was amiss.
There was a mix-up with his seat. In a hurry, Greer hadn't
even bothered to look at his ticket prior to boarding. He had been
assigned a seat in coach, while in the past he had always flown first
class. A twenty-three-year-old oil and gas company land surveyor,
Greer was doing all right for himself. He wasn't rich by any means,
but he made a decent living. He dressed well, drove fast cars, and
had nice girlfriends. His occupation also gave him the opportunity
to travel quite a bit. And when you traveled as much as he did, coach
would not do.

The stewardess corrected the seating error without a fuss, as she
was able to accommodate Greer in the nearly empty first-class section. Taking a seat next to the window, Greer glanced over the vacant

seats next to him and across the aisle to his right. There sat a towering male figure and his female companion. Greer wasn't much of a
baseball fan; in fact, he couldn't name more than a handful of players
in all of professional baseball. However, this man's face was familiar,
and at six feet five inches and 230 pounds, Dave Parker unquestionably had the build of a pro athlete. Whether Greer recognized
him for this reason or rather because Parker had been the subject of
nonstop media scrutiny recently for being awarded baseball's first
million-dollar-per-year contract, Greer can't say. But he was sure
that it was indeed Dave Parker.

══

It HAD been a long journey to the top for the twenty-eight-year old
Parker, who grew up two streets away from Crosley Field in Cincinnati, home of the Reds. As a kid he and his friends would play in
the parking lots outside the major league park. "I learned to slide on
concrete," Parker told *Sports Illustrated*. "We played in Levi's, and it
took some technique. I very seldom skinned myself." One day he saw
Reds outfielder Frank Robinson getting out of a car. "And Frank gave
me a glove. That tripped me out. I told my mother when I was nine
that I was going to grow up and play ball and buy her a house."

In 1970 Dave Parker was the fourteenth-round draft pick of
the Pittsburgh Pirates. He signed his first contract for $6,500 and
reported to Bradenton to play in the Florida rookie league. He was
initially listed as a catcher and a slow-moving one at that. He took
his turn in the mandatory sixty-yard dash, and 6.8 seconds later he
was told to lose the catcher's mitt; he was moving to the outfield. He
succeeded at all levels of the minor leagues, and by the 1974 season he
was in the big leagues to stay. In 1975 he batted over .300 for the first
time, and by 1977 he was the National League batting champion. He
won the batting crown again in 1978, along with hitting thirty home
runs and knocking in 117 batters. He also took home the 1978 NL
Most Valuable Player Award. During that season a newspaper poll of
baseball's general managers revealed that Parker was the most cov-
eted player in all of baseball. The Pirates management took notice,

and after the 1978 season they quickly signed him to a five-year contract worth seven million dollars. It made Parker the highest-paid athlete in all of team sports. The Pirates fully expected him to be the backbone of the team for the next ten years.

Parker would have been the first to boast how well deserved the contract was. In fact, he often did. Parker's on-field aggressiveness did not translate well to off-field interviews, where he came off as not only flamboyant but also brash and outspoken. But no one denied the man played with heart. In 1978, during a game with the Mets, Parker was intent on scoring from second on a base hit. Rounding third base at full speed, he collided with Mets catcher John Stearns with such force that both players were knocked flat on their backs.

After lying motionless on the ground beside home plate, Parker had to be helped from the field with blood oozing from both his mouth and left eye. The gash above his left eye required three stitches. His left cheekbone was depressed and cracked in three places. Surgery was necessary, and a permanent wire was placed in Parker's jaw. Incredibly, he returned to the lineup after only ten days, fitted with a uniquely constructed football-type helmet, with a face mask attached to it, to protect his injured cheek.

While his outspoken nature was often misconstrued, Parker's sound bites were not without a certain sense of humor. When asked why he played with a Star of David dangling around his neck, he flatly answered that he was a star, and his name was David. Another of his favorite lines was, "Two things are for sure: the sun's gonna shine, and I'm going three for four." A lot of people called him a showboat, but Parker, who admitted, "I'm kind of a flashy player," clearly felt his boasts were justified, pointing out, "I've popped off, and then I've backed it up. I've predicted two batting titles, and I've won them." He considered himself to be a highly verbal and outspoken player in the same way that the great Muhammad Ali was, to get himself up for the game. "The great Ali says the reason he talks a lot is that he puts himself on the line, and then has to go out and back it up. I push myself in that regard," Parker once said.

With all eyes on him, Parker wanted to make sure that he lived up to his fat contract going into the 1979 season. "The public needs to see a player who's gotten security and then still goes out and applies himself," he said, and he did not disappoint. Already known for his offensive prowess, the Gold Glove outfielder used the spotlight of the midsummer classic—the All-Star Game—to showcase his defensive skills. Twice runners tried to test his arm from right field, and twice those runners failed miserably. From the Seattle Kingdome's spacious outfield Parker made two legendary throws to nail runners out—one at third and the other at home plate. He picked up that game's MVP award despite having only an infield hit and a sacrifice fly at the bat.

Parker went on to have another good, if not spectacular, season at the plate. But more important, he led the Bucs back to the playoffs after a three-year absence and was instrumental in helping his team capture the championship.

═══

IN NOVEMBER 1979, fresh off the World Series win, Parker was traveling to Tokyo, Japan, to play in an All-Star Game. Denver was one of the flight's stops. As Shelby Greer settled into his seat across the aisle, he began to look for reading material. He wasn't about to make a spectacle of sitting near the famous athlete. Greer did notice—and found it strange—that the moment the FASTEN SEATBELT light went off overhead, Parker quickly undid his seatbelt and dashed toward the lavatory. A thought crossed Greer's mind regarding Parker's action, but he quickly dismissed it.

UPON PARKER's return from the restroom, Greer glanced in the star's direction. He probably should have been shocked, but he wasn't. His initial instinct had been correct. Parker's nose was a leaking mess, and he was making audible quick snorting sounds as he tried to control the drip. Greer smiled to himself and thought, "My turn."

Greer walked to the restroom, locked the door behind him, pulled some cocaine from his pocket, and did a couple of "bumps," one for each nostril. He thought about Parker seated outside the door and figured the product Parker was using was probably cut significantly and paled in comparison to his own. Dealers cut cocaine by mixing it with a similar-looking powder to give their product more weight and thus increase their profits. Cocaine has been cut with agents from benzocaine to common baking powder. Generally, the farther cocaine gets from its source, the more it has been cut. The cocaine that Greer held in his hand was straight off the boat in Florida and as pure as it gets. He had decided that if he was going to do cocaine, he would do the best he could get his hands on.

===

SHELBY GREER grew up in the Pittsburgh suburb of Thornburg. Located just four miles west of downtown Pittsburgh, Thornburg is an affluent neighborhood and the ideal suburb. It is situated close enough to Pittsburgh to reap its rewards yet distant enough to avoid the negative aspects of city life. He was one of two children, the other being an older sister. His parents split when Greer was a child, and as a result he bounced around between schools frequently before finally graduating in 1974 from Montour High School, where he had been a student for only one year. Former Montour superintendent Fred Ringer described Greer to the *Pittsburgh Press* as "more or less a loner. He didn't mix with any of the other groups." Others describe him as having grown up comparatively fast, "ahead of the curve," and "in a hurry." One of his teachers related, "Shelby was a nice kid, polite, good-looking, and always neatly dressed and groomed.... You didn't see many kids like that."

Upon graduation Greer jumped headfirst into the workforce, securing a job with Amax Inc., an energy resources firm in Elkins, West Virginia, where he worked for a year before entering his father's trade in the oil and gas business. He rented an apartment near the company's facilities in Denver. Although those who knew him described him as "a tall, blond, nice-looking young man with nice manners," his reputation as a loner stayed with him into adulthood. Greer became known "at some of Pittsburgh's most popular night spots as a well-dressed loner, who sometimes talked of women and gambling," the *Pittsburgh Press* reported, with one bartender noting, "I never saw him come in with anyone, but he knew the regulars here and would talk to them."

Greer first tried cocaine in 1976 at the age of twenty, and his use steadily increased. The more cocaine he did, the more he enjoyed it. As with everything else in Greer's life, the same rule applied: if he was going to do something, he was going to do it right. He became meticulous about cocaine, eventually buying a kit that tested its quality and purity. This led him to a realization: in order to get the best cocaine, he was going to have to take the horse to the water. Greer was headed to Florida.

As luck would have it, one of Greer's frequent business stops was Gainesville, situated about three hundred miles north of the Fort Lauderdale and Miami areas. He would rent a car, make the five-hour trip south, and make the necessary connections. It was that simple.

When Greer arrived in Fort Lauderdale he quickly set out to gather information. By this time in his life Greer had grown accustomed to mixing with strangers, and it didn't take him long to figure out where he needed to be and who he needed to make inroads with. A handful of trips later, and Greer had succeeded in making the right acquaintances, finding a product he approved of, and forming a business relationship with a supplier. He made his first small purchase in Florida in 1977. Before long he was buying and then transporting back with him up to a pound of cocaine at a time. There was no grand courier system; he would simply pack his raincoat full of drugs and board the plane.

===

SOME PEOPLE love a nice bottle of wine. They sample and seek out rare vintages and build extravagant collections. Others like to talk with friends about food and review the restaurants they discover. Greer just happened to be a connoisseur of pure cocaine. This is what led him to put together a nice little package for Dave Parker inside the cramped quarters of the airplane's lavatory. He wanted to show off his product. Greer admits that Parker's superstar status probably lent something to the equation, but more than anything else, this was about the cocaine. Down the road, Greer allows, his reason for continuing to seek out the star may have hinged on the heightened self-esteem that hanging out with and being accepted by a member of the social elite brought him. But at this point, Greer simply enjoyed turning others on to good shit.

Greer sealed up a small amount of cocaine for Parker and slipped out the restroom door. As he approached their row of seats, Greer realized that he didn't have anything to say. He tapped Parker on the shoulder and said off the top of his head, "Here's a little thank-you for the five hundred dollars I won off you guys last week." It was bullshit, of course, but it wasn't bad, he thought. Parker looked up at him, didn't say a word, and put the package into the pocket of his shirt.

Greer again took his seat by the window. He wondered how long Parker would be able to wait before he tried his stuff. Three minutes later he got his answer as Parker again shuffled off to the restroom. When Parker returned, he sat directly next to Greer. This time Parker had a smile on his face and a big one at that.

"Where'd you get that shit?" he asked.

"Oh, that doesn't matter," Greer answered, coolly.

"Sure it does," Parker said. "Because you just can't get that kind of stuff.... I mean, I haven't had shit that nice since I was in Venezuela." Parker had played winter ball in Venezuela during the 1976 off-season.

Greer nodded knowingly. "I know. Good stuff's hard to find," he said.

"Well, do you think I can get some more of it, or what?" Parker asked, eagerly.

"Sure," Greer replied, "but I don't have any more on me right now. But I don't live far from the airport in Denver. If you're interested, I'm sure we can work something out."

Greer felt sure there was no way that Parker was going to accept his offer, but he was wrong. Even though Parker was traveling through, he did have about an hour and a half layover. Upon approaching Denver he told his girlfriend to make her way to the next gate at the airport and that he would meet her there. Dave Parker, the previous year's National League MVP, was on his way to Shelby Greer's apartment. An unexpected alliance had begun.

Once at the apartment, Greer played the gracious host and laid out a line for Parker before asking him how much he was interested in purchasing. Parker requested two grams, to which Greer replied, "Sure, that'll be $120." Parker misinterpreted this to mean $120 for each gram—a little more than the going rate in Pittsburgh, but for the powder Greer was throwing down, well worth it.

"No, it's $120 for the two," Greer clarified.

Parker was taken aback. He couldn't understand how Greer could charge so little. Greer explained that he wasn't a dealer and wasn't looking to make money. He had a good job and made a decent living. This was just about one admirer of cocaine helping another. None of that mattered to Parker, however, who must have thought that he had just met Santa Claus. Parker quickly sought to continue the relationship, and the two men exchanged information so they could meet up in the future. Parker returned to the airport after giving Greer $120. The young oil and gas businessman had made a total profit of fourteen dollars. But that obviously didn't bother him, and at the end of the day both men felt they had made a good deal.

===

SHELBY GREER's new friendship with the Pirates' star right fielder soon allowed him opportunities to hobnob with the upper crust of Pittsburgh's social scene. He was invited, as Parker's guest, to an exclusive New Year's Eve party at Christopher's Restaurant on Mount Washington, overlooking the Steel City. The event was cohosted by Willie Stargell and Steelers quarterback Terry Bradshaw. Although Greer's "value" to the team and to other guests was not immediately evident and wouldn't be until the following season, the use of cocaine among some on the team and within baseball at large was slowly being revealed. Pirates pitcher Jim Rooker remembers players using the drug as early as the 1978 season, when he saw teammates return to the clubhouse from the lavatory with white powder dusted around their noses. Orioles infielder Billy Smith would later say that cocaine use was "very prevalent" in 1979 around Baltimore's clubhouse as well. Pirates outfielder Lee Lacy was even said to have had cocaine delivered to him during the 1979 Series via his agent.

While cocaine was for the most part still lurking in the shadows of professional baseball in the 1970s, that didn't mean that drugs were not a part of the game. Players had been using drugs—legal and illegal, medicinal and otherwise—for decades. The 1968 World Series was called a classic match-up, pitting the St. Louis Cardinals against the Detroit Tigers, Bob Gibson versus Denny McLain, in a showcase of two of baseball's finest hurlers. Before it was over, both men turned to pharmaceuticals just to keep themselves on the mound for competition. A year later, *Sports Illustrated* reported of the Series, "At times it seemed to be a matchup between Detroit and St. Louis druggists." The Cardinals' Bob Gibson was reportedly taking muscle relaxers to keep his arm loose, while Denny McLain said, "A few pills—I take all kinds—and the pain's gone." McLain also needed shots of cortisone and Xylocaine injected into his shoulder in order to pitch the sixth game of the Series on two days' rest.

The Cardinals' team surgeon at the time, Dr. I. C. Middleman, further added that the club's list of drugs also included on occasion the amphetamines Dexamyl and Dexedrine; the barbiturates Seconal, Tuinal, and Nembutal; and Triavil, Tofranil, and Valium.

Such medicinal use would later lead noted sports essayist Robert Lipsyte to comment in the *Nation* that by the time most athletes made it to the professional level, they had been given so many "pills, salves, injections, and potions, by amateur and pro coaches, doctors and trainers, to pick them up, cool them out, kill pain, enhance performance, reduce inflammation, and erase anxiety, that there isn't much they won't sniff, spread, stick in, or swallow to get bigger or smaller, or to feel goooood."

The most commonly used drugs in major league locker rooms throughout the history of the sport were amphetamines, better known in baseball circles as "greenies." First synthesized in 1887, amphetamine was sold in the 1930s in an inhaler under the trade name Benzedrine and later became a favorite of Jack Kerouac and the Beat Generation. Amphetamine and its derivatives were also used extensively during World War II by soldiers and fighter pilots in order to combat fatigue. According to Dr. Gary Wadler, author of the book *Drugs and the Athlete*, the drugs, also referred to as "uppers," induced "false feelings of power, strength, self-assertion, and enhanced motivation." Former Baseball Player's Association executive director Marvin Miller once remarked of the drug's prevalence, "In most locker rooms, most clubhouses, amphetamines—red ones, green ones, et cetera—were lying out there in the open, in a bowl, as if they were jelly beans. They were not put there by the players… they were being distributed by ownership."

During his inaugural season with the club, the new Pirates' mascot, Kevin Koch, took notice of such pills, particularly of the little green ones making the rounds through the locker room. Koch quickly realized that greenies were more common than aspirin and practically as widely used as the coffee the players were spiking the pills into. Feeling down? Pop a greenie. Had a rough night? Pop a greenie. Long road trip? Double header? Need a base hit? The answer for it all was the same: pop a greenie.

"Greenies were what everyone was doing," Koch says. "I remember coming in a couple of times, and some of the players saying, 'Hey, you look bad. You have a tough night?' I'd say 'Yeah, I have to climb into that suit again,' and they'd say, 'Here,' and they'd give me a couple of them with coffee."

Besides those occasional greenies, Koch wasn't in on any of the cocaine use or other drugs being consumed at the time. He was still nervous with his surroundings, keeping his eyes straight ahead and merely trying to fit in. Even so, he must have heard the "legend"—the locker room tale about pitcher Dock Ellis and his 1970 no-hitter.

=

DOCK ELLIS began his career with the Pirates in 1968. Flamboyant, controversial, and outspoken, Ellis was a man ahead of his time. He encouraged and led the way for a parade of young African American athletes to speak their minds and be themselves. Once when Pirates management complained about Ellis's haircut (he was known for wearing a variety of hairstyles), he greeted the objection by wearing hair curlers onto the field.

Because of Dock Ellis, guys like Dave Parker didn't feel the need to tamp down their true natures. The first time Parker saw Ellis, Ellis was strolling into the locker room wearing "white pants with a purple suede jacket with spangles hanging and a little band around his head." He was also "wearing about four rings," Parker said. It was Ellis's leadership, however, more than what he wore, that stood out and made a difference to young players. When Ellis thought his teammates had become fearful of their archrival, the Reds, he promised to bean every Reds batter he faced the next time the two clubs squared off. Sure enough, on May 1, 1974, in order to motivate and toughen up the young ball club, Ellis made good on his word, and down went Rose, Morgan, and Dreissan to start the game. Tony Perez managed to elude Ellis's pitches to draw a walk, and the next two pitches narrowly missed the head of the number-five hitter, Johnny Bench. After that, Pirates manager Danny Murtaugh decided he had seen enough; he walked to the mound to rescue the rest of the Reds lineup by relieving Ellis of his duties for the day. The first thing Ellis said upon his return to the dugout couldn't be considered remorseful: "You see how big [Bench's] damn head is? How did I miss that head?"

Ellis would later admit he was using greenies during this game.

"Dock Ellis was without question the most intimidating pitcher of his era," Parker told the *Dallas Observer*. "I call him my baseball father, but after I left the Pirates, he said he was going to hit me in the face. And every time I faced him, I was scared." Ellis had once beaned slugger Reggie Jackson in the face in retaliation for a home run Jackson hit against him.

Despite numerous achievements over his twelve-year career, it was a game on June 12, 1970, that Dock Ellis will be remembered for. That was the day Ellis pitched a no-hitter against the San Diego

Padres. The story begins, however, much earlier in the day, prior to the contest.

It was a Friday morning when Ellis awoke in the Los Angeles home of childhood friend Al Rambo. Since arriving on the coast a few days prior, Ellis's hours had been filled with pot, booze, and pills. That particular morning, the drug of choice happened to be Purple Haze acid. A few hours after dropping a dose, Ellis's girlfriend, Mitzi, called for Dock's attention from inside the folds of a newspaper.

"Dock," she said. "You're supposed to pitch today."

Dock had lost track of the time, having squandered a day by sleeping through Thursday. By 1:00 P.M. he was on his way to the airport to catch a $9.50 flight from Los Angeles to San Diego for the 6:05 p.m. contest against the Padres. He was the scheduled starter.

Ellis was no stranger to LSD, a weekend favorite of his at the time. So he was well aware that his buzz wasn't going anywhere soon; he was in it for the long haul. He prayed for rain. There was not a cloud in the sky.

Fortunately for Dock, a young lady with whom he was acquainted frequently came to Jack Murphy Stadium to see him pitch when he played in San Diego and arrived that day bearing a gift—Benzedrine—to share with Dock. Ellis ate a handful of White Crosses and went to the bullpen to loosen up his arm. "Damn. Looks like I'm gonna have to pitch," he finally said to himself.

The *Dallas Observer* described the game in 2005 after Ellis opened up about it in an interview.

Sometimes [the ball] felt like a balloon. Sometimes it felt like a golf ball. But he could always get it to the plate. Getting it *over* the plate was another matter entirely. Sometimes he couldn't see the hitter. Sometimes he couldn't see the catcher. But if he could see the hitter, he'd guess where the catcher was.... The hardest part was between innings. He was sure his teammates knew something was up. They had all been acting strange since the game began. Solution: Do not look at teammates. Do not look at scoreboard. Must not make eye contact. His spikes—

that's what he concentrated on. Pick up tongue depressor, scrape the mud, repeat. Must. Clean. Spikes.

Sometime in the fifth or sixth, he sensed someone next to him. Looking. He turned. It was rookie infielder Dave Cash.

"Dock," Cash said. "You've got a no-hitter going."

Ellis finished the ninth inning and walked off the mound with a true baseball rarity, that of the no-hitter. Although the game was far from perfect, as he did walk eight batters, while hitting another.

"I remember getting that last out," Ellis said. "And turning around and saying, 'A fucking no-hitter!' It didn't really hit me until the next morning, and I was less high, and I got a live call from CBS or ABC or something, wanting to interview me."

═══

As the 1970s came to an end, Chuck Tanner's hands-off philosophy, which had brought the city a championship ring, should have been vindicated. His style of managing had worked for decades. Carousing and less-than-wholesome extracurricular activities had always been part of the game's fabric. But for the most part, the players had policed themselves. Dave Parker asserts that among the Pirates' players of the 1970s, "we governed ourselves. Stargell was the leader—the stabilizer. I was the motivator and the enforcer. [Phil] Garner was the clubhouse lawyer."

Only now, a new variable was about to throw a wrench into the "live and let live" clubhouse atmosphere. It was a phenomenon that the easygoing Tanner, with his old-school mentality, may have never even known existed. After all, this was a man who once said, "If drugs were any good for you, God would have had it in you when you were born, because he made the perfect machine."

The 1980s would turn the page on all that. The days of baseball innocence had come to an end. Cocaine was about to sweep the nation.

PART II

THE 1980S—
HIGH TIMES

4

The Lefty

I LOVE BASEBALL, AND WHEN YOU LIKE A SPORT AS
MUCH AS I DO, THAT'S ALL YOU WANT TO DO.
  —ROD SCURRY, 1975

ROD SCURRY was a high school phenom. Blessed with an unhittable, some would say deranged, curveball, the tall, lanky left-hander from Proctor R. Hug High School in Reno, Nevada, was the first-round draft pick of the Pirates in 1974. Upon graduation, the eighteen-year-old, who was once voted shiest in his class, was immediately shipped off to Bradenton, Florida, for a brief stop at the Pirates minor league headquarters before beginning his pro career in Niagara Falls, where he would play in the Class A New York–Penn league. "He was drafted on a Tuesday, graduated on Thursday, and had to go to Florida that Sunday night," Rod's father, Preston, recounted to the Associated Press's Steve Wilstein.

Scurry quickly became Niagara Falls' top pitcher and found himself named to the league's all-star game. The future was bright for Rod Scurry. "I feel really good about my first season," Scurry told the *Reno Evening Gazette*. "I'm dedicating everything to baseball. I haven't had time to worry about college or other things."

Following his summer in A-ball, Scurry was sent back to Florida to play in a winter league in Bradenton. After that he was invited to the big league camp for spring training in February, and then on to another summer in the minors. Scurry wasn't joking about not having time for college. The teenager went directly from high school to a full-time career. In completing his first year in professional baseball, Scurry downplayed the demanding schedule. "We only had one day off all summer... except for the games that were rained out. But baseball is all I've ever wanted to do. That's what I'm happy doing." He did acknowledge the change in environment. "I have a lot more freedom, and I've met a lot of people. But it hasn't been that big of a change."

His coaches described Scurry as cool and reserved. His confidence in himself was obvious when asked about his ultimate goal of playing in the majors. "I'm not worried about making it now. I think it's just a matter of time before I get onto the major league club."

Salem, Shreveport, Columbus, Shreveport, Columbus—Scurry made his way up and down the minor league ladder. The year 1977 was pivotal in Scurry's ascent to the pros. Other pitchers were starting to pass him by on the Pirates' radar. Don Robinson, for instance, was drafted by the ball club one year after Scurry, in the fifth round of the 1975 draft. In 1977, when they met up in Bradenton, the two pitchers were practically on equal footing. Fellow left-handed pitcher and teammate Randy Brandt remembers that during a series that season, while playing for Double A Shreveport in Jackson, Mississippi, Scurry could sense the younger Robinson gaining on him. Manager John Lipon received word to get Robinson ready to hit, which Brandt says is a sure sign that a minor league pitcher is being groomed for the big leagues. (Pitchers in the low levels of the minors are instructed instead to focus on their pitching.) A call to the majors was the next apparent step for Robinson. An upset Scurry approached Lipon. Why wasn't he being given the chance to hit? Lipon tried to sidestep the truth—that Scurry was indeed being passed over for the younger Robinson, whom the team was pushing hard—by explaining that Robinson was a faster runner than Scurry and claiming that *that* was the reason Robinson was going to be allowed to do his own hitting.

With his teammates rallying behind him, Scurry demanded a running race. Out to the foul line in left field the team went. A foot-race would decide it. With Randy Brandt holding his cap high in the air to start the race, the two pitchers took off. At first they matched stride for stride, but Scurry pulled out a tight victory. Lipon granted Scurry's request: the young pitcher would start batting for himself as well.

By midseason, Scurry was doing all he could to earn his ticket. In July 1977, in front of scouts from other teams, including the Braves' Hank Aaron, not to mention the Pirates' pitching coach, Larry Sherry, Scurry threw a no-hitter in his Triple A debut for the Columbus Clippers, his final stop before playing for the big club in Pittsburgh. The papers back home in Nevada reported that Scurry was "just a hair away from the Big Leagues and the Reno left-hander is not doing anything to hurt his chances."

Nonetheless, when the 1978 spring training season ended, it was Don Robinson who was packing his bags for the majors, while Scurry was headed back to Triple A. The pressure must have been mounting for the young hurler. In an interview in 1977, Scurry showed a glimpse of his state of mind. "There was a lot of glory the way things worked out for me in the draft. I would feel I let a lot of people down [in Reno] if I didn't make it. If I referred that to the Pittsburgh organization, I would feel I let them down if I didn't make it."

In 1979, with the Pirates and Robinson in the midst of their championship run, Scurry was toiling through his sixth year in minor league ball. This time he was in Portland, Oregon, where the Pirates' Triple A affiliate was now located. Prior to being drafted, Scurry had only consumed beer on two occasions. In Portland, however, boredom and loneliness replaced the excitement and contentment Scurry had once felt as an eighteen-year old who actually got to play the game he loved for money. Scurry's father, Preston, who at one time had to take monthly weeklong trips from the family's home in Sparks, Nevada, to Las Vegas to sell stereo equipment to support the family, knew what life on the road was like and could sense what his boy was going through. "That's a lonely life when you live on the road out of a suitcase a week or two at a time, and you get back home to a lonely apartment," Preston Scurry said. "So, you've got two things to do—sit there by yourself or go out and raise Cain. And you're in the public spotlight, being compared to guys like Koufax. It's a fast-paced life and tough on a boy just out of high school put in with grown men who know he's looking to take their job. And you've got guys there who he looked up to that were doing things and giving him a bad influence."

Scurry, along with teammates Craig Cacek and Gary Hargis, began knocking back Henry Weinhard's beer every night in Portland, with Scurry drinking up to twelve a night. Yet the escape Scurry was seeking eluded him. He missed his family. He missed his home. Drinking wasn't helping. He searched for something stronger.

"I remember the first time," Scurry later told *Sports Illustrated*, speaking of his initiation into the world of cocaine use. "I went fishing at 5:00 A.M. I had one gram of cocaine with me. I just wanted to try it. It was kind of like having your first beer. The stuff I had that day wasn't that good. I wanted to try something better."

Scurry's habit started slowly, but as the season progressed, so did his coke consumption. He began spending time with infielder Dale Berra, son of New York Yankees legend Yogi Berra. The two became close. "You see Dale, you see Scurry. They were tight," recalls Dave Parker. In Portland, Scurry and Berra purchased coke from either a clubhouse attendant or a teammate's brother who was a long-distance truck driver. According to Craig Cacek, Scurry's buddy and Portland's first baseman and leading hitter, a handful of guys on the club were using coke. That same handful, plus a few others, were also into popping greenies for some pregame pep. As the players made their way into the clubhouse in the morning, the running joke was to shout out to the clubhouse attendant, "Hey clubbie, get the coffee on!" Those in the know knew this meant to get the greenies out, although coffee was indeed prepared as well, since it was the preferred drink with which to consume the amphetamines.

Minor league life was awash with greenies at the time—which isn't to say that everybody was using them, but players surely didn't have to look far to get their hands on some. Managers were said to look the other way when it came to amphetamine use. Craig Cacek says he used them for his last two years of professional baseball on a daily basis.

Cacek, who played in seven major league games as a member of the Houston Astros, was first introduced to the world of pregame uppers by outfielder Leon Roberts in 1977. Roberts, who hit .267 in eleven major league seasons, had run out of pills and was scrambling to find a substitute to get himself up for a game. So he took some over-the-counter caffeine tablets instead and gave Cacek five or six of them as well. Unfortunately, that many tablets made Cacek too shaky; by the time he entered the batter's box he was ready to jump out of his shoes. When a ninety-mile-per-hour fastball was fired his way, Cacek was so far out in front of it that the right-hander launched it preposterously foul, down the third base line and into the bleachers. In the dugout, Roberts was in stitches at the sight of his young, pepped-up teammate.

Going back to the 1940s, amphetamines were purportedly used in baseball to deal with the rigors of season-long travel. However, to the players, the real reason was evident, and greenie stories were passed through the minors like lore. The pills were quite simply the magical hangover helper. The culture of baseball has always been one of drinking, chasing, and partying. If Mickey Mantle could put up five hundred homers while hitting the town every night, every youngster who came along after him would give it a try as well. Never mind that Mantle probably could have put up another hundred or so homers had he taken better care of himself. The legend was cemented—whiskey and women were fine as long as you could drag your ass to the ball field in the morning. Legendary player-turned-coach George "Sparky" Anderson once said, "In the old days twenty-four of the twenty-five guys on every team were drunk."

Cacek says he and the rest of the minor league ballplayers heard all the tales, from the great "Yaz," Carl Yastrzemski, keeping a bottle of greenies labeled SUPERMAN in his Red Sox locker to Willie Mays and his "red juice" (liquid amphetamine). And everybody knew the real reason behind Steve Carlton's exaggerated facial expressions while on the mound for NBC's *The Game of the Week* on Saturday afternoons. It was the greenies turning his face inside out.

Once a player got hooked on greenies, it wasn't easy to play without them. The players dubbed this feeling "playing naked." Cacek described taking the field without greenies after a long stretch of use, saying, "It was like everything was in slow motion." The player would feel as if he weren't running, throwing, or simply moving fast enough, as though he were stuck in the mud. So while greenies weren't performance enhancing, it did seem that way to the players. They felt that the drugs got them back to what Cacek calls their baseline. Whether a guy had been out all night or had a day game or a doubleheader, greenies would get him back to where he needed to be. They got him back onto the field.

===

ON SEPTEMBER 1, 1979, Rod Scurry was at long last called up to the major league club. He made it to Pittsburgh in time to watch the Pirates make their playoff push and witness fellow pitcher Don Robinson take his star turn in the playoffs against Cincinnati. But Scurry observed it all from the bench. He never pitched an inning during the 1979 season. The Pirates had merely wanted their former first-round draft pick to wet his feet in his new surroundings.

As 1979 rolled along, Scurry's cocaine use became much heavier. Following his brief stint in the majors, Scurry was off for the Dominican Republic to play winter ball. He was joined by his Portland teammates Cacek, Gary Hargis, and Dale Berra.

While Cacek was keen to explore the island and broaden his horizons, Scurry's interests were confined solely to baseball and partying. "Rod was doing blow every day in the Dominican," Cacek says. Whether related or not, his performance in the winter league wasn't sharp. The *Pittsburgh Post-Gazette* called Scurry's pitching in the Dominican League "wild." Apart from going to the ballpark, Scurry and Berra hardly ever left the house. Instead they called in some local girls for company and snorted cocaine. "Scurry and Berra ran around like a couple of twelve-year-olds," Cacek says. The pair seemingly had no cares or thoughts about the implications or consequences of their actions. "Berra was out of his gourd," recalls Cacek.

Going into the 1980 season, Scurry was out of minor league options, which meant he either made the major league club or the Pirates risked losing their former number-one pick. Phil Musick of the *Pittsburgh Post-Gazette* documented the pitcher's precarious position, writing, "He is, at once, that most envied and lamented of major-league hopefuls, a player without options. If happiness is having alternatives, as more than one poet has suggested, Scurry is in trouble."

"Yeah, this might be a do-or-die situation for me," Scurry agreed. The Pirates had little time to make up their minds about the pitcher. "Decide to keep me or get rid of me.... Whatever," Scurry concluded to the *Post-Gazette* .

In the end Scurry made the club straight out of spring training. The now twenty-four-year-old from Nevada could finally call Pittsburgh his full-time home. Little did he know the timing couldn't possibly have been worse. The private dabbling in cocaine that Scurry had done around the small northwestern towns of Triple A baseball or on the islands of the Caribbean was nothing. He was now in the major leagues and in the city at the dawn of the 1980s, and everyone was doing coke—his teammates, the guys at the bar, even the corner butcher.

Minor league pitcher Randy Brandt had met Scurry when Scurry arrived in Niagara Falls directly out of high school. Brandt had seen a different side of Scurry than the hard-living drug user his teammates in Portland and the Dominican Republic had come to know. Brandt knew a soft-spoken, gentle young man who felt more at home in the hills of rural Pennsylvania or the mountains of Nevada than amid the crowded streets of the city. Brandt was an all-everything athlete from Newell, Pennsylvania, a small coal town on the outskirts of Pittsburgh. Newell was country, and Scurry loved visiting Brandt there. He felt like he was in his element—from fishing and groundhog hunting to knocking a few beers back and shooting pool at the Newell Moose Lodge.

One night, Brandt remembers, Scurry had car problems while leaving the small town, and Brandt's wife directed him to a local auto garage. After the Brandts hadn't heard from Scurry for a while, they decided to check on him at the garage. Time had gotten away from Scurry, who was sitting on the hillside conversing with the mechanic, his new friend. Just talking about life. But that was then.

Chuck Tanner used Scurry sparingly during the 1980 season. The manager preferred to work his rookie into the big leagues slowly, choosing just the right spots to work the pitcher. "We babied him," Tanner admitted. Scurry was the tenth pitcher on a ten-man staff. His first major league appearance illustrates the type of situations he was used in during his rookie season. With the St. Louis Cardinals leading 11–3 by the top of the seventh inning, the bullpen telephone at Three Rivers Stadium rang. Kent Tekulve picked it up. "You're going in, Scurry," he said after hanging up. Scurry held his own for two innings of work, giving up three hits and one run in his debut.

Scurry wound up the season having pitched only 37.2 innings in twenty appearances. His tortuously slow career was not lost on the Pittsburgh sportswriters. The *Pittsburgh Press*'s Bob Smizik, who was never known to sugarcoat anything, showed rare sympathy for the seldom-used pitcher: "Rod Scurry has worked hard to get to where he is today. He can only hope he gets other chances to show he deserves to stay."

===

DAVE PARKER and his new acquaintance Shelby Greer continued to meet up around the country during the 1980 season. Greer visited Parker in Florida during the Bucs' spring training and joined him and the rest of the Pirates at the annual end-of-Grapefruit-League party at the Sarasota Holiday Inn. Then in early May Greer and Parker once again ran into each other on a flight from Pittsburgh to Denver. Parker and the Pirates were en route to San Diego to face the Padres for a three-game series. Before landing in Denver, Parker asked Greer if he would be able to score some blow and bring it to San Diego. Greer purchased half an ounce in Denver from a couple of Venezuelan college students he had dealt with previously. He then flew to San Diego and met up with Parker at the Sheraton Harbor View Hotel. There he was paid for the drugs and reimbursed for a portion of his airfare by Parker, who, Greer said, paid him partly out of his own pocket and partly with funds collected from his teammates. He stayed the night in one of the rooms assigned to Parker. It was this trip that prompted other players on the Pirates to regard Greer as not only Dave Parker's cocaine connection but also someone who could also furnish *them* with cocaine. "He got to know Dale Berra and Scurry and some of these guys pretty good, and so he kind of increased his market more or less by knowing more athletes. Then he latched onto players on other teams," Parker says. "It came to the point where Shelby was selling directly in front of the ballpark after the games."

During this same period another man began to supply the Pirates with cocaine, both in Pittsburgh and on other East Coast stops. Curtis Strong was a former life insurance salesman from Philadelphia who put his love of cooking to work and began a career as a caterer. The short, plump, boyish-faced Strong worked out of Philadelphia's Richard's Tavern and Lounge. His business cards read simply, Chef Curt. His favorite dish was fried chicken wings, and people from all over Philly flocked to taste his creations. Strong became familiar with a few members of the Philadelphia Phillies. Soon he began to associate with other ballplayers from around the National League. He was introduced to Parker in May 1980 by Los Angeles Dodgers Dusty Baker, Steve Howe, and Derrel Thomas when the Dodgers came to Pittsburgh to face the Pirates. Parker in turn introduced his friend and teammate John Milner to Strong later that month at the Franklin Plaza in Philadelphia, and the two purchased an eight ball (one-eighth ounce of coke) from Strong after a game against the Phillies.

Milner was a key contributor to the Pirates' championship team. A feared pinch hitter who platooned with Bill Robinson in left field, as well as made the occasional start at first base to give Stargell a rest, Milner hit sixteen home runs, with two coming as grand slams, and had sixty RBIs for the Series winners. Milner was first introduced to cocaine during the 1976 off-season at a bar in New York City, when a stranger approached him and asked him if he would like to try some. Milner proceeded to the restroom, where he unwrapped the cocaine from an aluminum foil seal, took out a house key, and experimented.

In a June 1980 game against the Astros, Milner was seated in front of his locker just after the game had begun when he saw Curtis Strong walk through the clubhouse. "The clubhouse was pretty much wide open at the time. If you knew one of the players, you could enter," Milner said. Milner was not starting that day and would only be used later in the game as a pinch hitter, if needed. So he asked Strong if he had any coke on him. They went back to the restrooms inside the Three Rivers Stadium clubhouse, and "that is where we exchanged money and package," Milner said. The sale was for two grams at the price of two hundred dollars.

Strong continued to network that season and would ultimately make cocaine sales to Enos Cabell of the Astros and Dale Berra, among others. In the years to follow, his clientele would grow to include Jeffrey Leonard of the Giants, who would share with team-mates Chili Davis and Al Holland, and Lonnie Smith, who would purchase for himself and Keith Hernandez. Strong's new business venture took him not only to Philly and Pittsburgh but also to Atlanta and New York.

Shelby Greer met up with Parker in Pittsburgh once more in September. From that point forward he spent a lot of time with the star. He tried in vain to get a few of the Pirates interested in legitimate oil and gas investments, claiming to have spoken with Bert Blyleven, Bill Madlock, and Lee Lacy on the subject, without success. On occasion during the off-season Parker would purchase cocaine from Greer, who would sell it to Parker at cost, which was about fifty or sixty dollars per gram. But Parker rarely had to pay for the drug when he hung out with Greer. Instead, the two would wager both money and cocaine on backgammon, a game that Parker taught Greer. Parker could usually win as much cocaine as he needed.

With Stargell and Parker both playing with injuries that made their knees swell to the size of grapefruits, the Pirates fell from pennant winners to third place in the National League East after the 1980 season. Besides the injuries, could the increased cocaine use among players have been a factor in the Pirates' diminished place in the standings? Dock Ellis described cocaine's effect on ballplayers, telling the *New York Times*, "It gives them the feeling they can do anything, 'I can conquer the world,' like Superman." But while players may have *felt* invincible, Ellis concluded that "down the line it will affect you negatively."

5

Big League Call-up

YOU ALWAYS GET A SPECIAL KICK OUT OF PLAYING
OPENING DAY, NO MATTER HOW MANY YOU GO
THROUGH. YOU LOOK FORWARD TO IT LIKE A BIRTHDAY
PARTY WHEN YOU'RE A KID. YOU THINK SOMETHING
WONDERFUL IS GOING TO HAPPEN.

—JOE DiMAGGIO

"THE BUTTERFLIES have already started," said Rod Scurry on April 18, 1981, in anticipation of his first major league start the following day in Houston. The season was almost two weeks old, and Scurry had yet to make an appearance on the mound. In fact, he hadn't pitched more than four innings in a single outing in two years. He was only getting the break now because Pirates ace Jim Bibby was injured; still, Scurry was excited and was hoping not just to start but also to finish his own game. "I'll be trying to go nine," he said.

GROWING UP, Rod Scurry never doubted he would play in the majors, if not as a pitcher then as a hitter. In high school he once hit a five-hundred-foot home run. But despite his batting prowess, he had always been a pitcher at heart. In the 1960s, when he was just a child, he stacked mattresses against the wooden fence in the backyard of his Nevada home and hurled fastballs at it. He had always had power. But then there was the hook. He could sweep his curveball in at such an angle the ball would bend between a batter's legs. Frequently compared to the preeminent lefty of all time, Sandy Koufax, Scurry drove himself to live up to the compliment. This desire propelled him out of bed at 5:30 A.M. to jog to school through high mountain air and sometimes freezing temperatures just so he could get extra pitching practice in at the Hug High gym before the opening bell rang. On game days, when his teachers believed him to be studiously tending to his work in the classroom he would in fact be poring over index cards he had made that listed the tendencies of the opposing team's big hitters.

===

SCURRY'S ASPIRATION to pitch a complete game nearly came to fruition. He pitched seven strong innings, shutting out the Astros on four hits, while adding seven strikeouts. Lifted for a pinch hitter in the top half of the eighth in a scoreless game, Scurry was forced to pace the clubhouse floor, listening to the final innings on the radio, anxiously rooting for his club. His teammates cooperated, as the Pirates finally picked up a pair of runs to make the score 2–0. Reliever Eddie Solomon completed the shutout, going the final two innings to secure the victory.

Although he didn't close the game, Scurry had made a superlative debut start that lived up to his pedigree and reminded many of the days when he struck out eighteen or nineteen per start back at Hug High. "I'm excited," Scurry said. "My first big league win is a big thrill. I've dreamed about this day. Winning my first big league game is the highlight of my career. I never complained about relieving last year, but I've always wanted to be a starter."

"Last year was frustrating," Scurry admitted. "I understood the situation. They were world champions, and they had to go with the pitchers who won. I wasn't thrilled too much with sitting around, but I didn't get down on myself."

Across the diamond, the Astros took notice of what they had seen thrown against them. "The kid has an outstanding curveball," the opposing starter, Joe Niekro, commented. "Sometimes a pitcher has to wait a long time to get his chance. I know how it feels." A poll of scouts echoed Niekro's assessment, declaring that Scurry's curveball was not just good but the finest in the major leagues.

"Scurry Can't Sleep on Major Success," read the *Pittsburgh Press* sports page the day after the game, playing off Scurry's remark that he had been "too excited to sleep" the night before his start and had in fact slept little at all in the two days leading up to the outing. Pitching coach Harvey Haddix defended the young pitcher, saying, "You don't need sleep to pitch. I did it many times in the days we rode trains between cities. In fact, it may help. You take it out on the other team's hitters."

What Scurry failed to mention to Haddix was that it wasn't merely adrenaline keeping him up at night—it was cocaine, which he also used before the game. His memorable first big league start and win were accomplished while he was high.

———

By this time, Rod Scurry and Pirates mascot Kevin Koch had become friends. The trail to friendship started in 1974 when Scurry met Randy Brandt in the minors. Koch landed the mascot position in 1979, and a short time later Brandt married Koch's sister, Jackie. Koch and Brandt were now brothers-in-law, and before long, Scurry and Koch were running around together as well. "It was like [Scurry] was my brother-in-law, too," Koch said.

Soon, the circle expanded to include Koch's high school buddy Dale Shiffman. It was a dream come true for the local boy Shiffman, who fit right in with the baseball crowd. He had always loved the game, but as he reached high school in the 1960s he didn't have time for baseball anymore as his interests ran to "beers, cigs, and slicked-back hair." In the army during the early 1970s Shiffman picked up baseball again and played at a high level while based at Fort Devin, Massachusetts. By the 1980s Shiffman had become a three-sport season ticket holder in the 'Burgh. He was the type of guy whose awareness of the four seasons was determined not by the temperature outside or the leaves on the trees but by the particular sport being played in his city. Fall was all about the Steelers, in the winter he followed the Penguins, and his summers were devoted to the Pirates. So when Koch started inviting Shiffman down to the stadium to hang out with the team before games, the outgoing Shiffman was in his element. When the invitation was extended for him to take to the field for batting practice and a chance to shag a few fly balls, Shiffman was in downright heaven. "I got to stand out there in right field with my heroes," Shiffman said. "A few would even invite me to meet after the game to have a beer. Life could not have been better."

Shiffman's 1969 high school yearbook describes him as "a real car buff... enjoys a good laugh... dependable pal... carefree." Shiffman stayed true to his character in the ensuing years, particularly to being "carefree" as he spent much of his time bowling, golfing, and playing softball. "Dale's not interested in working," a friend later told the *Pittsburgh Post-Gazette*. "Dale doesn't want to grow up. All he wants to do is have a good time."

Shiffman was employed only sporadically in the photography business when he made his entrance on the major league scene. Without a full-time occupation, he felt a certain validation in being able to say he knew and spent time with prominent sports figures. Right or wrong, "hanging out with athletes made your pride go up," Shiffman admits. Instead of being just another guy struggling to hold down a job, he now felt important. He was being invited to golf and barbecue outings with different players. When he took a date down to the ballpark, all the ushers would know his name, and a player or two might give him a shout-out following the night's contest, which would duly impress his female companion, not to mention Shiffman himself. "It made you feel like a somebody even if you really were a nobody," he says.

Shiffman and Koch, like so many others in the early 1980s, had recently discovered cocaine. The drug was making the rounds through their softball league, alongside the other party mainstays beer, pot, and Percodan. "Everyone we hung out with at the bar and from our end of town—everyone was into [cocaine]," Koch says.

When Koch and Shiffman hit the city's nightclubs and bars after Pirates' games, they typically ran into some of the players. Inside Pittsburgh-area nightspots such as Heaven, the VIP, Sophie's Saloon, or the Sunken Cork, things got interesting for the pair. Koch explains, "Berra or somebody would say, 'Hey, do you guys party?' Then one thing led to another, and the players found out that Dale [Shiffman] could get stuff, and that's how it kind of snowballed from there."

Koch says that the players, mostly Scurry and Berra, began to call him prior to games to ask if he could pick some blow up from Shiffman and bring it down to the ballpark. Shiffman purchased the cocaine from various locals. He cut the coke, not to increase the weight but rather to replace the cocaine he was taking out for his own personal consumption. Shiffman says his motivation wasn't to make money; it was to get his party favors without having to pay for them. He figured he was not only scoring free coke but also greatly expanding his social circle, now filled with local sports figures. He could have hardly asked for more.

Typically Shiffman wrapped up a gram or two, or sometimes an eight ball, then Koch swung by and picked up the drugs on his way to work. The transactions between Koch and the players usually took place deep within the corridors of the stadium, such as in the runway outside the clubhouse or sometimes in the parking lots. The men never had any run-ins with Pirates officials; in fact, as cocaine use became more prevalent, Koch even suspected that those in charge had to know what was going on.

"It seemed like no one really cared," Koch says. "I mean, I think Major League Baseball even knew itself that it had problems, like, years before, when they had alcohol problems with a lot of guys."

After a while Koch realized that with Shiffman frequenting the games, maybe his own role in these transactions was superfluous. Beyond that, despite the fact that he was in a drug- and alcohol-induced haze much of the time, Koch could still see the precarious position he was putting himself in. Something in the back of his mind wouldn't let him rest. "When you're raised by a mom and dad that care about you, you start to put one and one together," he says.

Koch tried to distance himself from his middleman position, telling the guys that they had one another's phone numbers and could set things up for themselves. A few of the players began to call Shiffman's house directly, or Shiffman met them outside the clubhouse after the games, where they made their exchanges. These callers were usually Scurry and Berra, although Shiffman was also becoming close with the Pirates reliever Eddie "Buddy J." Solomon. A pretty low-key guy, Solomon sometimes invited Shiffman over to his apartment, where they would do a couple lines and just hang out. Occasionally Shiffman received calls to bring some blow to a downtown hotel room for some of the visiting National League teams' players.

"I remember some of the other teams all of a sudden started to get involved," Koch says. "They'd say, 'Hey, can you get your buddy to do this or that?' And I'd call Dale, and he'd come down, and we'd party with just about everybody; it was pretty bizarre. It was pretty out of control in the eighties."

Yet Koch insists it wasn't all about the cocaine all the time. More often, he says, it was just a bunch of guys getting together, and if someone had some on them, then sure, they would all do a line. "Now, we *would* be in the clubs every night drinking and stuff," Koch admits, "but it wasn't like 'Hey, let's all get together because of cocaine.'"

Whenever there were requests made of Koch, however, he found it very hard to decline them. "Imagine guys that are making that much money, and now you're partying with them. After a while you don't think anything about it. You almost think you're untouchable," Koch says. If players were looking to hook up, and Shiffman wasn't going down to the game that night, Shiffman called Koch. They both lived in the South Hills, so Koch could easily swing by Shiffman's residence and pick up a couple grams for the boys that night. Other times the players would ask Koch to call Shiffman for them. Koch says he would think about the job that had opened up a whole new world to him, a job he cherished. He would think about how the people within the organization treated him so well. He had been welcomed into the family; he was well liked and appreciated.

He knew he wasn't doing the team any favors by bringing drugs to the stadium, but in the end, he always agreed.

"I'd say all right," Koch says. "I couldn't say no. What are you gonna do? It's almost impossible to say no. These were your heroes. Guys from when you were a kid. I remember sitting down with Willie [Stargell] going, 'I remember your first game, Willie. It was in '63 at Forbes Field. I was like nine or ten years old.' And with other guys, we'd talk sports together, and I would tell them this or that; and they'd say, 'Man, you were there that night?' Like Gene Garber, I said, 'I remember you pitching your first game against the Chicago Cubs. You had three perfect innings going at Forbes Field, then in the fourth Billy Williams jacked that ball.' And Garber would be like, 'Oh my God!'"

Koch wasn't a mere fan. Baseball was a game he loved. And whether Dale Berra or Rod Scurry were stars or not, it didn't matter to him. Or to Dale Shiffman. It was the name on the front of the jersey, not the back, that was important. For guys raised in the South Hills who grew up with baseball in their blood, anyone who donned the black and gold sat on a pedestal and was worthy of reverence, and it would be damn hard to say no to them.

Koch's baseball memories are part of who he is, and more often than not his stories always come back to the Pirates previous home at Forbes Field in Pittsburgh, otherwise known as the House of Thrills. "What a ballpark to go to. Ah, that was the park. That was heaven to me. When that ball was hit at Forbes Field in a night game, it would literally disappear into the darkness. There were no stands to see it bounce around in or people to grab it. It went straight into Schenley Park. You would see it going, and then once it went past the lights, it was gone; it was into the night."

=====

ON JUNE 12, 1981, a strike by the Major League Baseball Players Association caused a work stoppage and the cancellation of 713 games. During this time, according to Shelby Greer, he and Dave Parker spent a great deal of time together. Greer had moved back to Pittsburgh in 1981, and following the strike, which ended the last day of July, he became something of a regular in the Pirates clubhouse, frequenting the players' quarters between ten to fifteen times during the tail-end of the 1981 season. This was Greer's peak period for selling to major league ballplayers. He had also been in Houston for Rod Scurry's first victory against the Astros and delivered, at Parker's request, a quarter ounce of cocaine to the Shamrock Hilton, where the Pirates were staying.

Scurry made six subsequent starts following his debut victory. The youngster pitched well, but as a member of the pitching-heavy Pirates, it wasn't long before he was back in the bullpen. By 1982 his role as a full-time member of the Pirates bullpen was cemented. His starting days were behind him.

For somebody who was quiet to begin with, Scurry talked even less when using cocaine at the ballpark. He feared his mouth would betray him. He had begun living his life in secret. By his own account he became a con artist of sorts and "got to be pretty good at it." He couldn't let the outside world know that his life was now controlled by cocaine, and he became even more introverted. His future wife, Laura, later described to the Associated Press how tough it was for Scurry to deal with stress. "He had a hard time with pressure, and I think that's why he started doing what he was doing," she said. "It was the pressure of waiting and not knowing. The drugs made him quiet, shy, and scared. When he wasn't on them, he was normal and fun and happy."

In 1982 cocaine use had become routine for many major league ballplayers. The Pirates' John Milner would later say that he, Parker, Scurry, Berra, and outfielder Lee Lacy shared up to seven grams a week with one another during this time. "If I had it, I shared it; if they had it, they shared it," he said. In fact, it was so common that the first thing Scurry and Berra thought about prior to the season's home opener was making sure someone had called Shiffman for easy home game delivery. Nothing said opening day like the sound of Pirates organist Vince Lascheid banging out a few notes of "Let's Go Bucs," the smell of hot dogs wafting through the stadium, or the prospect of an eight ball of cocaine to take it all up a notch.

6

The Kings of Pittsburgh

WHATEVER THE PRICE, BY WHATEVER NAME, COCAINE IS BECOMING THE ALL-AMERICAN DRUG.... A SNORT IN EACH NOSTRIL AND YOU'RE UP AND AWAY FOR 30 MINUTES OR SO. ALERT, WITTY, AND WITH IT. NO HANGOVER. NO PHYSICAL ADDICTION. NO LUNG CANCER... INSTEAD DRIVE, SPARKLE, ENERGY.
—*TIME* MAGAZINE, 1981

THE NEIGHBORHOOD of Garfield was settled on the hills above the Allegheny River in Pittsburgh's East End. Up until the 1960s Garfield was home to predominately Catholic, working-class families. Its earliest inhabitants worked the mills along the Allegheny River and shopped locally from the merchants along Penn Avenue. Neighborhood activist Aggie Brose recalled to the *Post-Gazette* that Garfield was once a place where "you sponsored each other's kids, you went to all the weddings and funerals, you never wanted for a babysitter.... When you put the kids to bed, the women went out on the stoops."

In the latter half of the 1960s and early 1970s, Garfield's citizens moved to nearby suburbs. Soon, the small businesses in the community were boarded up, and public housing projects sprouted up in the area. As more and more residents continued to flee, twenty-four-year-old heating and cooling repairman Kevin Connolly and his family remained.

Connolly was an all-state baseball player at the sports power-house Central Catholic High School, the alma mater of Hall of Fame quarterback Dan Marino. Connolly himself later played semipro football as a member of the Pittsburgh Tri-Ward Rebels.

If anyone could attest to what a slippery slope cocaine use could be, it was Connolly. Early during the 1982 baseball season, he was introduced to Rod Scurry on a double date arranged by the pair's girlfriends. During the evening the talk turned to cocaine. Up until this point Connolly had only tried the drug a few times. "That night we all pitched in and got some," Connolly says. "Then we went out again the next Friday."

Before long the foursome was hitting the town three nights a week, when Scurry wasn't out of town with the Pirates. Doing coke became an integral part of the evenings, with Connolly struggling to match funds with the well-to-do pitcher. From fifty dollars on the first occasion, the price of admission seemed to grow with each ensuing outing as the group's drug consumption increased. After a month or two the evenings were costing the young repairman a minimum of $100 or $150. "I couldn't afford that," he says. "After going out three nights a week and pitching in every time, I couldn't do it, you know. Then I got this brilliant idea."

Connolly was having the time of his life hanging out with Scurry and the girls, and he had to find a way to make things work. He had to "find somebody that had [cocaine], get it at cost, then sell it." That was the key to staying in the game.

Initially, he didn't know exactly how or where to go about enacting his plan, but it didn't take him long to figure out. The East End was Connolly's turf. His business, Budget Air Conditioning and Heating, was located on Penn Avenue. He also played softball in the neighborhood. He knew people there, and he knew people who knew people. If he was going to find cocaine, the East End would be where he would find it.

Connolly began to regularly buy a quarter ounce of cocaine, which he would usually split, keeping half for himself and selling the other half to Scurry or sometimes a few other acquaintances or contacts. His new enterprise yielded hardly enough to make a profit. But he was doing free cocaine, and that was the whole point, anyway. On top of that, he was introduced to Dale Berra around this time, which was even cooler to the young sports fan. "Early on we didn't hang out that much," Connolly says, but he remembers it being a big deal whenever Berra did come around.

Connolly soon realized that his quarter-ounce purchase wasn't sufficient to keep up with the group's growing appetite for cocaine. It was time to up the ante. His next purchase was for a quarter kilogram. However, once initiated into the world of cocaine, it didn't take him long to realize the extent of the money-making opportunities now open to him. A quarter kilogram wasn't going to cut it either. The demand around him necessitated yet another increase in weight.

=====

NINETEEN EIGHTY-TWO was Rod Scurry's career year. If the switch to the bullpen bothered Scurry, he didn't let it show on the mound. He had the season of his life in 1982, saving fourteen games coming in as a reliever and posting a minuscule 1.74 earned run average, the lowest in the league of anyone with at least twenty appearances. The Pirates finished the season in fourth place, eight games off the pace.

Despite the fact that Connolly was emerging as a new supplier for Scurry, Dale Shiffman continued to receive calls from the pitcher throughout the season. Even on the road Scurry managed to hook up. In Philadelphia there was Curtis Strong. In Atlanta he ran into Shelby Greer at a club and scored from him. He snorted a gram before a game against Houston, and then went on to hold the Astros scoreless. From that point on, he figured drug use wouldn't hurt him when he pitched. Scurry's career ascent brought him an abundance of money and with it an abundance of cocaine. "Finally," he would later tell the *Pittsburgh Press*, "it got to the point where I couldn't quit."

Come opening day 1983, scoring coke had become paramount to Scurry. Personal matters were arranged first, before any baseball would be played. Once more the season began with a call to Shiffman.

===

A YEAR after meeting Rod Scurry for the first time, Kevin Connolly came to a realization: *This shit is everywhere*. Going out to clubs or parties with his new Pirates buddies, he saw cocaine use so out in the open, so common, that he looked around and quipped, "Cocaine is legal, isn't it?" This pervasiveness made him feel like he wasn't doing anything wrong by partaking, but now he was going to get in on the real action. By 1983, Garfield's Kevin Connolly was heading to Miami to trade forty thousand dollars for two kilos of cocaine.

The deal was arranged through a girl he knew from the Pittsburgh area who was dating a supplier in Florida. From there a regular hook-up would be cemented. The suppliers taught Connolly the ropes, including how to pack his product for safe airline travel. The cocaine, which came in a large chunk, was placed in a plastic bag. The bag was then placed inside another bag and dipped in mustard. This package was placed into "another bag that had coffee grinds in it," Connolly explains. "So we had three bags going.... Then we just sewed it into my jacket, and I'd walk through the airport."

The experience tested Connolly's mettle as his heart raced with fear; oddly enough, he found it to be an enjoyable fear. Transporting drugs gave him a rush he would come to love more than using the drug itself. He always stayed straight for the transactions and the transport. But that didn't stop him from getting high. These deals became Connolly's new source of adrenaline, and physiologically they took him places cocaine never did. If, for instance, a group of police dogs stood ahead of him, Connolly would not change his course; instead, he would walk straight toward the dogs, pushing the thrill as far as it could take him.

The scene in South Florida was like something out of a movie for the novice drug trader. Deals went down anywhere, from inside beautiful yet bullet hole–riddled houses to aboard *Miami Vice*-style cigarette boats. Other times, if his connection happened to fall through, he could score kilos in the parking lots of Miami's or Ft. Lauderdale's after-hours clubs.

"There was like ten or twelve people there who all had kilos in their car," he recalls, "and they'd say 'Try my stuff.'" One person's loss was another man's gain, and somebody was always more than happy to help out an out-of-towner.

"It was just a joke," Connolly says. "There was just so much down there. I'd go out to the car, and they'd open up the trunk and they'd have like five keys [kilos] in it. Then another guy would say, 'Hey, look at my stuff, man; I'll give it to you for a hundred cheaper.'... It was like how you could get ounces in Pittsburgh, you could buy keys down there." He could walk into a bar "knowing nobody," and kilogram transactions were still guaranteed. "What a joke," Connolly repeats.

Back in Pittsburgh, not much changed for the repairman. He kept up appearances. He ran his business with the help of his childhood friend Tommy Balzer. Growing up, Balzer and Connolly's lives had revolved around sports, and they had played on a variety of sports all-star teams together. By the 1980s, with their friendship still intact, Balzer began to work with his old friend, and since Connolly's business now ventured into the drug world, Balzer helped out in that arena as well. Connolly called his friend's role in this area more of an administrative position. "He was more like a secretary," Connolly says. "All he was in charge of was watching me. He would write down who we owed money to, stuff like that."

They did their work and ran a legitimate business, and by day everything remained the same. Nearby residents never suspected a thing. "They don't have anything," said Tom Balzer's neighbor John Hughes, referring to the pair's modest lifestyles.

"You should have seen my place," Connolly says. "What a dump. But then you'd have a Mercedes or something like that pull up; it didn't make any sense."

"He was a steady worker," Hughes said of Balzer. He "would come home every night dirty black, like a coal miner." Balzer sometimes drove a beat-up red truck labeled BUDGET AIR CONDITIONING AND

HEATING, and when he arrived home after a long day of work he appeared to be nothing more than a regular family man. "He and his wife and their two small boys would jump in the car and go out together all the time," Hughes told the *Pittsburgh Press*. "Nobody would come to his house much. He was a quiet guy, a nice fella." Hughes also commented that Balzer was a regular on the basketball courts of Butler Street during the summer.

Connolly's neighbors described a similarly unremarkable scenario. "[Connolly] would work all day, then come home, and you would not see him until the next morning when he went to work again," said neighbor Terrence Carney.

It was when darkness fell that Connolly felt like the king of Pittsburgh. When he walked into a club and hung out with his new Pirates buddies, people turned to look. But it wasn't just to check out their local sports heroes anymore. Connolly was making his own mark. He could hear the whispers—*Hey that's Kevin Connolly*—and see the patrons gawk. Connolly says the club Heaven was where the in-crowd gathered. It was Pittsburgh's answer to Studio 54 or the like—the club everyone talked about and went to be seen. Known for its grand marble staircase and white interior, Heaven also had private lounges and held events such as beach night or hot tub night. Connolly often joined a number of the Pirates and Steelers there. "[Lynn] Swann was there all the time, Mel Blount, Franco [Harris] too. It was the only place in Pittsburgh where everyone went," Connolly says.

Despite making his own name for himself, Connolly could not deny the benefits that came with hanging out with athletes. Rod Scurry, for example, was known to attract a particular crowd. "Yeah, all the girls would know who he was," Connolly says. This was a definite bonus for the lighthearted and good-natured Connolly, who was also not dumb to the allure that the little white powder he carried possessed. Right or wrong, he employed this magnetism to his advantage. *Let me buy you a drink*, he would say while reaching into the "wrong" pocket for his money. He religiously kept his coke in one pocket and his money in the other, always the same ones so that he would never make a mistake in front of the wrong people, such as law enforcement. Pulling out his abundant supply of blow, which was obviously much larger than most, he would make his female companions weak in the knees. *Whoops*, he would innocently declare, finger on his lip like a schoolboy. Needless to say, Connolly and his buddies were not short of company most evenings.

One thing Connolly's baseball acquaintances *weren't* doing for him was making him any richer. Ballplayers are notoriously slow to their wallets. While some of them had voracious appetites for cocaine, this hunger did not translate to much money for those supplying it. There was a sense of privilege embedded in the athletes, as if they thought it should be enough for others to merely be around them. Other times they would adopt the stance, *What's the problem? You know I'm good for it! I'll get you later.*

"We never got paid," Connolly remarks. Berra always seemed to be broke and even had his own particular excuse at the ready. "I get my check next week," he would say.

"His checks were like $6,200, and he couldn't even pay me," says Connolly. Nor did Scurry. "You couldn't get it off him, either." Particularly if Scurry happened to already be holding; then it was an absolute certainty "you'd never see your money."

Tom Balzer hated dealing with the ballplayers, Connolly says. He didn't like them to begin with and couldn't care less about what positions they played or what the names and numbers on their backs read. He didn't like how they always expected shit for free, and he wasn't about to buy Scurry a beer every time the gang stopped at a bar. Balzer would rather sling bags on the street than sell to Berra and consequently have to chase his money for the next few weeks. That was what it amounted to when trying to get paid by these guys—chasing. Berra would at times end up paying by check, which even to the most uninformed observer seems an ill-advised move. Selling cocaine should be a cash business. Nobody wanted to have to explain what he was doing with a handful of Dale Berra's checks, written out to "cash."

It was inside Pittsburgh's after-hours clubs, selling to patrons rather than ballplayers, where Connolly was truly making his money.

"We had a nice little round," Connolly explains. "There was like five of them, and we'd hit them all starting at 2:30 A.M. The Allegheny Club was our first hit. Then we'd go *dahntahn* to Joyce's, or JJ's. After that we'd go up to Brookline, to the BYM Club [Brookline Young Men's Club], a little higher class, nicer place. From there we'd go to the Perry Social in East Liberty, and our last stop would be at the BBC down in Bloomfield."

All told the late-night rounds brought in around $2,800 on both Fridays and Saturdays. Add another thousand dollars or so during the day, and the weekends netted Connolly over seven thousand dollars. He puts his weekly gross profit at an estimated $13,000 at its peak. He would store the twenties and hundred-dollar bills in a shoe box and spend the rest. He blew through cash on women and partying as well as by charging the players less than he should have. For instance, many times he asked only two hundred dollars for five hundred dollars worth of coke. Connolly wasn't exactly maximizing his profits. He knew the money was dirty, that it wasn't really earned, so he felt no obligation to hold on to it. Still, he was having a damn good time.

=

Seven miles south of Pittsburgh, just through the Liberty Tubes, sits Banksville Road, a bastion of strip malls that cropped up in the 1970s as families migrated from the city to the bedroom communities encircling Pittsburgh. At 3105 Banksville Road, inside one such plaza, sat a nondescript tavern named Michael J's. It was the type of comfortable suburban bar where one could drink and talk and get something to eat. The Pirates' John Milner loved it for the chicken wings. Dale Berra loved it for the people.

Milner discovered the place in 1980, and he quickly turned teammate Berra on to it. "Michael J's is the type of bar like the ones I go to in New Jersey. It's a sports-oriented bar where a lot of guys gather around and talk football, baseball, and hockey," Berra said. "All my life I would think, drink, and eat sports. The people there were similar to my friends in New Jersey. I adopted it as a place to hang out."

Milner advised Berra, who in 1980 had not met Connolly or Shiffman, that if he wanted to score some blow he could do so from the bartender, Jeffrey Mosco. "I asked him to get me some," Berra remembered. Mosco made a phone call, and a half hour later Berra had his drugs. The relationship continued, with Mosco charging Berra what he had paid for the coke—fifty dollars for a half gram, one hundred for a gram. "I have no idea who gave it to him," Berra said, but he called Mosco his first cocaine source in Pittsburgh.

The bartender at Michael J's was a bear of a man who had worked his whole life in the service industry. An affable, easygoing, gentle giant, Jeffrey Mosco entered the workforce after dropping out of Peabody High School in the ninth grade. He eventually obtained his GED from Connolly Trade School. His first job was as a vendor at Forbes Field, which he did for a few years before becoming a bartender. He began working at Michael J's at the age of eighteen and made between $170 and $200 a week. In 1983 Mosco was twenty-eight years old and resided with his mother, with whom he split payments on a four-thousand-dollar car loan, in the community of Morningside, near Garfield in the city's East End.

Mosco and Berra grew close. "He was a good friend of mine... a personal friend," Berra said of the bartender. The two became so tight that in time Berra leased his luxurious townhome in the North Hills to Mosco and another friend for a nominal fee.

The bar wasn't much, but John Milner loved Michael J's and spent as much time as he could there. During the offseason, not having to play baseball meant Milner had time to kill at the nightspot. "I used to go there every day," he said. In late 1982 Milner met Robert William McCue at the establishment. Milner said McCue, like himself, used to frequent the pub every day. McCue was an accountant who worked as the comptroller for the Easter Seals Society. He was five feet ten inches tall and weighed 205 pounds. He wore a red devil tattoo on his left biceps and tinted prescription glasses. His friends called him Rav, and when the accountant would moonlight as a disc jockey at different nightspots around the city, including Michael J's, he would go by the moniker of Ravishing Rob. McCue had served a tour in Vietnam before entering college late. It took him only three years to graduate, at the age of twenty-six.

In 1983 McCue, like Mosco, lived with his mother. After the thirty-six-year-old two-time divorcee discovered the Banksville bar, his life started to revolve around its social scene. During the winters he coordinated a fantasy football league for the bar's patrons, including Milner and Berra. He organized barbecues and picnics at nearby South Park, as well as golf outings at Lindenwood Golf Club or South Park Links.

Milner joined in on all of the events. Not much of a golfer, he would take the opportunity to get some fishing in, spending his time on the links alone at a pond near the seventeenth hole. At Steelers games, Milner and the other denizens of the South Hills crew would regularly establish their presence at the Wall, a standing-only section of Three Rivers Stadium located beyond the end zone. Once, driving his Mercedes-Benz, Milner even chauffeured a carful of Michael J's wrestling enthusiasts, McCue among them, downtown to the Civic Arena for a night of wrestling action. On the card that evening were such "squared circle" legends as Hulk Hogan, Junk Yard Dog, Rowdy Roddy Piper, Big John Stud, Sgt. Slaughter, and the Iron Sheik.

For guys like McCue, as well as other suburbanites such as Shiffman and Koch, the drive from the South Hills to downtown Pittsburgh elicited a personal metamorphosis. Driving through the Liberty Tubes, they emerged from the tunnel shed of the skin of their old personas. Now amid the U.S. Steel Building and other sky-scrapers, they were no longer just one of the guys. On this side of the river they shined under the bright lights of the city. They walked the streets, shuffled through the clubs, as men of importance. "We thought we were somebodies," Shiffman admits.

McCue said he first experimented with cocaine in 1983, a result of working two jobs. Out late as a disc jockey and up early for his career at the Easter Seals, he turned to cocaine. "The feeling that it gave me was that of like, I guess, a strong cup of coffee," he later described, also noting that his jobs took him "quite a few hours into the nights. And there were times I was working during the weekdays till two and three o'clock in the morning, then having to get up and to work at nine o'clock the next day. So, this is the time I remember when I first used the drug."

McCue described a communal setting at Michael J's, an environment where cocaine was distributed with a carefree give-and-take attitude. Speaking specifically about Berra and Milner, McCue said, "If I had my own special, just small little quantity, I would share it with them. Give it to them and say, 'Here. Pay me back later on, another time when you get some.' It was just a constant, you know, 'Here. You can have mine or I can have yours.' ... Nobody was trying to make any money out of it. ... I sort of lost money."

Whether it was perceived as having been bought or sold, given or borrowed, cocaine was exchanged for money, from McCue to Milner, twice in the fall of 1983. Both times the hook-up took place at Three Rivers Stadium during Steelers games: first on October 16 against the Browns and then again on November 6 against the Chargers.

McCue, like Connolly, was also the beneficiary of checks from Berra, although what exactly the checks were written for would later come into dispute. "He gave me checks for borrowed money," McCue said. "He borrowed money off me at least thirteen times... fourteen times." This could have been one more shining example of the big happy family sharing and giving at the Banksville Road tavern, or not, as Berra later stated that he had never borrowed money from McCue.

While Berra considered Mosco and McCue to be sources, McCue saw the landscape somewhat differently. When talking of the two Pirates, Berra and Milner, McCue said, "They weren't the only sources, I guess. There were two or three other people down there that also used it." He also made clear his feelings as to whether he himself was a supplier.

"I am not a dealer. I never was. I wouldn't know how to do it."

Rod Scurry later shined a different light on the accountant when he claimed that McCue introduced himself to Scurry in a restroom at a Station Square bar and told the pitcher that the product Scurry was receiving from Shelby Greer was "junk." According to Scurry, when he asked McCue how much of the drug "he could handle, McCue answered, 'Up to $50,000 worth of cocaine.'"

===

In his book *The Wrong Stuff,* pitcher Bill Lee writes, "The problem with groupies—or Annies, as they are sometime called—is that they can give you an inflated sense of yourself. They go into orgasm if you just look at them and can really make you believe that you're the second coming in the sack. It's rarely true. We're just regular human beings with excessively greased hormones."

Encounters with baseball Annies were usually enjoyed by the visiting team's players. Pirates mascot Kevin Koch didn't travel with the team, but in Pittsburgh even the Parrot earned his fair share of admiration. Growing up, Koch had been described as the typical "nice, regular all-American boy." As he grew into adulthood, local papers painted a similar portrait, albeit one with a bit more edge. As the *Pittsburgh Post-Gazette* put it, he was "the sort a mom would like her daughter to bring home, an earnest yes-ma'am kind of guy with a bit of the devil in him." An apt description. One Pirates' player who wishes to remain anonymous remembers Koch coming into the clubhouse one afternoon shaking his head with a sly grin. When asked about it, Koch opened up to the player, telling him that the girl he had met the previous night had an unusual request before they slept together. She had wanted him to don the Parrot head during the proceedings. Koch acquiesced. "Even *I* was able to 'bed' and drink anything I wanted," he admitted on HBO's *Real Sports* in 2006.

"The Parrot is a genuine local celebrity," wrote the *Pittsburgh Post-Gazette.* And with celebrity came the perks. "I pretty much had carte blanche wherever I went," Koch says. "Never asked for it, but that's just the way it ended up. Like owners of a nightclub or whatever—I'd come in, and they'd get to know me, and I would get the keys to the VIP room.... It was pretty crazy."

One evening he was chosen to judge a bikini contest at a local club. Blasted out of his mind, he spent the night alternating between a private upstairs room where lines were thrown out on the table like candy and then back downstairs amid the girls for his bikini-arbitrating responsibilities.

Then there were the "Pirettes," the Pirate ball girls, who were arguably among the most beautiful women in the city. "Drop-dead gorgeous," Koch's pal Dale Shiffman says. Both Shiffman and Koch hung out at the stadium with the Pirettes prior to games. In time Koch became close with the young women, sometimes too close. "I used to roll around a lot with them in the outfield until they told me to cut it out," he said. But overall Koch's performances continued to be well received. As *USA Today* put it, "His many antics at Three Rivers were legendary—from singing at second base with umpires to popping wheelies while flying over the mound on a motorcycle."

Shiffman, too, was living the high life on the Pittsburgh sports scene, from the green diamond of summer with the Pirates to the white ice of winter with the Penguins. "Dale's a great guy. He was always at the games," Penguins forward Kevin McClelland said. Added team captain Mike Bullard, "I think he more or less knew a bunch of us—ten of us. He probably knew everybody on the team to say hi."

Shiffman wasn't getting rich as a result of his role as a supplier. But it wasn't about the money for him anyway; it was about hanging out with his heroes and having fun. He didn't need much. He split his rent with a roommate or two, and when he needed money he found a freelance photography gig. Whatever money he was making from blow tended to go right back up his nose.

While there were some in the medical community who were still arguing in the 1980s that cocaine was "a safe, nonaddicting euphoriant," Shiffman probably should have known he was headed for trouble the first time he tried the drug, an experience he describes as "love at first sight." He slowly became addicted. The days of a little fun, in-control partying were long gone. He was now firmly in cocaine's grip and wanting more, more, more.

7

Strung Out

HE SAID HE WANTED HEAVEN
BUT PRAYIN' WAS TOO SLOW.
SO HE BOUGHT A ONE-WAY TICKET
ON AN AIRLINE MADE OF SNOW.
—HOYT AXTON, FROM "SNOWBLIND FRIEND"

A LOOK THROUGH the newspapers of the early 1980s would reveal a nation under the spell of cocaine. What started out in the 1970s as an amusing and polite party offering among the so-called glitterati crossed over to the mainstream in the following decade. No longer strictly for the rich, famous, or even the white-collar class, cocaine could just as easily be found in the nation's heartland among doctors, nurses, construction workers, pilots, schoolteachers, or students. It was, quite simply, America.

But where did this drug come from?

"*Erythroxylum coca* is a peculiarly ordinary-looking shrub native to South America," writes Dominic Streatfeild in his book *Cocaine: An Unauthorized Biography*, which provides a thorough examination of the drug's history. The shrub most closely resembles a camellia plant and would be of no real significance were it not the source of cocaine. "A less distinctive plant would be hard to find," Streatfeild writes, "yet coca has started wars, prompted invasions, embarrassed politicians, toppled governments, filled prisons, created billionaires, and bankrupted countries, and both taken and possibly saved thousands of lives."

Peasants in Peru and Bolivia have been chewing coca leaves for thousands of years, "long before the gringos arrived... and will continue for long after they leave." Ironically, the coca leaf is chock-full of vitamins. "Two ounces of coca chewed daily provided the chewer with all of the vitamins he needed (A, B2, E, calcium, iron, and phosphorous)." This was important in the Sierra region of South America, which is lacking in fresh fruits and vegetables. Sources of milk are scarce as well.

Cocaine, the active ingredient, was first isolated from the plant in 1862 by European scientists. Among the first to experiment with the drug was a young Sigmund Freud, who wrote enthusiastically of the new wonder drug, "It's as though the need for food and sleep were completely banished." Freud was smitten with cocaine and wrote of the drug in love letters to his fiancée: "And if you are forward you shall see who is the stronger, a little girl who doesn't eat enough or a big strong man with cocaine in his body."

When cocaine hit American markets in the 1880s the world's first coke craze was underway. During this period medical firms and drug companies started advertising campaigns promoting the drug. The nation's largest drug maker, Parke, Davis, and Company, claimed cocaine was "a drug which, through its stimulant properties, could take the place of food, make the coward brave, the silent eloquent, and free the victim of alcohol and opium habits from their bondage." Herman Guttmacher, editor of the *Vienna Medical Press*, wrote, "A whole new field has been opened up by the availability of Parke's cocaine, a reliable, effective, and purer cocaine. This is a beautiful white powder."

In 1884 cocaine was credited as the world's first local anesthesia. It didn't stop there, as it became a cure-all for late nineteenth-century Americans. Around this time the *Boston Medical Journal* reported that "the moderate use of coca is not only wholesome, but beneficial." Marketers in all areas of commerce recognized cocaine's earning potential and jumped onto the drug's bandwagon. Soon companies were hawking cocaine salve, cocaine cordial, coca lozenges, coca cigarettes, and cocaine wine. No matter the occasion or the ailment, cocaine was seen as the elixir.

One of the men chiefly responsible for introducing coca to the masses was the French chemist Angelo Francois Mariani. His contribution to society was Vin Mariani, a coca wine made by adding two ounces of fresh coca leaves to a pint of Bordeaux wine. The result was a smashing success. Pope Leo XIII, William McKinley, Ulysses S. Grant, and Thomas Edison were among those singing the drink's praises. Even baseball players took to the wine in the 1880s. In what could be considered an early endorsement of drug use in sports, Mariani's chief competitor, Metcalf's Coca Wine, touted in its ad: "Athletes… and baseball players have found by practical experience that a steady course of coca taken both before and after any trial of strength will impart energy to every movement."

In 1886 J. S. Pemberton took alcohol, the controversial substance of the time, out of the popular coca wine beverage. He then added syrup, kept the coca, and called his new beverage Coca-Cola. That year Coca-Cola flowed from soda fountains across the country. Bottled in 1894 and marketed with the slogan, "The ideal brain tonic," it was also said to relieve exhaustion.

As Streitfeild points out, the truth was that, excluding its use in "anesthetic surgical procedure, cocaine was not really curing anything, it was just making people feel great for a while."

Around the turn of the twentieth century the pendulum started to swing. From paranoid delusions to insomnia to malnutrition, the dark effects of cocaine were beginning to show. While use of the drug was still widespread, the benign veneer associated with having a cocaine habit was slowly cracking. Spurred by stories circulating in the South involving crime, rape, and unstoppable, cocaine-crazed black men, the temperance movement targeted the drug, and almost as quickly as it had been lauded, cocaine suddenly became feared. Users were classified among the ranks of low-brow society. "The bohemians, gamblers, prostitutes, burglars, racketeers, and pimps" were the new face of cocaine. In 1903 the Coca-Cola Company dropped the ingredient from its formula and became coke-free. (Today it uses a cocaine-free coca leaf extract.)

The Pure Food and Drug Act of 1906 was the first law to step in against cocaine. The act did not outlaw the sale of drugs but forced drug manufacturers to list potentially harmful ingredients such as narcotics or alcohol on their labels. But it wasn't until the Harrison Act of 1914 that the drug was officially banned and listed as a narcotic. While the entertainment industry clung to the drug they called "stardust" for some time afterward, cocaine essentially went into hibernation in America from the 1930s to the late 1960s.

Going into the 1970s, a new generation had no recollection of the drug's previous surge and burn. Unbelievably, by 1971 it was reported all over again that cocaine was nothing if not good for you. *Newsweek* magazine quoted a female student from the University of Tennessee who said, "Orgasms go better with coke." In the same article the Chicago Bureau of Narcotics deputy director reported, "You get a good high from coke and you don't get hooked." Streatfeild summed up the article, writing, "Together, these assertions—that cocaine is fun but not dangerous, that it's worth $125,000 per pound, and that it makes co-ed students at the University of Tennessee have better orgasms—are pretty much enough to make me stop writing this moment, leap out of my house, and score some right now. It would be hard to concoct a more positive piece."

Jill Jonnes, in her book *Hep-Cats, Narcs, and Pipe Dreams: America's Romance with Illegal Drugs*, explains that "the original 'war' on drugs in the early years of this century was so successful that we have no collective memory of that era." In the 1970s that certainly seemed to be the case. In 1974 the *New York Times Magazine* called coke "the champagne of drugs," contributing to the journalistic chorus claiming that it was a harmless and chic drug, a drug without a downside. A century's worth of documentation on cocaine's effects was ignored by the public, not to mention the medical community. Jimmy Carter's future drug advisor, Dr. Peter Bourne, described cocaine in 1974 as "probably the most benign of illicit drugs."

By the early 1980s the Colombian families in charge of cocaine distribution saw their profits soar to over thirty billion dollars. In time, however, they became *too* successful, as they began shipping too much of their product to the States, glutting the market and forcing prices downward. In Miami the price of a gram fell from one hundred dollars to fifty dollars. Suddenly, cocaine was affordable to the middle class, which was happy to join a party once reserved for the elite. As coke made its way into the suburbs it was welcomed by a generation fervently chasing power and status. Cocaine and the 1980s were a match made in heaven. Soon, cocaine was not only in again, cocaine was "it," and it was everywhere. Not even the death of John Belushi or the near-death of Richard Pryor—the result of a freebasing accident—could put a damper on the party. By 1982 over twenty-one million Americans had tried the drug, up from 5.4 million just eight years prior. Everyone was rolling bills. It reached the point where officials in Miami reported that not a single dollar bill passed through their banks without containing some trace of cocaine.

===

DAVE PARKER saw the cocaine rage as a passing fancy, calling it "something that was a fad." It was a fad that baseball players were not going to miss out on. "It was so prevalent in society that, you know, we *had* to be doing it too," Parker said in 2006. Of course, being a professional athlete who earned millions of dollars made such experimentation easier, but that wasn't always the case. Years earlier, once the season was over, many professional ballplayers had to take on second jobs to make ends meet. In the late 1960s and early 1970s Pirates infielder Richie Hebner had famously been employed as a gravedigger during winters back home in Massachusetts. Players from the so-called golden age of baseball simply could not have afforded a cocaine habit, nor was the drug as readily available. But as the 1970s came to a close, cocaine's popularity was skyrocketing right alongside players' salaries, beginning with Parker's million-dollar contract in 1979, creating the perfect storm. Adding to the storm were the trappings of celebrity itself. "I think anybody who's in the public eye and making any kinds of substantial money is going to be targeted to purchase or try cocaine," Parker says.

Former Yankees and Twins relief pitcher Ron Davis told the *New York Times* he never had to look far for cocaine, especially in New York. "I have seen a lot of cocaine around, not that any of our players took it. But it was there if you needed it. A guy would come up to you and say, 'Let's go into the back room, I got some stuff.' He was giving it to us for free if we wanted it."

Left-fielder Tim Raines of the Montreal Expos also spoke of cocaine's prevalence at parties, telling the *Times*, "Anytime there's a big party, there's going to be drugs around. That's the easiest thing to do, to meet someone."

But just as fans sought to ingratiate themselves with their home-town sports heroes, ballplayers had their desires, as well. They wanted to experience the same social diversions and be perceived to be as hip as their fellow "entertainers." Jack Nicholson and Waylon Jennings were prominently featured in *People* magazine as part of the 1970s "coke generation." Philadelphia Phillies pitcher Al Holland heard about cocaine use in high-profile clubs around the country and about celebrities using it. Shortly thereafter, he began using cocaine recreationally. Young athletes who suddenly found their pockets overflowing with money instinctively wanted to do what the other millionaires were doing at the time. Dr. Gary Wadler, an expert in the world of drugs and sports, described the situation: "Fame, for-tune, free time, and feelings of invincibility put athletes at risk."

Dave Parker noticed how the drug was spreading throughout society. "You got people in the front office [team management] who were probably doing cocaine too.... All branches of life used it. I know doctors that had problems.... It's not only athletes and enter-tainers.... Lawyers lost practices because of it.... It was a situation where if you didn't have a strong will, you had no business partici-pating in it."

Parker says he gave up cocaine on his own in 1982, after the birth of his oldest daughter. "I didn't want it to be a part of my daughter's life." Following the 1983 season, he left the Pirates via free agency for his hometown Cincinnati Reds. It had been a rough ride for him in Pittsburgh. The 1979 championship honeymoon was long gone. In fact, the glow from that season didn't last long at all.

===

ON JULY 20, 1980, the Pirates were taking on the L.A. Dodgers for a hot and humid afternoon doubleheader. Temperatures were expected to reach the nineties. More than forty-three thousand fans were on hand to honor their star first baseman as part of Willie Stargell Day. For forty-five minutes between games, tribute after tribute was made to the great slugger. A teary-eyed Stargell accepted gifts and thanked the fans. A short time earlier, prior to the top of the eighth inning of the first game, Dave Parker was also nearly brought to tears by a fan, but for much different reasons. Staking out his usual spot in right field, a black-and-copper Duracell battery flew past his head from the stands, possibly from the upper deck of the bowled coliseum. The three-ounce battery came at Parker with such velocity it bounced nearly two hundred feet upon hitting the outfield turf. Parker noted that he could hear the battery as it buzzed by his head. "Long lasting," he joked. "That's what I want to do... last longer than it." Despite the attempt at levity, Parker was deeply unsettled by the incident. On a day when the stadium was filled to honor one of his teammates, this was the tribute paid to Parker. "Man, it's my life; that could kill you. I've got a lot of good years left. I'm looking forward to them. I can't understand that."

Parker was making a million dollars a year in a blue-collar town. He wore a diamond in his ear and walked with a swagger. He was hardly soft-spoken. He understood that he wasn't for everybody. "You pay your money, you've got a right to do something, verbally," he said. "But this... it's getting unbearable.... That was too close.... When you can hear it, it's too close."

Parker had experienced objects thrown at him before. In fact just two weeks prior in New York something was whipped at him while he was in the batter's box. But Three Rivers was his turf; these were his fans. As *Pittsburgh Post-Gazette* columnist Phil Musick put it,

Pittsburgh was "Home. Where they've watched him win two bat-ting titles and play a peerless right field. Home. Where a year ago, they watched him help fire a pennant race that led to a world cham-pionship. Home. Where for more than two weeks, he played every day with a shattered face. Home. Where even the most ignorant among them understand that he is irreplaceable, that he plays the game as hard as it can be played, that he has a history of producing under pressure."

Nonetheless, following the battery incident Parker reportedly demanded a trade. Thereafter, injury led to surgery, which led to weight gain. He would battle both injury and weight issues the remainder of his time in Pittsburgh. He became a lightning rod for criticism. Bob Smizik of the *Pittsburgh Press* lightheartedly described Parker's plight by writing that he could hit three home runs and drive in eleven runs in a lopsided Pirates win, but after the game, "of the forty-two talk show calls, twenty-seven complain bitterly that Parker struck out with a man on third in his last at bat."

Smizik later wrote, "The town has never understood the man. The man has never understood the town. It's a pity."

Following the 1983 season Parker went home to Cincinnati. For his fellow players who had, unlike himself, continued down the cocaine road, he could only sympathize. "Some of the guys that did have major problems with it... you felt it. Poor Rod Scurry."

=

KEVIN CONNOLLY had just returned home after an afternoon of fishing. At his back door to greet him was Rod Scurry. Connolly had expected him but not until later. Connolly thought the Pirates had a game but simply figured it had finished already.

"Hey, what's up? What happened with the game?" Connolly asked.

"Ah, fuck that shit," Scurry answered.

"Why, what's going on?" Connolly inquired.

"Ah, they're assholes," Scurry said.

Connolly invited Scurry inside, not fully understanding what his friend was upset about. He then headed to the shower to get cleaned up. After he came out and got dressed he found Scurry seated on the couch in the living room. Connolly flipped on the television and was shocked to see the Pirates game on.

"I was like, *oh my God!* And it was the end of the game, too." Just when the team might have been calling on the relief pitcher. Connolly looked on in disbelief. He listened as the announcer called the action: "It's the ninth inning, and there's a lefty in the on-deck circle. I wonder why Scurry isn't warming up."

Connolly turned and laid his eyes on the pitcher, who was anxiously waiting to purchase some cocaine. In response to the announcer's query Connolly silently shouted to himself, *Because he's in my fucking living room, that's why!* But Scurry didn't bat an eye.

"He didn't care," Connolly says.

Connolly knew Scurry was in trouble. He had been acting strangely all season. In fact, all around town things were getting weird. Prior to his departure from Pittsburgh, Dave Parker had been woken up one night by a phone call from Shelby Greer. It was 4:00 A.M., and the dealer couldn't get rid of Dale Berra, who was searching through the house, flipping through flour cans and other items, scouring the place for cocaine. Parker got Berra on the phone. "We've got a game tomorrow," Parker said. "Why don't you get home?"

At the ballpark, too, clues were popping up concerning a link between Scurry and Berra's drug use and their play on the field. "The signs were there," *Pittsburgh Press* sportswriter Bob Hertzel opined. "Dale Berra couldn't perform the simplest task. He was picked off first base with a 3-and-0 count on the batter." This is an inexcusable act for a base runner and the sign of a player lacking concentration. Berra wasn't alone. While he was daydreaming on the base paths, Scurry was in the bullpen snoozing away. He later told *Sports Illustrated* he fell asleep in the bullpen between twenty and twenty-five times during the 1983 season and had to be roused when he was called on to pitch. His cocaine habit had him so run down, he said, he even fell asleep while standing up in the outfield during pregame batting practice.

Scurry's teammates said nothing. "I didn't think there was a problem," fellow reliever Don Robinson says, explaining that Scurry never really talked much to begin with. At the ballpark Scurry's social interactions amounted to some brief small talk with Robinson and fellow pitcher Jim Bibby while in the outfield during batting practice. At spring training Scurry lived at the beach alone. Off the field the only teammate he really mixed with was Berra, who was also using. So in this respect, according to Robinson, it would have been difficult for any of the other players to ascertain whether something was amiss in Scurry's life.

Scurry's performance suffered in 1983. The young lefty had a terribly disappointing year on the mound, finishing the season with a 4–9 record to go along with an inflated earned run average of 5.56. He pitched only 68 innings, down from 103.2 the previous year. *Press* writer Bob Hertzel later noted of Scurry, "He was talkative one day, withdrawn the next. He lost concentration and his ability slipped." With the lousy performance came Pittsburgh's boo birds. The 1983 season delivered a blow to Scurry's self-confidence. In response he turned even more to cocaine.

In Scurry, Kevin Connolly saw a man who hated his job. "The only reason he was playing the game was for the money. He didn't care about baseball," Connolly says. But Connolly had only known Scurry for a brief amount of time. He hadn't seen the boy who had devoted his life to making it to the big leagues, the young man who gave everything he had to the game, playing ball every day for months-long stretches and loving every minute of it. That kid was long gone. Connolly saw someone different, and that person was falling quickly. "He couldn't control himself," Connolly recalls. "He was using during the game. There's a line, where it goes from partying— but this was way over partying."

What had started out as a gram-or-two-a-week habit quickly escalated. Dale Shiffman said Scurry's requests were now reaching "seven, eight, nine grams a night" and costing the pitcher between five hundred and one thousand dollars per evening. "I just saw him get so sloppy sometimes," Shiffman told the Associated Press. "Where he was actually snorting coke in bars and restaurants and coming out of the bathrooms. I told him, 'Hey man, you've really got to cool it.'" Because of Scurry's indiscretion, his local connections began to steer clear of him. "It got to the point where Rod used to call me, and I would end up lying to him or avoiding his phone calls because I knew he had a big problem," said Shiffman.

Kevin Koch recalls, "I never saw something overtake somebody like it did [Scurry]. He was such a good guy, such a quiet guy. Fun to be around. He had that shy laugh; he was just a super guy. And then to see him just not be able to have any control at all. He had no control."

Shiffman filled his friend Koch in on all the late-night calls and unannounced knocks at the door, which, for as low as Scurry was sinking, still came as a surprise to Koch. "I knew it was bad," Koch says. "But I didn't know that it had gone to that level."

Scurry took off for Sparks following the 1983 season. Maybe some time with the family was just what he needed. During his minor league days he used to call his parents up to three times a day as he struggled with homesickness. Scurry loved being around his family. His father remembered the day Rod left to start his career, directly out of high school. "I'll never forget that expression on his face when he turned around and looked at his brother Rick. It was a feeling of family devotion," Preston Scurry told the Associated Press's Steve Wilstein. "He just hated to leave home."

"It was horrible," Scurry's mother, Betty, added. "He wanted to play ball, but he did not want to leave home. After he signed he said, 'I'm not going. I can't leave home.' I said, 'Rod, Pittsburgh owns you now, you have to go.'"

Each ensuing spring the family relived the separation pains anew. "It was just as hard on us as it was on him," said younger brother Rick. "Every time we went to the airport, or when he was driving, everybody cried. It never changed."

This time when Scurry arrived home, however, things were different. His priorities had shifted. He stayed in a hotel room the majority of the time so he could get high freely and uninterrupted, which was about four times a week. He never slept there, though. Instead he stayed up late watching television and doing coke before returning home in the morning, when he knew nobody would be there. He did everything in his power to keep from talking to people, including avoiding telephone calls.

One night in February 1984 Scurry reached his breaking point. Following yet another coke-filled evening, he sat alone in his hotel room desperate for help, crying and hoping someone would mysteriously appear to save him. He finally decided the best way to quit his drug use was to quit drinking. The next morning, as he later recounted to *Sports Illustrated*'s Ivan Maisel, he returned home, where he told his parents that he was quitting baseball as well. Four days later he was drinking again. His declaration to give up baseball did not keep either.

====

SHELBY GREER made a dozen trips to Florida in 1983 for the sole purpose of purchasing cocaine. Sunshine, bikinis, and piña coladas were not part of the scene for Greer. Instead his Florida trips meant money scarcity, rental car worries, and nights spent sleeping in his car on the side of the road. He took night flights through People Express Airlines or American International Airways for anywhere from $98 to $139. Greer, who was later obliged to detail his cocaine enterprise in court documents, wrote, "The minimal traveling expenses permitted me to travel to Florida even though I could occasionally only afford to purchase quarter-ounce amounts of cocaine. Providing I had at least six hundred dollars, I was able to purchase seven grams for four hundred dollars, which allowed me to spend two hundred dollars on my airfare and rental car expenses."

Sometimes, despite the precise planning, things didn't always work out to the penny. "On several occasions I was forced to borrow twenty dollars from my supplier for return expenses," he said. Other times even a loan from his dealer wasn't enough to get him back home. On one occasion, Greer recalled, "Upon arrival in Pittsburgh, from West Palm Beach, via Newark… I realized I did not have enough money to pay the eleven dollar airport parking fee. I paid the attendant eight dollars and left my watch for collateral.

Later that afternoon I returned to the airport parking office and paid the general manager three dollars, at which time my watch was returned. I frequently experienced a shortage of funds throughout my travels to Florida. I continually borrowed money from friends and my bookmaker."

Greer was now dealing with a supplier in Florida known by the name of Ted. Ted gave Greer his pager number, and unless Greer called from a number with a 305 Florida area code, Ted would not return his call. This meant that on several occasions Greer had to fly to Florida without even knowing whether Ted was in town and they would be able to hook up. This caused a logistical nightmare for the tight-fisted Greer, who often rented multiple cars during a single trip in order to save a few bucks. "On the January 29 through February 3 trip I rented three cars during the five-day period.... I returned the second car because I could only afford to pay for one additional day's rental charge." Three times Greer returned to Pittsburgh empty-handed, as he was unable to locate Ted.

Greer rarely paid for lodging. "I ordinarily arrived in West Palm Beach after 3:00 A.M. I either stayed at one of my two friends' houses... or if I arrived after 4:00 A.M., I ordinarily slept in the car I rented, which I parked on the shoulder of Interstate 95 between West Palm Beach and Ft. Lauderdale. On a few rare occasions, I stayed at the Trade Winds Hotel, which cost me less than twenty-five dollars per night during the off season." A couple of times he stayed at the Holiday Inn, which had a rate of fifteen dollars for late-night arrivals. But that was the extent of his hotel stays. He wrote that he was staying at the Marriott on his car rental agreements, but that was just a cover to make him seem more respectable. "I have never stayed there, nor could I have afforded the expense to stay there. Even if I could have afforded the expense to stay at a Marriott hotel, I would not have wasted my money extravagantly on Marriott lodging."

Hypothetically, dealing cocaine should have led to an opulent life on easy street. Jerry Jensen, former West Coast regional director of the Drug Enforcement Agency, told the Associated Press at the time that "for an investment of $10,000 and an airplane ticket, you can buy a kilo of cocaine in South America, bring it back here, cut it, and sell it for $2 million."

But Greer, despite having rich baseball players as some of his clients, was hardly living the flashy life of a coke dealer portrayed by Hollywood. In April 1983, in fact, Greer's roommate kicked him out of their apartment, keeping Greer's watch and television in lieu of the cash Greer owed for rent and bills. Greer had also been a recent victim of a burglary, with the thieves making off with 126 grams of cocaine. To top it off, he was also either getting paranoid or he was, in fact, being watched by authorities. He noted an incident near the Ft. Lauderdale airport, after he had just met and obtained cocaine from Ted. Greer was unhappy with the quality of his purchase and paged Ted to discuss the situation. "As I waited for Ted's return call," Greer recalled, "I called Dave Parker in his hotel room… to let him know that I was still planning to meet him in San Francisco approximately ten hours later [the Pirates were in L.A. playing the Dodgers that night]. As I talked to Parker, I noticed a man watching me from a parked car. I then suspected the police had listened to Ted's pager radio frequency, recorded the number of the phone I was using, cross-referenced the number, determined the location, and notified agents at the airport of my location. Ted never called back. I hung up, drove away, and then realized I was definitely being surveilled. I then went into a video/book store on U.S. 1, where I hid the one-and-a-quarter ounces of cocaine…. I returned the rental car and flew to Pittsburgh rather than San Francisco." There went another thirty-five grams of cocaine without a profit for Greer.

By the fall of 1983 Greer had reached a crossroads. "I became broke and frustrated because I always consumed more cocaine than I could afford. I decided to quit selling cocaine." However, just as in the case of Rod Scurry, the resolution didn't last. "I later decided to go back to Florida in October," he wrote, "to buy cocaine primarily for myself." Soon Greer was not only still selling but also buying and transporting more cocaine than he ever had before.

═══

NINETEEN-EIGHTY-FOUR WOULD prove to be a pivotal year for not only Shelby Greer but also for Pirates mascot Kevin Koch and his buddy Dale Shiffman; young heating and cooling repairman Kevin Connolly and his childhood friend Thomas Balzer; accountant and DJ Robert "Ravishing Rob" McCue; Michael J's bartender Jeff Mosco; and Philadelphia caterer Curtis Strong. The good times, the high times, would soon come to an end as friend turned against friend and scenes of backbiting and traitorousness unfolded. The dominoes were about to fall, with Rod Scurry playing a decisive role in knocking over the first one.

PART III

THE HEAT

8

A Night in L.A.

BASEBALL IS TRYING TO SOLVE ITS DRUG PROBLEMS, BUT IT'S GOING ABOUT IT THE WRONG WAY. AS LONG AS THERE IS NIGHT BASEBALL, 162-GAME SCHEDULES, AND LONG, BORING ROAD TRIPS, THERE ARE GOING TO BE DRUGS IN THE GAME.

—BILL LEE, FROM *THE WRONG STUFF*

THE PIRATES opened the 1984 season with a seven-game West Coast road trip. The club had played well in 1983 and finished the season in second place. However, Rod Scurry was one Pirate hoping to put a disappointing 1983 campaign behind him. After his stellar 1982 season, during which he had been showered with accolades, Scurry was considered one of the league's top relief pitchers, and the Pirates looked at him as a star in the making. His 1983 performance had been dismal as Scurry's addiction worsened, but good left-handed pitchers were hard to come by, and big things were still expected from him.

Scurry was slated to start the 1984 season as the Bucs' top left-handed reliever. In *Sports Illustrated*'s season preview on April 2, the stage was set: "If left-hander Rod Scurry can get the finest curveball in baseball over the plate, the pen will be even better." Still, if anyone had cared to look, it shouldn't have been difficult to see that a problem was brewing for the young Scurry. His appearance upon arrival at spring training should have been one telltale sign, as his weight was down a staggering twenty pounds.

On Tuesday, April 3, the Pirates began their season with a 5–1 loss to the San Diego Padres. In the game, Scurry pitched well with a scoreless inning of relief. After an off-day, the two teams met again on Thursday. In the bottom of the fourth inning with the bases loaded, Scurry was summoned from the bullpen to protect a 6–3 lead. Scurry quickly walked the only two batters he faced before exiting the game. However, it wasn't just that he walked the batters; he hadn't thrown a single strike. Eight straight pitches with none of them coming remotely near the plate. In fact, three of his pitches almost hit Padre third baseman Graig Nettles. The Pirates went on to lose the match-up 8–6, with Scurry picking up the loss. After the game, Scurry told reporters that "the plate was jumping," before adding, "I was wild. There's not much more to say."

The team traveled to Los Angeles after the game, set to take on the Dodgers the following night. Scurry retreated to his room at the Biltmore intent on forgetting about his poor performance. He had a coke connection in town, but he needed to be careful. A few friends on the team had recently begun keeping a close eye on him and making it difficult for the pitcher to hook up. They were regularly checking up on him and even kept their doors open to watch over Scurry's room and ensure that he received no visitors. However, in an example of how far addicts and dealers will go to conceal their enterprise, Scurry had his blow delivered to him inside the webbing of a new Rawlings baseball glove. Players were always receiving new gloves and equipment to try out, and even though the deliveries were usually made to the ballpark, not to a player's hotel, the glove's arrival aroused no suspicion. With Scurry's guardians satisfied that no contraband had entered the room, doors were shut, and players went to sleep for the evening. Scurry went on to party alone late into the night.

During the course of the evening, Scurry called his parents at their Nevada home. His behavior quickly caused alarm. "He was talking to us, and he blacked out," his father, Preston, recalled. "I called Don Robinson and had him go check Rod's room."

In the confines of his room, Scurry had begun to hallucinate. He saw snakes crawling around and became convinced that cameras had been planted inside the television set, watching him. Such hallucinations and paranoid thoughts are consistent with a condition known as cocaine psychosis, first described by Freud in 1884. Most users who snort powdered cocaine through the nose never experience psychosis. However, if the drug is used for many years or in day- or night-long binges—both true with Scurry—the condition becomes much more common.

Agitated by this perceived spying, Scurry fell into a rage, tearing the TV apart and turning the room inside-out. By the time Robinson, who had enlisted Dale Berra's assistance, arrived at the room, it was a complete mess. Robinson and Berra quickly summoned Chuck Tanner for help. Hotel security, having seen people frantically coming and going from the room, joined them as well. But the security guards were quickly whisked away, and despite the commotion and the fact that a pile of cocaine was found in the room, the pitcher managed to skirt any sort of legal trouble. Scurry later told *Sports Illustrated* he had snorted between fifteen and twenty grams of cocaine during his two-and-a-half day binge. Placed on the disabled list and ordered to a drug rehabilitation center, he flew out of Los Angeles later that morning.

In the papers in the ensuing days, the whole episode took on a slightly different hue. "Scurry Asks for Help, Admitted to Drug Center for Rehabilitation" read one headline in a local Pittsburgh paper. The story presented to those who had not been present at the Los Angeles hotel room ascribed somewhat heroic qualities to Scurry. "I'm proud that he came to us seeking help," Pirates GM Harding Peterson said. Pirates captain Bill Madlock joined in, adding, "It takes a big man to step forward the way he did." The tale from that night forward was that Scurry, with the help of friend and fellow Pirates pitcher Don Robinson, had walked into Chuck Tanner's office, admitted his problem, and asked for help of his own accord. The party line was evident, and the Pirates were sticking to it.

Scurry's West Coast scandal sent shockwaves throughout the city of Pittsburgh. "When the Scurry thing happened, it was over," Kevin Koch remembers. Dale Berra filled Kevin Connolly in on the story when the team returned from the road trip. "Stay away from Rod," Berra told him. "He's lost his mind.... He was taking apart the TV." Dealers, players, and friends alike knew that Scurry's transgressions meant only one thing—the party would quickly be coming to a halt.

After twenty-eight days at the Gateway Rehabilitation Center in Aliquippa, Pennsylvania, Scurry emerged re-energized and was officially declared clean and sober. The Pirates decided that the next step for a shy and introverted twenty-eight-year-old who was trying to stay clean was to stick him in front of a roomful of reporters and cameras. In a news conference on May 9 Rod Scurry finally let the whole country in on his secret. Admitting that he had almost died three times during the past year, Scurry was ashamed and remorseful but at the same time thankful and even displayed a hint of hopefulness.

"I was ashamed every time I went out and pitched," Scurry said. "Cocaine had a hold of me, and I couldn't quit. I hated myself." He admitted to using during games, before adding, "I didn't care about nobody. Cocaine was the number-one priority in my life. It came before my family, before baseball. In the winter I lived in a hotel room. I had no control over what I was doing."

Kevin Connolly, while not a cold-hearted man, couldn't help but look at the teary-eyed Scurry and slip out a chuckle. The whole scenario just seemed so unbelievable to him. He was at work, putting up some duct in a client's home, when the Pirates' press conference came on the television, pre-empting the afternoon's soap operas. Connolly knew what had really happened in Los Angeles, and with all of the backslapping congratulations going on, the whole affair struck him as staged and phony. The Pirates and the media made it seem like Scurry had just up and decided it was time to go to rehab, when Connolly knew that the night had ended somewhat differently.

Besides that, Scurry had stayed in the rehab facility for only twenty-eight days; it seemed a bit premature for him to be proclaiming he was saved from drugs. Not after a five-year affair with cocaine. "I'm working at it" or today's adage, "One day at time," would have seemed more appropriate. But in 1984 institutional drug treatment was still in its infancy. Dr. Alan I. Leshner, the former director of the National Institute on Drug Abuse, described early treatment.

"We didn't have a prescription or protocols of how you go through a treatment process. It was much more day to day, 'Figure it out as you go, use your own personal experience,' as the backdrop. It worked, but not nearly as well as our current techniques," Leshner said.

Scurry's parents had visited him at Gateway Rehabilitation and had come away less than impressed.

"My husband and I went back to see him, and I was very disappointed in the rehab center because I felt they were treating him as a big major league star and not as a drug addict," Betty Scurry told the Associated Press. The center even came equipped with a pitching mound for the pitcher to practice on and stay sharp.

"When my husband and I got there, we were greeted like we were coming to a big party. I cried all the way home because I felt they weren't doing the job.... I was very disappointed in it," she said.

Scurry's brother, Rick, also visited the center, but he came away more worried by what he had seen in his brother than by the surroundings. Rick felt Rod's attitude suggested he thought his addiction was behind him, that he could just put in his time and be done with it. Rick could sense that his brother's use of drugs and alcohol was tearing the two of them, who had always been so close in the past, apart. "When addiction becomes a problem, you start to become a dysfunctional family," Rick says. "The walls go up, even within the family, the walls start to go up a little bit."

After rehab and the press conference, Scurry was credited with a clean bill of health and was back in the game action by May 13. His return to Three Rivers Stadium, however, nearly triggered a good old-fashioned donnybrook inside the clubhouse. It turned out that Scurry's arrival at the stadium coincided with a visit by Shelby Greer, which was the last thing the vulnerable young man needed. A member of Pirates management and a nameless Buccos player learned of Greer's visit, and both became irate. The two searched the stadium for Greer, intent on provoking an altercation and removing Greer from the clubhouse permanently. In the end, however, the men's paths did not cross.

On the surface Scurry's release from rehab was good news for all those involved. It would also prove to be quite beneficial for a couple of FBI agents who had been patiently biding their time for a chance to speak to the pitcher.

9

The Agents

BASEBALL'S DRUG CULTURE GREW BECAUSE PEOPLE
LOOKED THE OTHER WAY, OR LIED ABOUT ITS EXISTENCE.
—*SPORTS ILLUSTRATED*, 1985

AGENTS WELLS Morrison and William "Bob" Craig began working together in 1981, while they were both in the special oper-
ations group (SOG), a surveillance unit of the FBI. Based in
Pittsburgh, the agents then both moved to the organized crime/drug
squad in 1983. The pair made a great team, with Morrison playing
the straight man Abbott to Craig's Costello. Morrison was matter-of-
fact, with nary a wasted word, while Craig liked to stretch his legs a
bit, taking the time to make a wisecrack or share a story. Regardless
of their techniques, they were known to get results.

In March 1984, prior to Rod Scurry's stint in rehab, a drug case
from Huntington, West Virginia, had been sent Morrison and Craig's
way for follow-up in Pittsburgh. The FBI agents were instructed to
interview Dale Berra and Rod Scurry. The Pirates were in spring
training at the time, so Morrison and Craig decided they would
delay the interviews until the team came north for the season.

U.S. Attorney for the Southern District of West Virginia Dave
Faber and his assistant, Wayne Rich, handled the Huntington case.
The story revolved around Pirates pitcher Don Robinson and dealt
with events surrounding some of the Pirates' activities during spring

training in Brandenton, Florida, the prior year. A resident of Huntington, Robinson had his friend Harry Severino drive his car south for him so he would have transportation while he was in Florida. In return, Robinson offered to put Harry up at his place. Severino happened to be a coke user who also sold a little on the side.

He also must have had some of the worst luck around, because during his brief stay in Bradenton, he managed to get himself caught up in the middle of an FBI drug sting. Once pinched, Severino did what Craig and Morrison said happens all the time: he started cooperating with the authorities and giving up the names of the people he was involved with. In this case, he just so happened to mention that he was partying with Dale Berra and Rod Scurry during spring training and selling drugs to the two.

Back in Huntington, while the Pirates were on their 1984 season-opening West Coast road trip, another piece of evidence turned up for Faber and Rich. They received a taped phone call from a Pirates player to the manager of a Huntington bar and restaurant. During the conversation the player, still in San Diego at the time of the call, expressed interest in buying cocaine. The bar happened to be owned by Don Robinson, who was ultimately cleared of any wrongdoing. Agent Craig later described him as "about as straight and narrow as you could expect a ballplayer to be." His choice in company was perhaps another story. Faber and Rich sent all their information north to Pittsburgh so that the agents there could follow through on this Pittsburgh Pirates theme.

On May 23, Morrison and Craig made their first foray into the world of pro baseball as they sat down with Dale Berra and his lawyer at Berra's North Hills apartment complex known as the Mews. Berra, however, was less than open with the agents, and the pair left the apartment with little useful information. They felt that Berra was in denial about the seriousness of the situation, including his obvious involvement.

On that same day, the agents heard from Pirates management for the first time regarding its players and cocaine. The timing of the call didn't go unnoticed. "That's gotta be more than a coincidence that the day we interviewed Berra, the Pirates call the office and say, 'By the way, there's a guy that's a friend of Dave Parker who's been hanging around the clubhouse and traveling around with the team,'" Craig recounts. The man in question was none other than Shelby Greer. Pirates officials were clearly signaling that they weren't ignorant about cocaine use on the team, and now that the FBI was investigating, they were ready to lend a hand.

On June 22, the agents finally got their chance to speak with Rod Scurry. They met him and his lawyer at Scurry's home, also located at the Mews in the North Hills. Scurry turned out to be much more forthcoming than Berra. He named five sources from whom he had bought cocaine: Dale Shiffman, Shelby Greer, Kevin Connolly, Jeffrey Mosco, and someone Scurry knew only as Curtis. He also named five players from the Pirates whom he believed were using: Dale Berra, Dave Parker, Lee Lacy, Lee Mazzilli, and Jim Bibby. (Bibby's name was later cleared by the agents, as he was found to have no involvement.)

Rod Scurry's allegations formed the foundation for the FBI's investigation into drugs and the major leagues, which proceeded in two directions. On one front, they continued to interview the players named by Scurry; on the other, they set up surveillance on the dealers.

With the baseball season in full swing, setting up meetings with all the players proved taxing. "We chased these guys for months," Craig says. When Dale Berra was hospitalized at Passavant Hospital in the North Hills with an infected elbow near the end of the 1984 season, the agents thought they might seize the opportunity to talk with him again and see if he would disclose any information. Agent Craig even brought along a gift, a book about Dale's father, Yogi. When the agents arrived at the hospital, though, they discovered that Berra had already flown the coop. He was at Kevin Connolly's house within three hours, eager to make up for lost time and hook up with some coke. Berra wanted nothing to do with the FBI. According to Agent Craig, he fought them at every turn and admitted nothing. Finally the agents issued a warning through his attorney. "We understand he's in denial. That's fine, but it's going to come to a crashing halt eventually. So you might as well start talking to him, if you haven't already," Craig told Berra's attorney.

But Berra was nothing if not loyal and refused to give up his friends. In the FBI's 302 report (a written summary of an interview) of their June meeting with Berra, the agents wrote that he "refused to identify his suppliers of cocaine, stating that these people are small time and would have to make a special effort in order to obtain cocaine after Berra asked for it. Quite often these individuals would be personal friends of Berra's."

After the initial Berra and Scurry interviews, the agents discussed their case with U.S. Attorney J. Alan Johnson. Johnson in turn contacted Scurry's attorney, and the issue of immunity was discussed and proffered in exchange for information. On September 21, the agents returned to Scurry's house, where he was living alone. Even with the offer of immunity, Agent Morrison wasn't particularly optimistic.

"I don't think we knew what to expect. We'd done so many interviews before. You never know what you're going to get from people, so I don't think we had any particular expectations," Morrison says. Not to mention that Scurry had clearly put his newfound sobriety behind him. It had been only a couple of months since Scurry left rehab, but, according to Agent Morrison, it was evident within minutes of their arrival at the interview that Scurry seemed wired and was struggling to keep a grip on himself. Agent Craig sums things up bluntly. "Poor Rod, he was just a wreck. Even on his best days, he was a wreck."

Initially, Scurry provided the same information he had given in his June interview. The agents pressed him, but the group, which included Scurry's lawyer, continued to cover the same ground over and over again. Finally the agents figured they were finished, and everybody stopped talking. After a prolonged silence, Scurry's lawyer finally spoke up. He understood that the immunity the U.S. attorney and he had discussed was contingent upon Scurry divulging everything he knew. It was up to the attorney to prod Scurry into giving up the dirt. The lawyer looked at his client and said, "Rod, this is what we talked about."

"I know— I know," Scurry said.

"This is the time we talked about," his lawyer said, again.

There was another long pause before Scurry spoke.

"I'm ready to tell you—what the story is. There's a network of drug dealers servicing the National League."

The agents were stunned. Still, they were cautiously optimistic. It wasn't a bad start, but, Craig remembers thinking to himself, "It's one thing to declare it," but to back it up was a whole different ball game. Yet back it up he did, as name after name of dealers, players, and locations came pouring out of Scurry's mouth. The fact that other National League teams were involved came out in the open for the first time. The name Curtis, which the agents had learned about during the first Scurry interview, now had a last name to go along with it.

Scurry described how the Philadelphia caterer Curtis Strong traveled to Pittsburgh to sell cocaine to the Pirates through his Phillies connections whenever the Phillies played at Three Rivers Stadium. The agents also learned that Shelby Greer had traveled with the Pirates to various National League cities selling to teams around the country.

Upon leaving the Scurry residence, both agents felt that, judging from Scurry's condition, there was little doubt the pitcher's playing days were nearly over. (He may even have been losing touch with reality, illustrated by Pirates GM Harding Peterson's call shortly thereafter to FBI offices to advise that Scurry had refused a urinalysis test because, in Scurry's words, he was "working for the FBI.")

The agents went directly from Scurry's house to a pay phone outside an Eat 'n Park restaurant to call U.S. Attorney J. Alan Johnson. When Johnson casually asked him what the pitcher had to say, Agent Craig relayed Scurry's statement regarding a network of cocaine dealers selling to players across the National League. Johnson promptly cut the conversation short. "Get in here now," was all he had to say.

The agents immediately began setting up surveillance on the suspected dealers. A pen register, which lists the numbers dialed from a phone, was placed on the pay phone outside Shelby Greer's apartment on Mt. Washington. On September 27, a call from Greer to

Dale Berra led Morrison and Craig to send some agents over to watch Berra's North Hills home. Sure enough, a deal quickly went down at Berra's front door, which he answered clad only in a towel around his waist. Money and drugs were exchanged, though not with Shelby Greer, who the agents had expected to see. The FBI learned of a new face in the game—Robert William McCue.

McCue, the DJ from Michael J's and comptroller who was presently on the clock at the Easter Seals Society, was doing a lunchtime cocaine delivery. The agents would later learn that it was actually Berra and McCue's second transaction of the day, and it wasn't even three o'clock in the afternoon yet. The multiple daily deals were something else Morrison and Craig were quickly coming to understand was typical ballplayer behavior. The pampered and skittish athletes never liked to carry a lot of drugs on them at once. Instead, they called their local connections to come and meet them usually before and after games. For some of the players, though, their habit was beginning to necessitate around-the-clock service.

The agents continued to piece their case together. Thanks to the Scurry interview they knew that McCue was part of the Michael J's crew at the Banksville Road bar, along with Jeffrey Mosco, Dale Berra, and John Milner. SOG agents quickly set up surveillance on the bar and soon spotted McCue and Milner together.

On October 5 the FBI moved on Kevin Connolly and Thomas Balzer. A week prior, Connolly had received a tip to play things cool for a while. "I just got a call that I was being watched, to not go to Florida. Well, I didn't want to hear that," Connolly says. "I had already set it up. So I just pretended it was a prank call."

Kevin Connolly was fighting reality. In 1984 his coke habit had increased dramatically. He had once gone through a seventeen-day stretch consuming an ounce of blow each day except for one—he had needed a day off. Despite all of the partying and the late hours, Connolly continued to keep up appearances and didn't slack off at work. While his coworker and friend, Tommy Balzer, played the part of the family man and retired to his home after work, most nights saw Connolly out at the clubs until two or three o'clock in the morning. After that he would head home and party there for a few more hours, until around 5:00 A.M. "Then," he says, "I'd go wake up for work at 8:30."

Some vague phone call was not going to slow Connolly's momentum. He was sliding down the same icy hill as Rod Scurry, and not even Scurry's well-publicized crash in the Los Angeles hotel room made a difference to him. He did have the sense to attempt to steer clear of Scurry after the pitcher returned from the West Coast. "Everybody was staying away from him," says Connolly. The word on the street was that Scurry was being closely watched.

But there was nothing Connolly could do to prevent Scurry from showing up at his house. The pitcher's cooperation with the FBI didn't mean his cocaine addiction was suddenly resolved. Connolly did his best to ignore the knocks at his door. On one particular evening this obvious brush-off struck a nerve with Scurry, who took out his frustration on Connolly's vehicle, landing a brick through Connolly's windshield. For good measure, he also ripped off the antenna. Within a few weeks, however, Connolly relented and let Scurry back into the circle. "I thought I was doing a good deal," says Connolly. "I'd rather that than him going out and people taking advantage of him. He didn't have nowhere to go; I figured if I kept him company, stayed up with him and talked with him, that he wouldn't do as much. I'd keep an eye on him, just watch out for him and give him a little bit instead of him buying a ton, and we'd talk about baseball n'at."

Connolly made his trip to Florida. During a layover at the Atlanta airport on the way home, he spotted someone watching him. The alarmed Connolly ditched his flight and jumped on a train. Feeling the heat, he stopped at a friend's place in Jeannette, Pennsylvania, outside of Pittsburgh, where he buried part of his stash prior to returning to his residence. Neither Agent Craig nor anyone from the Pittsburgh office was aware of or took credit for the suspicious character in Atlanta who had spooked Connolly. However, Craig did acknowledge that suspects often "heated up," or became suspicious, during the course of an investigation. Adding cocaine to the mix surely only intensified such feelings.

In the fall of 1984, Rod Scurry was laid up following knee surgery at the North Hills Passavant Hospital. Shortly after Connolly returned from Florida, he received a phone call from Scurry, who was requesting an eight ball of cocaine from his hospital room. Connolly didn't feel like going out, so he sent an acquaintance in his place. When Connolly's associate did not return with the money, Connolly realized he had been set up. First by Scurry and then by his friend, who, according to Connolly, got pinched delivering the coke to the hospital and quickly gave Connolly up.

"The kid was no good," Connolly says of his friend. "He was always a con artist."

Shortly thereafter, the agents obtained search warrants and conducted searches of both Connolly's and Balzer's residences. At Connolly's Garfield home, FBI agents began trashing the house, causing such a mess that Connolly felt he couldn't stand idly by. He finally showed the agents what they were looking for, taking down a plate of cocaine from the top of the refrigerator. All told, the agents confiscated around nine ounces of cocaine, along with various drug-measuring devices, from Connolly's home. At Balzer's Lawrenceville house the haul was lighter but no less damning as agents collected two ounces from the master bedroom, as well as the accompanying scales and paraphernalia. Just days after the search, both Connolly and Balzer began cooperating with authorities.

Morrison and Craig were intent on next gathering hard evidence on Shelby Greer. They knew that Greer was actively dealing at the local Station Square watering holes Houlihan's and Chauncy's, and they set up surveillance. But it took the agents a couple weeks just to understand Greer's behavior at the bars. They observed that Greer would go to Houlihan's, grab a barstool, and order a drink at the bar. He would put his money down in front of him and then suddenly rush off his stool. The agents figured it was simply a matter of nature calling, since he would leave both his money and his half-finished drink on the bar. However, when his disappearance continued for fifteen or twenty minutes, the agents grew perplexed. Finally Greer would reappear momentarily, and then he was off again.

"He was driving us nuts," Craig admits.

In time the agents discovered that Greer's actions made perfect sense. What he was doing was heading over to Chauncy's, his other hangout, where he would grab a seat, buy a drink—usually a gin and tonic—stay for a few minutes, and then head back to Houlihan's, just a minute's walk away. Back and forth he would go, all night long. As the agents would learn, Greer's actions were intended to let patrons know that he was available for business. He was simply keeping his face in the game at both establishments.

Between Michael J's and Greer's hangouts at Station Square, Morrison and Craig were spending the majority of their time rotating between different Pittsburgh nightspots throughout the fall of 1984, chasing and watching the dealers. "We were making our living in bars," Craig says. Still, that piece of hard evidence they were searching for on Greer continued to elude them.

═══

JAMES ROSS was a rookie. As a recent graduate from Ohio Northern University College of Law, his only legal experience so far was as a law clerk for United States District Judge Alan N. Bloch in downtown Pittsburgh. That changed in October 1984 when Ross, at the age of thirty, was sworn in as assistant U.S. attorney for the Western District of Pennsylvania. His motive for taking the position was simple—he wanted to learn how to prosecute. The day he was sworn in, his new boss, J. Alan Johnson, gave him his first assignment. "I'd like you to work with me on this case," Johnson told him, referring to the cocaine investigation headed up by Craig and Morrison. Johnson was grooming Ross to try his first case, which, as luck would have it, turned out to be followed by millions of people and to make front-page news across America.

While Morrison and Craig continued to watch the dealers and interview players, the attorneys began to present evidence to a grand jury. Their case thus far revolved around seven men who had begun dealing to major league ballplayers in late 1979. While in some cases the amounts sold were not large, the number of transactions, the attorneys argued, was excessive. Dale Shiffman was said to have sold on the same day as every Pittsburgh Pirates home game of 1983. The majority of the evidence, prosecutors claimed, would come from the ballplayers themselves.

Federal cases work differently than those at the local level, where law enforcement officers see local criminal activity and charge suspects on the spot. In local cases, the officers bring the case to the district attorney, who moves forward after the charges have been filed. A federal case, on the other hand, begins when federal agents (from the FBI, DEA, and so on) learn of criminal activity taking place. The agents then go out and investigate. If they determine that there is indeed criminal activity afoot, they take their findings to the U.S. Attorney's Office, where someone is assigned to the case to work with the agents. Search warrants, pen registers, and any other tools needed to conduct their investigation are supplied to the agents by the U.S. Attorney's Office. The agents check in with the U.S. attorney as the case progresses, and they work together to strengthen the case. Once enough information is gathered, the U.S. Attorney's Office will present its information and question witnesses before a grand jury, which meets three days a month for eighteen months. The grand jury hears the U.S. attorney's information on an ongoing basis, and the agents and U.S. attorney will then subpoena additional witnesses as needed to build and prove the case. The grand jury makes a decision as to whether to indict or not and is the body that actually issues charges.

The witnesses in this particular case were the ballplayers. They had two choices once subpoenaed. They could cooperate and answer the questions asked of them, or they could invoke the Fifth Amendment, which states that nobody may be forced to testify as a witness against him- or herself.

James Ross didn't have any illusions that the players were just going to waltz in and unburden themselves of their transgressions. "There was a significant problem in terms of cocaine usage by not only Pittsburgh players but with players throughout the league," Ross says. "We knew Pittsburgh was one city where cocaine was readily available to players, and the only way you were going to verify and support that was by getting the people who were purchasing the cocaine to cooperate with you. And the only way you were going to get them to cooperate was by first letting them know they could be the subject of the grand jury and then if they were willing to cooperate, they could get immunity depending upon what they were willing to say."

Simply put, in order to get to the cocaine suppliers, the government intended to go through the cocaine purchasers, who in this case just happened to be young kids' heroes, as well as millionaires. This was the standard way in which the Western District of Pennsylvania handled such cases. J. Alan Johnson, known as Jerry by his colleagues, had a reputation for being tough but also honorable and fair. His predecessor as U.S. attorney, Robert J. Cindrich, described Johnson this way: "Jerry will go after a guy; he'll try to get a conviction, and he'll try to put the guy away. But he won't bend or break any rules. Jerry is a stickler for playing by the rules, even those that work against him." Johnson had repeatedly pointed to narcotics prosecutions as one of the top priorities of his office. However, going after and prosecuting the users was not something that his office or his predecessors had done in the Western District in years.

Ross said he and his colleagues were operating according to standard procedure; if these had these been street dealers, then his office would have granted immunity to the purchasers in exchange for their cooperation in naming their sources, so ballplayers shouldn't be treated any differently. This logic turned out to be quite ironic because, in the coming months, as news surrounding the case became public, this belief in treating the players the same as anyone else was one thing the government was *never* accused of. The players were in fact perceived to be receiving special and preferential treatment.

J. Alan Johnson, who had attended only two professional baseball games in his life and knew few of the players' names, said his lack of baseball knowledge helped him to treat the case like any other. To him it was simple. "When you have a drug deal, you have two persons—one bought and one sold. It's a clandestine transaction. If you decide to prosecute the case, you have to give one or the other immunity," Johnson said.

Even though Johnson's stance would prove to be controversial, Ross applauded his boss's gumption and openness, saying, "It wasn't like he hid behind it. He just said, 'I made this decision for these reasons, and I stand behind it.'"

Johnson said as much himself, dismissing the notion that fear of controversy might cloud his choices. "I'm not in a public relations battle. If I was, I wouldn't have pursued this case. If you let public opinion bother you, you can't perform the job of U.S. attorney. Once you let everybody's opinion bother you, you become indecisive," he said.

In early October the first player, protected with the promise of immunity, was subpoenaed to appear before the grand jury: Pirates pitcher Rod Scurry.

==

AGENTS MORRISON and Craig continued to press the dealers throughout October. With Kevin Connolly now in the fold, the agents sought ways to use his cooperation to their advantage. On Tuesday, October 16, they had Connolly call his Florida connection, a man known only as Roland, to set up a buy. Connolly was able to arrange a deal between himself and Roland that would go down right in Pittsburgh. The agents were expecting big things from the meeting with Connolly's supplier and arranged for one hundred thousand dollars to be provided for show money. On Friday, October 19, Agent Craig, Kevin Connolly, and Special Agent James Benedetto from the SOG arrived at the Pittsburgh International Airport to pick up their guest from Florida.

Parked in front of the terminal at the airport, Agent Craig waited in the car while Agent Benedetto and Connolly went in to meet Roland. Agent Craig went through a quick mental checklist, making sure there was nothing on him to connect him to the FBI and blow his cover. *No ID, no badge, no gun.* His mind then shifted to the car itself. He had borrowed a rental car from a fellow agent for the airport buy because his own Bureau car was outfitted with the usual FBI radios, antennas, and so forth. The car should have been "clean," but at the last minute Craig felt the need to give the car a final once-over. *Overhead visor—check. Glove compartment—check.* But what about the trunk? Roland was going to need to put his luggage away. Craig made his way behind the car, unlocked the trunk, and popped it open. The first thing he saw was a large, conspicuous SWAT bag. His fellow agent must have left it behind.

Roland was due to appear at any moment, and there Craig stood with a bag full of guns, radios, and other FBI-related items. Craig looked around and spotted an Allegheny County Police Department sign. There was a subdivision office at the airport, and it wasn't more than a couple hundred feet away. Craig grabbed the bag and made a run for it. He swung open the station's door and dropped the bag on the floor.

"This is going to sound crazy, but I'm an FBI agent, and I'm right in the middle of something going down. Can I leave this bag here?"

Of course it wasn't going to be that easy. "Can I see your identification?" the officer requested. Agent Craig tried to explain to her that he was presently undercover and that time was of the essence, but to no avail. Finally he gave her the number to his office and hoped for the best. The officer put the call in to FBI headquarters, explaining that there was a man in her office claiming to be an FBI agent by the name of Bob Craig. When asked what the gentleman looked like, the officer replied, "Oh, I don't know, Jack Nicholson, I guess."

Agent Craig, who was nicknamed Wolf after the movie by the same name starring the famous actor, overheard the reply, "Yeah, that's him." He was permitted to leave his bag of guns so he could get back to his drug buy, which he did—in the nick of time.

In the end, the big deal the agents were expecting never transpired, although a smaller exchange between the agents and Roland for three thousand dollars' worth of cocaine was conducted in an airport hotel room later that evening. No arrest was made, though, as the agents still hoped to make a larger buy.

Since meeting Rod Scurry on their double date in 1982, Kevin Connolly had been running in the same cocaine circles as his friend and many of his fellow Pirates. Those circles also included Shelby Greer, and that's where the agents were headed next. J. Alan Johnson had let the agents know that he would authorize an indictment on Greer without Greer's being caught red-handed holding drugs and based solely on testimony if need be. This piece of news made little difference, however, to Morrison and Craig, who knew only one way to do their job: they gathered evidence. They were going back to Houlihan's in an attempt to use Connolly to set up a couple of con-trolled buys from Greer. Paired with undercover agent Benedetto, who occasionally wore a hard hat to the bar in his role as Connolly's construction-worker buddy, Connolly spent the next week making introductions and laying groundwork at Houlihan's.

On October 29 Agent Benedetto met with Greer for the second time that week to discuss drugs. On the same day he was introduced to Robert William McCue, from whom he tried unsuccessfully to score some blow. Two days later, on October 31, Kevin Connolly secured a one gram bag from Greer for one hundred dollars. The FBI now had drugs on the table in the case against Shelby Greer, but the agents were not letting up. The next day, November 1, Morrison and Craig told Connolly to discuss weight with Greer, who usually sold in gram amounts. Later that night Agent Benedetto and Con-nolly tried for the second time to purchase cocaine from McCue but were again spurned. This meant they would have to back off McCue. Two tries was the general rule of thumb; after that, if you continued to press someone to sell drugs and did eventually succeed, a good defense attorney could easily claim entrapment.

On November 5, FBI Special Agent in Charge Walter Weiner clued the agents in on one possible reason they were having no luck with McCue. Pirates Vice President Joe O'Toole had told Weiner that it had come to his attention that Jeffrey Mosco knew about Kevin

Connolly's cooperation with the FBI—which meant that McCue probably knew as well. The FBI presumed that the information was coming from Dale Berra, who was most likely trying to keep Mosco out of the mix and steer him away from trouble. By all accounts Berra considered the Michael J's bartender, who had attended Berra's wedding, a good friend.

10

The Wire

MY PUNISHMENT IS GREATER THAN I CAN BEAR.
—CAIN TO THE LORD, GENESIS 4:13

IN EARLY November thirty-two-year-old Dale Shiffman sat in his car outside a bar known as the Theme in the borough of Whitehall near Pittsburgh. It was almost three 'o clock in the morning, the temperature was low, and the thermometer was still dropping. Despite the frigid conditions, Shiffman continued to sit alone, staring out the window in a daze. His mind was focused on the phone call he had received earlier in the evening from Rod Scurry. Scurry had wanted to apologize and give Shiffman a heads-up.

"I don't know what you know or don't know," Scurry said, before revealing that he, along with several other baseball players, had been talking with federal agents. "And I'm telling you flat-out, we gave you up. You might want to leave town," Scurry said.

Shiffman knew that leaving town wasn't an option. This was a federal case; they would get him no matter where he went. He let Scurry's confession sink in and tried to get his head around what it meant. It wasn't entirely a shock. His instincts had told him that with Rod being in and out of rehab the player was probably being closely watched. Still, Shiffman felt that the two of them had become close acquaintances, and he had been unsure what Scurry might do if push came to shove. Now he knew. Shiffman decided that, although the ride had been great, he would no longer have anything to do with professional baseball players from that night forward. Maybe if he just cooled it, things wouldn't be so bad after all. How much could they have on him, anyway? It wasn't like he was a major drug dealer, he reasoned to himself. He had bought and sold coke basically for his own consumption and that of a few close friends. An eight ball here, an eight ball there.

"I wasn't getting rich off of it.... What [dealing] amounted to was that I was essentially getting mine for free," Shiffman says.

Shiffman drove away from the bar stricken with uncertainty.

Rod Scurry's drug problem was bad, Shiffman knew, but he didn't grasp how bad until Scurry, having warned Shiffman that he was at risk just a few days earlier, appeared at Shiffman's door hoping to buy cocaine. Shiffman was shocked, yet more than anything he felt sorry for the troubled Scurry, who was clearly in bad shape. And even if there hadn't been the issue of the grand jury hanging over their heads, there was still no way Shiffman would have sold to Scurry that day. It would have been like putting a loaded gun in the hands of a man on the brink of suicide. Obviously Scurry's other contacts were steering clear of him as well, Shiffman thought, and the addict must have been scrambling. Scurry continued his attempts to contact Shiffman for cocaine for weeks to come.

On the afternoon of Thursday, November 8, Shiffman received a phone call from Kevin Koch. Unlike Scurry and the other athletes that Shiffman had sworn off, Koch was an old friend, someone Shiffman trusted completely. If Koch needed something—money, food, clothes, or whatever—and Shiffman had it, it was as good as Kevin's. So when Koch asked his friend to hook him up, it was definitely not a problem. Koch hadn't been around for a while, but that didn't arouse suspicion in the now very careful Shiffman. He wrote it off as "Kevin just being Kevin." Koch was aloof like that. He had frequently been incommunicado for weeks at a time and then suddenly was back by your side like he had never left.

That Thursday evening was cold and rainy, and Kevin Koch felt as gloomy as the night. He had asked Shiffman to set him up with a couple of grams that afternoon. Koch told his friend that he had a promotional appearance as the Parrot lined up that weekend. "I just want to pick up a couple for myself, maybe stay awake on the drive back to Pittsburgh," Koch had explained to his friend. Nothing out of the ordinary.

When Koch arrived at Shiffman's house in Bethel Park, Shiffman and a handful of other friends greeted him, but Koch was in a rush, and the exchange was over in fifteen minutes. Koch bought two grams from Shiffman for two hundred dollars. When the two men parted company Shiffman was smiling, as usual, while Koch was fighting back tears. He had just put the last nail in his best friend's coffin, and as he walked back out onto the dark and damp Pittsburgh streets, he shamefully wondered if it was all worth it.

Earlier that morning Koch had been awakened by a knock at the door. Agents Morrison and Craig were following a lead. They had received information that the Pirates mascot had facilitated drug deals for some of the team's players. This led them to Koch's apartment.

Answering the door was something Koch would never forget. "It was two agents," he recalls. "They said, 'We have you on federal charges of carrying narcotics,'" and presented him with a subpoena. The agents then offered Koch an out. They made a pitch for his cooperation and asked him to accompany them to the federal building to get started working with them right away.

Koch's thoughts immediately turned to April 1984 and the Scurry incident in Los Angeles. He had heard that Scurry said it was Koch who had originally brought cocaine into the Pirates clubhouse. Even though Koch had steered clear of any drug transactions for some time, he could see the writing on the wall.

Koch stalled for time. He wasn't sure how to handle the agents standing in his doorway and their request for cooperation. He didn't give them an answer right away, and the agents didn't press. They played it cool, leaving Koch their card and telling him to give them a call.

Koch was stunned by the turn of events. He had been riding high as the Parrot and loving every minute of it. In fact, the gig was the best thing to ever happen to him. Between all the women and the parties and the good times, Koch believed being the mascot was the next best thing to being an actual player. He was earning a thirty-thousand-dollar salary and performing at nearly three hundred additional appearances each year. No way was he ready to give it all up.

"I was grasping for that last straw, to save my career."

Koch contacted an attorney and walked into the Pittsburgh Federal Building later that morning. The agents made things simple for Koch, but in doing so they could not have made things any more difficult. It was either wear a wire in a controlled buy from his best friend, Dale Shiffman, or go to prison. "They said, 'We basically have Dale, and if we have to go after you and put you in jail, we will. Unless you wear a wire for us.'"

"[Go to jail] for what? Doing a favor?" Koch had replied, disbelieving. He then looked to his attorney for verification. There was no getting around it. The feds had Koch and could without a doubt put him away. It was time for Koch to make a decision. Would he join sides with the government, or would he join his friend Shiffman in prison?

The agents presented the evidence they had against Shiffman, reassuring Koch that they already had a bulletproof case against his friend and that they were just making sure they had him pinned. The fact that Koch had served mainly as a facilitator of the coke deals and was not making any profit off them went a long way toward the government's willingness to protect him. But, they warned, if he chose not to cooperate, that leniency would evaporate.

"It was brutal," recalls Koch. "Here's a friend of mine. They have a lot against him.... He's pretty well screwed. Why am I going to take a hit like this? Here I am stuck between a rock and a hard place. And I'm thinking to myself, *What am I going to do time for? If it's any time, even a week, I ain't doing a week. Why should I? I didn't make any money off it. I wasn't getting no drugs for it. I was basically doing a favor for guys that I knew.* I thought the hell with this. I said, 'All right.'"

Koch's attorney and J. Alan Johnson quickly ironed out the details for an exchange between Koch's cooperation and immunity from prosecution. At this meeting the authorities also expressed an interest in the issue of gambling. They wanted to know if Koch had been placing bets on games using his inside information, for example knowledge of a starting pitcher for an afternoon game stumbling into the stadium that morning with a hangover. But Koch dismissed the notion. "A guy like myself who has that 'in' and is in that clubhouse—am I making phone calls or whatever? That's what they wanted to know," Koch says. "But that was way out the window. I was in half a haze. I couldn't have dialed a phone number if I wanted to half the time."

Agents Morrison and Craig put their new informant into action immediately. "They wanted to hurry up and get it done," Koch says. Koch detailed what he knew about Shiffman's cocaine sales to the ballplayers. Once the agents ascertained that Koch and Shiffman's relationship was still intact and that Koch was still "viable" on the street, they enlisted his help in making a buy. Koch called Shiffman to set up a meeting for that very evening. It was the biggest decision of Koch's life, and he couldn't believe how fast everything was moving. In a matter of a few hours his whole life was being turned upside-down.

Later that night, Koch met FBI agents in Bethel Park, behind a shopping center a few blocks from Shiffman's house. The parking lot was nearly deserted, with only a handful of cars around. "There was hardly anyone out, because the weather was so bad. Inside the agent's car, they put the wire on me. It was a rainy night. A bad night.... They gave me the money. They said, 'We want you to walk in. We want you buy it for us, and we'll get it on a tape. And it'll be a done deal.'"

Koch returned to his own vehicle and slowly drove away. He was in front of Shiffman's house in just seconds. As he exited his car and walked toward the door, the rush of second thoughts nearly stopped him in his tracks. It was as though he had hit a wall. "It was horrible," Koch says. "But something in the back of my head kept saying, *Why should I take the hit? For what? For a bunch of guys in a bar to say, Wow, what a guy!* Piss on that."

Once inside Shiffman's house, things did not get any better for Koch. "It was brutal," he says. "I'm trying to keep it together. I know these guys are outside. I can feel the wire on me. It feels like a time bomb. I feel like a terrorist." He sensed that Shiffman could tell something was up. Shiffman knew his friend well. They had been so close. Shiffman asked him if everything was all right. Koch shrugged off the question and went ahead with his act. "I just wanted to get in and get out," he says.

And just like that it was over. Koch had no idea how or where things would go from there, but for what he had done, Koch would get to walk away from the experience as an innocent man. A free man. Yet the guilt would never leave him. "It was the worst feeling I think I ever had in my life. Everything had just bottomed out at that point. It was horrible. I did something I didn't want to do."

11

Grant Street

> I HAD IT IN LITTLE GRAM BOTTLES THAT I KEPT IN MY
> POCKET. ACTUALLY, A LOT OF TIMES, I WOULD PUT IT
> IN MY BATTING GLOVE AND THEN IN MY POCKET. I WAS
> TRYING TO FIND WAYS OF NOT GETTING CAUGHT. . . .
> USUALLY, WHEN I CARRIED IT IN MY POCKET, I'D GO
> IN HEADFIRST.
> —TIM RAINES DISCUSSING HIS BASE-SLIDING TECHNIQUE
> WHILE CARRYING COCAINE

THE SECOND player subpoenaed, on November 9, and granted immunity was Pirates shortstop Dale Berra. Assistant U.S. Attorney James Ross described Berra as unapologetic. "He was almost like, *How dare you question me about this stuff?*" Ross says.

Ross is a Pittsburgh native who also happens to be a diehard and lifelong baseball fan. He idolized Roberto Clemente growing up and insisted on sitting in the right field bleachers as a kid, just so he would have a clearer view of the great number 21. Upon meeting with Berra he took the opportunity to argue with the shortstop about his notoriously bad fielding. Berra and second baseman Johnny Ray had signed big contracts with the Pirates the previous year and were widely considered to be the double-play combination of the future for the team. Yet Berra, who had just finished hitting .222 at the plate in 1984, was having an even tougher time in the field, having made thirty errors in each of the last three seasons, with that mark tied for the league lead among National League shortstops in 1984.

Ross suggested that cocaine might be the reason for Berra's fielding woes—a suggestion that Berra denied. Yet if one were to glance through the sports pages that year, there were certainly some interesting clues as to what might have been affecting his play. Team captain Bill Madlock, who was able to observe Berra closely from his perch at third base, commented on Pirates fans' constant booing of the shortstop in the summer of 1984. "His only problem is his concentration," Madlock told the *Pittsburgh Press*. "I do a lot of talking to him. You got to keep talking to him every play just to keep him in the game. I keep telling him, 'Don't make those funny errors.' He makes so many errors that he doesn't have to make." Taken in the context of what Berra was about to tell the grand jury, Madlock's statement was quite telling.

Despite all the difficulty the feds had had getting him there, once Berra finally did talk, he certainly opened up. At the grand jury he admitted to having purchased cocaine that year, 1984, from Greer, Shiffman, Connolly, McCue, and Mosco. He also named twenty players in more than 140 pages of revealing testimony. An attorney for one of these twenty players offhandedly described Berra as having named practically every person he had ever played with. Agents Morrison and Craig surely could not have been delighted to hear that there seemed to be no end in sight to the player interviews, for each player named in Berra's testimony would have to be questioned and their stories corroborated. And the named players would no doubt lead to even more names. The investigation seemed to be far from over.

===

By the winter of 1984, the Pirates team as it was currently constructed bore nary a resemblance to the 1979 family, let alone to major league champions. Dave Parker was gone. Willie Stargell had retired following the 1982 season. Now with the trade of Dale Berra to the Yogi Berra–managed New York Yankees and the free-agent departure of Lee Lacy in December, the number of ties to the championship season was less than a handful.

By this time, drug use in baseball was increasingly becoming public knowledge. Former commissioner Bowie Kuhn, who was having difficulty not only protecting the image of his sport but also dealing with the contentious players union, put it simply. "The problem," Kuhn said, "is serious." New commissioner Peter Ueberroth echoed those statements upon taking office in October 1984, the same month the first player, Rod Scurry, was subpoenaed by the grand jury. When asked to name some of the issues facing the sport upon his hiring, Ueberroth said, "Drugs in baseball are a problem as they are in society generally. But in dealing with the problem, baseball has to fight the drugs, not the players."

The seedier underside of baseball had actually first become apparent in October of the previous year, when four members of the Kansas City Royals were caught in a Missouri federal sting. Pitcher Vida Blue was charged with possession of cocaine, while fellow Royals Willie Wilson, Jerry Martin, and Willie Aikens were arrested on charges of attempting to possess cocaine. The four ultimately pleaded guilty to the charge, a federal misdemeanor. As a result, Wilson, Martin, Aikens, and Blue became the first active major league ballplayers to be imprisoned on drug charges. Commissioner Kuhn suspended Wilson, Martin, and Aikens for one year; however, the suspensions were reduced after appeal. Blue was suspended separately for the 1984 season.

Vida Blue, a six-time all star and the 1971 Cy Young and League MVP award winner, felt that he and his teammates were being singled out for a leaguewide problem. "I am not bitter," Blue later said in *USA Today*. "The public thinks the three [convicted] Kansas City players and I are the only athletes in professional sports who used drugs. Let me tell you something: if you were to make a case against everybody who uses drugs in pro sports, you might have to close down some of the teams."

Supporting Blue's point, Los Angeles Dodger Steve Howe, in particular, was having ongoing problems staying clean. Commissioner

Kuhn described Howe as his "most persistent and difficult drug problem." The 1980 National League Rookie of the Year, Howe would go on to star in the Dodgers 1981 World Series triumph over the rival Yankees. In 1983, with a brand new child in his life, Howe spent the majority of his season alternating between drug treatment centers and the ball field. After his initial problems were disclosed to Dodger officials, he was ordered to take periodic drug tests. He failed three of the tests before Kuhn finally, in November, stepped in and suspended him for the following season. While the players union decried the suspension, stating that it was "clearly not likely to improve his chances of a successful rehabilitation," Howe later called the year off "the best thing that ever happened to me."

Also in November 1983, the Major League Baseball Players Association dismissed its executive director, Kenneth Moffett, after he had served just eleven months on the job. This followed the sixteen-plus-years tenure of the previous executive director, the legendary Marvin Miller. Miller was appointed to replace Moffett on an interim basis.

Players and management were due to begin negotiations on a new labor agreement in 1984. By rehiring Miller, who was seen as a hard-line, tough negotiator, as opposed to the "centrist" Moffett, the Players Association signaled to the owners that the upcoming negotiations would not be as easy as the owners might have believed. The players also questioned whether Moffett had even had the requisite interest in the job for taking on the labor contract, alleging that Moffett had put in neither the time nor the effort required of the executive director position.

Moffett, for his part, had no question where his ouster had originated. He put the blame squarely on the shoulders of Marvin Miller. "There's no doubt Marvin was involved," Moffett told the *New York Times*. But there was another reason that Moffett and others pointed to. "Moffett cited opposition by other association officials to his efforts on the joint drug and alcohol committee as a reason for his ouster," wrote the *Times*.

The joint drug and alcohol committee was formed in September 1983 by the Players Association and the owners to deal with this pervasive issue. They were scheduled to meet again the week after Moffett's dismissal. The Players Association obviously didn't want Moffett at that meeting. Moffett felt he understood why. As he later explained to the Associated Press, "I think that we were getting close to hammering out a tough, impartial drug policy was the thing that triggered my firing."

Moffett expected to receive a proposal from the owners, as the committee had been working out a plan on how to deal with drug violations by players. Moffett contended that other high-ranking officials in the players union, including general counsel Donald Fehr, did not agree with his views, particularly with Moffett's opinion that the union should have a role in the disciplining of players. Moffett said he felt Fehr and Mark Belanger, special assistant to the executive director, would rather retain the right to file grievances against management.

Summing up the situation later to *Sports Illustrated*, Moffett said, "Drugs aren't a win-lose type of situation. There are kids who are messed up and need help, and there are ways to do this short of confrontation.... My sense was that management was making an effort to be conciliatory. I felt this was the way to go.... I think it's about time people came to their senses."

In February 1984 things only got worse for Moffett. With seemingly nothing left to lose, at a sports-journalism seminar in Washington, D.C., Moffett declared that "an awful lot" of players were using cocaine and that many were involved and cooperating with federal investigators. He said that he had come to this conclusion after speaking with a combination of FBI agents, players' agents, and the players themselves. The purpose of these meetings, which took place shortly after he took his post in the union, was to determine what could be done to stem the players' widespread drug use. Moffett said he believed the FBI had "telephoto pictures of players using in the bullpen and clubhouse during games." In a follow-up to his statements in

D.C., he later told reporters, "Some of the player reps felt there were four or five [cocaine users], on average, on their clubs."

Donald Fehr, who had by this time replaced Miller and had become the acting executive director of the players union, downplayed Moffett's statements, as well as the problem of drugs in baseball in general. "I've been around baseball players since 1977, and my personal opinion is that baseball players in particular are going to mirror the society in which they are a part," Fehr told the *New York Times*. Yet for every opinion like Donald Fehr's there was a dissenting view being voiced in baseball circles. This view contended that highly paid young athletes were at greater risk of drug abuse than the general population. As Montreal Expos GM John McHale told *Sports Illustrated* in 1984, "We produce the blueprint of a user—young, wealthy, unaccountable for his behavior because of his athletic ability, and unable to handle pressure."

In response to this sentiment Major League Baseball officials sought professional medical advice. The data showed there was indeed a discrepancy in cocaine use between players and society at large. At the time the average cocaine user was white and middle class, whereas eleven of the sixteen baseball players named thus far were either black or Hispanic.

Baltimore physician Torrey Brown, who was a medical consultant for the NBA, felt there was another unique aspect to drug use among athletes. "I think most athletes believe, 'I can beat anything,'" Brown told *Sports Illustrated*. "They're always better than the next guy and the next team. And they extend that attitude to drugs."

Whichever side of the fence Kenneth Moffett sat on, he was by this time probably sorry he had ever opened his mouth. During his speech in Washington, Moffett had mentioned that Keith Hernandez was one of the players he had spoken to and recounted a story about drug use on the St. Louis Cardinals, Hernandez's team at the time. Moffett shared what Hernandez had told him about Manager Whitey Herzog issuing a warning to the team, suggesting that if the drug users on the team did not step forward voluntarily, they would be dropped from the team. In June 1983, Hernandez was one of two players who was traded, with Hernandez going to the New York Mets. Moffett also noted that Lonnie Smith asked to be admitted to a rehab center the same month.

Hernandez was said be incensed over the inclusion of his name in the speech. He accused Moffett of "spreading trash" and said, "The innuendos are not true. My lawyers are reviewing this for possible libel action, and that's where it stands." Hernandez had the full backing of Mets GM Frank Cashen, who called Moffett's remarks "hearsay."

Hernandez's lawsuit threat clearly made an impression; Moffett was forced to make a formal apology to not only Hernandez but also Detroit Tigers pitcher Doug Bair, another ex-Cardinal who was unhappy with Moffett's remarks. The apology was negotiated by lawyers after an initial, more informal apology by Moffett was not accepted by the Hernandez camp, which noted "his retraction in some papers was small and in the back."

Moffett's formal statement read that he "deeply regretted" having said anything that "could have been construed in any way as linking Keith Hernandez with illegal drugs." He went on to say that he had "no knowledge first hand or otherwise" as to why Hernandez had been traded or that he had ever been a drug user. The statement concluded with Moffett praising Hernandez as being "not only a fine baseball player, but a fine young man as well." With the release of his statement, Kenneth Moffett was officially out of Major League Baseball for good.

═══

WHILE THE issue of cocaine use in the major leagues had been hitting the media here and there in the preceding year, in Pittsburgh, as 1984 drew to an end, still not a word had leaked to the general public of a grand jury investigation involving drugs and major league baseball. In a time before the Internet and around-the-clock news and sports channels, print journalism was the main avenue for breaking news. Reporters kept an ear to the ground and worked their stories doggedly. But so far, besides some buzz among the players, who were noticing the law enforcement activity going on around them, things had remained relatively quiet in Pittsburgh, a situation that was obviously preferred by all those involved. However, a string of events near the end of the year and the beginning of the next would change that.

Former *Pittsburgh Post-Gazette* reporter Jan Ackerman blames this quiet time in Pittsburgh on her and her *Pittsburgh Press* counterpart Toni Locy's inexperience on the job. Both had been covering the federal courthouse for less than a year, and Ackerman would be the first to admit that they hadn't yet caught on to the intricacies of the position or even the geography of the courthouse. "We were both pretty green," Ackerman allows.

Ackerman, who was thirty-one at the time, says she was particularly naive about the secretive grand jury process. However, through good old-fashioned "dumb luck," her Pittsburgh readers, as well as the nation's, would soon discover the extent of baseball's little secret. Her big break occurred while she rode the courthouse elevator one November day, along with another courthouse employee and two rather large men whom Ackerman failed to recognize. It wasn't until later, when someone filled her in on one of the men's identity as that of Pirates shortstop Dale Berra, did she realize her good fortune. When she called the news in to her boss, Assistant City Editor Fritz Huysman, he became pretty excited and instructed her to keep her eyes open at the courthouse. Still, Ackerman wasn't expecting to discover anything that would cause too much of a stir.

On January 8, 1985, Ackerman and Locy were covering a routine proceeding in Judge Gustave Diamond's ninth-floor courtroom when they heard a commotion coming from the hallway outside the doors. As they peeked out they saw federal marshals in the process of blocking the courtroom windows. The marshals then refused to allow them or anyone else to leave the courtroom until a witness had finished passing through the halls.

Talk about setting off a journalistic alarm. The "feisty" Locy found an exit from the courtroom and snuck down to the seventh floor, hoping to catch a glimpse of whoever it was that was causing such a clamor. Locy had learned in her short time on the job that whoever was on the ninth floor was most likely there to receive immunity in Judge Carol Los Mansmann's courtroom and that his next move would be down to the seventh floor, where grand jury proceedings were held. Locy ducked into the restroom, keeping the door ajar, and waited.

Unfortunately for Locy, her stealthy moves were caught on the courthouse security camera. When the time came for the witness to depart the grand jury chambers, marshals were dispatched to the seventh-floor lavatories and told to block the exit of the women's room until the witness was safely out of sight. Now trapped inside the bathroom, Locy was furious and, befitting her character, she let her objections be known, screaming from behind the door as long and as loud as she could.

Back at the *Pittsburgh Press* offices, Locy's superiors were equally upset. They lodged a formal complaint that was brought to the attention of J. Alan Johnson, who blamed Locy's detainment on a "breakdown of communication between the courthouse guards and the U.S. Attorney's Office." He also said that steps had been taken to "remedy the situation."

Nevertheless, the damage was done. The two local newspapers went into full stakeout mode. If only such a commotion hadn't been made, Ackerman says, she doubts that she would have even recognized the witness, later confirmed as the Pirates' Lee Mazilli, passing through the halls, let alone looked out into the hallway in the first place.

Post-Gazette reporters David Rapp and Carl Remensky were sent with Ackerman to troll the courthouse corridors and assist the young reporter in putting names to the faces of any future witnesses. Locy was joined by ex-Pirates' beat reporter Dan Donovan for the *Press*. There was strength in numbers, the reporters reasoned, and should federal officials try any more shenanigans, it was doubtful they would be able to shield both the men's and women's restrooms, as well as all other views of the grand jury chambers. The seventh-floor hallway at 700 Grant Street would not go unattended again until spring. Assistant U.S. Attorney James Ross would call the scene a "monthly vigil" of reporters.

On January 23, 1985, the grand jury proceedings in Pittsburgh finally became public knowledge. Pitching in on the story with Ackerman was legendary Pittsburgh sports writer Charlie Feeney. The story in the *Post-Gazette*, headlined, "Drug Probe Calls Berra, Scurry Here," reported that Berra and Scurry, along with at least one other unknown Pirates player, had been subpoenaed and had testified before a grand jury investigating possible violations of drug laws. It also said that it was "not known whether the players are background witnesses or targets of the investigation."

Berra denied testifying. "I don't even know where the federal courthouse is in Pittsburgh. I've never been before any grand jury. I don't know how a story like this could have started," Berra said from his racquetball club in Montclair, New Jersey. Rod Scurry, meanwhile, declined to comment on the story.

The next day the *Post-Gazette* ran a second story on the probe. A piece was also written in the *Pittsburgh Press*. The third, previously unknown Pirate to have testified was identified as outfielder Lee Mazilli, who at first also denied he had testified. He changed his story, however, as his agent, Tony Attanasio, confirmed the outfielder's involvement. Attanasio quickly clarified his client's role at the grand jury by declaring that Mazilli was not the target of the investigation and was merely called as a background witness to answer questions regarding local restaurants and nightclubs frequented by Pirates players.

One day after declaring he had never testified, Dale Berra, too, retracted his denial and admitted that he had appeared before the grand jury panel but said he was not the focus. "I now confirm the fact that I was called to testify, and I want to make one thing emphatically clear: I was called as a background witness, and in no way, shape, or form was I a target of this or any investigation."

Pirates' GM Harding Peterson stood behind his former shortstop, saying the next day that he had no knowledge of Berra taking drugs. He urged the public to read between the lines of what was being printed. "I think if people read these stories and understand what they are saying, they'll see that the players are not involved with drugs," Peterson said. Never mind that the Pirates management had called the FBI in April 1984 concerning cocaine use or that Chuck Tanner and trainer Tony Bartirome had identified a photo of Shelby Greer for Agents Craig and Morrison on June 6, 1984. It appeared that those in baseball were attempting to spin events as quickly as they unfolded.

With the FBI taking the time to speak with each team during spring training on the dangers of drugs, and with memos concerning drug use being sent around the league from the commissioner's office, this investigation should not have come as a shock to anyone within the league. In fact, Lonnie Smith remembers being approached as far back as 1983 by an opposing player who warned him the feds had "a list of guys they believe are all involved with Curtis. All involved with drugs."

While the investigation certainly wasn't welcome among players, it should have come as a relief to a lot of them to know they weren't going crazy for suspecting they were under surveillance. Pirates captain Bill Madlock expressed this sentiment when he said in the *Pittsburgh Press*, "Last year, a number of our guys were getting paranoid, thinking they were being watched. I guess they were." He then added, "They know who is using drugs. Why don't they just bust 'em? That would stop it. Why bring up guys to testify who aren't using drugs and put them through this?" Madlock finished by saying that he was unsure which Pirates were using and which weren't. "If we had a team like we had a couple of years ago, I'd know. We were close then. We ran together. It was family with Will [Stargell] in charge. But we've brought in all new people, and when you do that everyone goes his own way. There's the chapel group, the guys who went alone, other cliques. It is not a family team."

=====

SHELBY GREER was on his way to Houlihan's on January 11, 1985, when FBI agents raided his apartment and secured between one and two ounces of cocaine as well as drug packing and selling materials. Thanks to Kevin Connolly, the agents had also succeeded in making three controlled buys from Greer to go along with the evidence from the raid.

Although Greer had toyed with the idea of stopping the sale of drugs completely in 1983, his operation had in fact expanded tenfold over the past year. According to his calculations Greer sold 31 grams of coke between 1979 and 1982, 48 grams in 1983, and 573.5 grams in 1984. He had never intended to become a drug dealer, but in the past year Greer had certainly graduated to that role, reaching a point where he was transporting up to a pound of cocaine from Florida to Pittsburgh. Even so, Greer wasn't getting rich. Despite winning over fifteen thousand dollars in football bets throughout the 1984 season, Greer was still borrowing money from both his bookie and friends for his trips to Florida and was able to finance his purchases only by taking advantage of his dealer, Ted's, price reduction and consignment program, in which Ted fronted Greer the cocaine and allowed him to pay later.

One of the key pieces of evidence obtained during the raid was Greer's rental car receipts, which gave the authorities a record of his travels in Florida. Greer had saved each of the approximately two dozen receipts to take advantage of Alamo's frequent renter program, which allowed renters to turn in accumulated receipts for their choice of gifts. While others were getting rich from the cocaine business, Greer was hoping for a free watch.

Agents Morrison and Craig approached Assistant Special Agent in Charge Pat Laffey with a proposal in February 1985. With the majority of the East Coast National League teams set to descend upon Central Florida for spring training, the agents suggested to their boss that a trip to the Sunshine State would be beneficial to their investigation, as they would be able to knock off the majority of their player interviews in one trip. It was a time-saving tactic, said the pair of agents. In response Agent Laffey asked Morrison and Craig if they thought he had been born yesterday. With the temperatures in Pittsburgh hovering around freezing at the time, the trip seemed more like a vacation to their boss, especially on the heels of Agent Craig's trip to Florida three months earlier, in November, when Craig, Agent Benedetto, and Kevin Connolly had again tried to nab Connolly's Florida connection, Roland, and again failed to produce results. Not to mention Morrison and Craig's December stay in Los Angeles to interview former Pirate and current Baltimore Oriole, Lee Lacy.

Nonetheless, Laffey eventually signed off on the idea, and Agents Morrison and Craig hit the spring training circuit in mid-February. They traveled from camp to camp to speak with various ballplayers, from the Pirates in Bradenton to the Phillies in Clearwater, and so on down the line working through all the names on their list.

At the St. Louis Cardinals camp in St. Petersburg the agents met with outfielder Lonnie Smith and pitcher Joaquín Andújar. According to Agent Craig, Andújar came away from the interview impressed with the agents' knowledge of his previous actions and whereabouts, summing up his experience: "There are two people you can not hide anything from—God and the FBI." Smith remembers the agents showed him a list with nearly one hundred players identified as cocaine users. But the focus of his meeting was on his interactions with Curtis Strong from Philadelphia. Smith admitted buying coke from Strong, saying, "I explained to them how I purchased it, how I used it, and that was it." Much of the agents' work, however, turned out to be nothing more than chasing down rumors, as a good number of the athletes they spoke with had nothing to do with drugs.

Many of the players were clients of baseball agent and attorney Tom Reich. Once they were subpoenaed, Reich referred players to his brother and fellow lawyer, Sam, whose office was located in Pittsburgh. When Sam Reich, who would go on to represent a number of Tom's clients, heard about the grand jury investigation, the first words that popped into his head were *Kansas City*.

====

KANSAS NATIVE Mark Liebl's story began much like those of Dale Shiffman, Kevin Connolly, Robert McCue, and the rest of the

Pittsburghers who became involved with professional baseball players. Having been sentenced to six years in prison in early 1984 for conspiring to distribute cocaine and using a telephone to conspire to distribute cocaine, Liebl reminisced to the *New York Times* from his cell at the Fort Worth Correctional Institute in Texas in 1985.

Late in the evening on a Sunday night in April 1982, Liebl was on his couch when a friend called and asked if he could stop by Liebl's for a visit. There was somebody he wanted Liebl to meet. A short time later, Liebl was greeted at his front door by his friend and the Royals' Vida Blue. A long-time baseball fanatic, Liebl was blown away by the presence of the big league pitcher at his home. The three men shared some cocaine that evening. Blue invited the thirty-two-year-old Liebl to a Royals game two days later, after which Liebl and Blue finished off the evening once again using cocaine at Liebl's house in the Kansas City suburb of Overland Park. "Vida and I struck up a real good friendship right off the bat," Liebl said. The situation was almost identical to Kevin Koch's experience during his initiation into the Pirates' clubhouse.

"I could tell him every number that every Oakland player ever wore," Liebl said regarding the former Athletics pitcher. "Gosh, he was amazed. Just as much as I was amazed about him being there, he was amazed at how much I knew."

In time, Liebl was introduced to all the familiar big league perks: free tickets, women, clubhouse access, and road trips with the team complete with all-night cocaine parties in hotel rooms. Liebl got to know other Royals—Jerry Martin, Willie Wilson, and Willie Aikens—as well as members of the Red Sox, A's, White Sox, and one player from the Minnesota Twins. Liebl's home soon became the postgame party stop for the players. And why not, considering Liebl's straightforward party rules? Any cocaine done on the premises was free. Anybody wishing to obtain cocaine for the road was charged eighty dollars a gram. In time Liebl not only went through a lot of money, he lost two homes and a business as well.

The baseball commissioner at the time, Bowie Kuhn, found Liebl's case important enough to take a trip to the federal prison in

Texas in order to interview him. Kuhn noted in his memoir *Hard-ball: The Education of a Baseball Commissioner*, "I suspect it was the first time a sports commissioner had ever 'gone to jail' in pursuit of his duties." Kuhn came away from the meeting impressed with Liebl and deemed him credible, commenting, "Oddly enough, Liebl is a real baseball fan. He wanted to make the players happy, so he supplied them with drugs. But he was concerned about what was going on. It was a paradoxical thing."

Liebl watched the Royals lose games following their nightly benders. During one particular road trip he joined the team in Anaheim, where the Royals lost 9–1 to the Angels after a night of partying. This game convinced him that cocaine was indeed affecting the team's performance. The Royals finished the 1982 season in second place, three games behind the Angels in the American League West standings. The Royals had gone to the playoffs during the previous strike-shortened 1981 season.

Liebl, as was the case with Kevin Connolly in Pittsburgh, spoke of the irony of not exactly getting rich from his dealings in the drug trade despite the enormous salaries of his clients. Describing an evening he spent with members of the Chicago White Sox, Liebl commented, "You talk about the greediness of some these guys. We snorted till about four in the morning, and when they got ready to go, they wanted to get one-quarter ounce, seven grams, they said it was going to be for other players, too. I gave it to them, and they said, 'Well, we don't have the money on us, but we're going to be here till Sunday, and we'll get the money to you.' They never did get the money to me. I often wonder, who do they think they're fooling? You don't forget that you just bought five hundred dollars' worth of cocaine and you haven't paid the guy. Boy, they were just a couple of jerks about it."

Liebl also noted the seeming prevalence of cocaine use among pitchers around the league. "That's what's so damn dangerous about it—those are the guys throwing the damn ball," Liebl said.

The party in Kansas City continued throughout the 1982 season with members of the Royals averaging two or three visits per week to Liebl's house. However, it was during the winter prior to the 1983 season that drug use in Liebl's circle really spiked upward, and the quantity of Liebl's cocaine purchases and sales grew accordingly. Coincidence or not, the Royals registered their worst full-season record in nearly ten years.

"It's all over baseball," Liebl said, regarding cocaine use in the game. In fact, said Liebl, talk of drug use was often at the center of many of the conversations taking place in his "Cooperstown Room," which was the tag given to the basement area of Liebl's home where his all-star guest list gathered. The gossip often revolved around which players in the league were into cocaine, as well as the routine use of amphetamines. "Like I said," Liebl remarked, "they didn't get their start from a friendly pusher man. They all got their start from another baseball player."

In 1983 a federal investigation began in Liebl's hometown of Dodge City, Kansas, and soon after a wiretap was installed at Liebl's home. On June 20, 1983, the house was raided by authorities with guns in hand just as Liebl was about to depart for a Royals game. Liebl greeted the agents with relief that the whole ordeal had finally come to an end. "That's how bad that whole thing had become for me," Liebl said. "I was relieved."

Liebl was the centerpiece of indictments and drug charges against seventeen people later that year, including four Royals. Aikens, Wilson, and Martin were charged with attempting to possess cocaine after their phone calls to Liebl were "intercepted by federal agents." Blue was charged with possession of cocaine.

Willie Aikens's attorney, James E. Kelley Jr., suggests that the geography of the investigation influenced the tactics and the handling of the case by the defense attorneys for the four Royals players. Had the case been in the Eighth Circuit Court of Missouri, where, precedent suggested, offenders would be charged with a misdemeanor for such conduct, then the attorneys would have had options. However, Kelley says, because the case was across state lines in the Tenth Circuit of Kansas, where there was a history of felony charges levied against nonselling drug users, it left the defense attorneys in a difficult position. Unnerved by the prospect of his client facing felony charges, Kelley had little alternative but to make a deal in which Aikens pleaded guilty to misdemeanor drug charges. The three other Royals did the same.

Kelley hoped his client would receive probation when it came to sentencing. The attorney went through all the expected steps, including pleading leniency due to the stature of his big league client. No active major league players had ever received prison sentences, he argued. In addition, this was Aiken's first offense. Needless to say, Kelley was surprised when Aikens was sentenced to a ninety-day prison term, as were Blue, Martin, and Wilson.

By 1985 only Willie Wilson remained in a Royals uniform. Willie Aikens, the 1980 World Series hero who became the only player to ever hit two home runs in the same game twice during the same Series, was traded to the Blue Jays following his arrest. (April 30, 1985, was his last day in a major league uniform. He would spend the remainder of his baseball days in the Mexican League.) Vida Blue, who was convicted, sentenced, and suspended separately from his teammates, rode out his suspension playing winter ball in Puerto Rico for the Ponce Lions and was hoping to hook up with the Giants for the 1985 spring training. Jerry Martin wound up in Columbia, South Carolina, and in a career in the insurance business. His attorney, Bill Simpson, left no doubt as to the reason for Martin's early retirement, telling USA Today, "I definitely feel he was blackballed" from the league.

Willie Wilson summed up his experience. "We were examples," he said. "I've accepted that.... What made me feel bad was that other guys got caught and nothing happened to them."

BACK IN Pittsburgh, the "example" Wilson described sent shivers down the spines of some. The events in Kansas City were of great concern to attorney Sam Reich. He didn't know all the facts surrounding the Royals case, but he did believe the prison terms were somewhat unusual because, in his words, "the policy of the federal government usually is to prosecute dealers and to use customers as witnesses." To Reich it seemed quite possible that the players had done something to aggravate the investigators in Kansas City and brought the charges down on themselves. He didn't want that to happen in Pittsburgh. "But now the precedent was set—players were going to jail," Reich says, and they needed to be cooperative.

Reich let the U.S. Attorney's Office in Pittsburgh know that he would recommend to his clients that they not testify without immunity, and he was successful in securing it. Once more it seemed to come down to the luck of geography, as the policy of the Western District of Pennsylvania was to target the suppliers of drugs while making the users witnesses in their investigations.

With immunity granted, Reich's next task was perhaps more arduous—getting the players not just to talk but to talk truthfully about their participation in the drug world. Reich spoke of the tradition of players not giving up dirt on other players, "sort of like in the ranks of the men in blue.... You protect your own." Tom Glavine, longtime Atlanta Braves pitcher and soon-to-be Hall of Famer, echoed this sentiment, telling ESPN's T. J. Quinn, "Everybody, from the minute they get to the clubhouse, it's, 'What goes on in the clubhouse stays in the clubhouse.' And that's team fights or team arguments or team meetings. All that stuff is supposed to remain in-house. That's the culture of the game."

In order for Reich to do his job, he had to ask players to turn their backs on this tradition. "We knew this was going to be an intensive interrogation. 'Who were your sources? How often? Who else was involved?' And all of that," Reich says.

Sam Reich probably knew more about the game of baseball than anyone else involved with this case. Something of a baseball historian, he would later put his love of the game and specifically his interest in the Hall of Fame selection process to use in his book *Waiting for Cooperstown*. As for drugs, Reich didn't consider it shocking that athletes in major league baseball were using cocaine. He, like others, pointed to the rest of society and wasn't naive enough to think that baseball players would be immune to the temptation. What he did find shocking was that cocaine had been allowed to reach epidemic proportions in baseball. He pointed to the strike season of 1981 as the genesis of the problem, asserting that a lot of rich players sitting around with nothing to do and feeling anxious about the future began spending all their time "palling around" together. One player would get another involved with drugs, and before anyone knew what was happening, "it became an epidemic."

Many players later shared their own explanations for their drug use, citing "boredom" and "peer pressure." Some, perhaps difficult to sympathize with, blamed the problem on having too much money. "Money *is* the problem." Lonnie Smith said. Other players pointed to the playing of eighty-one games on the road "away from family, friends, and home" as another cause.

Now, with their appearances due at the grand jury in Pittsburgh, some players would be spending even more of their time traveling.

———

BECAUSE OF his sports expertise and former beat as *Pittsburgh Press* baseball reporter, it was assumed that Dan Donovan had an astute eye for identifying players. And when Donovan was sent to the federal courthouse to accompany fellow *Press* reporter Toni Locy he seemed up for the task. Silently, however, he worried whether he would be able to put names to all the faces he encountered on the reporters' seventh-floor stakeout. Donovan was expecting to see a parade of B-list players and knew it was one thing to be able to point out, for instance, the backup catcher for the Astros during a game, with the benefit of a numbered jersey, but it was quite another thing to pick him out inside a federal building wearing a suit and tie. Inwardly he feared that he wouldn't be able to do any better than Locy at identifying players.

Donovan realized that his fears were moot when assuredly A-list players Dave Parker and Montreal Expos base path thief Tim Raines arrived at the courthouse in February 1985. Also testifying that month were the Pirates' John Milner and Lee Lacy. In March these four were followed by St. Louis Cardinals All-Star Lonnie Smith,

Houston Astros captain Enos Cabell, and former League MVP Keith Hernandez. The Pittsburgh courthouse was beginning to look like an All-Star Game batting practice. But despite their presence at the grand jury, the players continued to publicly deny any wrongdoing, and they were seemingly always backed by their team's managers or executives.

"Who? Enos?" Houston Astros president Al Rosen scoffed at the suggestion that Cabell used drugs. "Absolutely not," Rosen said.

Even when players were willing to tell the public the truth about their drug use, they were urged by team management to word their admissions with utmost care, as was the case with Lonnie Smith. Smith was approached by management before going in front of the press to speak about his rehab visit of 1983. "They told me that I had become a 'chemical dependent,'" Smith says, explaining that the phrase was emphatically preferred over "just telling them I was on cocaine."

With the April 22 testimonies of former Phillies and current Pirates pitcher Al Holland and San Francisco Giants outfielder Jeffrey Leonard, the number of players at the grand jury grew to at least twelve.

On May 14 Shelby Greer made a statement to agents Craig and Morrison. Word had gotten back to him that his pal Dave Parker had already talked, so Greer decided to try to help himself. Still, even after Parker had turned his back on Greer, Greer held no ill will toward Parker. "I guess I can understand—he had a whole lot more to lose than I did," Greer says.

Wells Morrison points out that the stars weren't given much of a choice. "I don't think the ballplayers—no one wanted to give up some drug dealers who they considered their friends," he says. "They just didn't want to be exposed themselves."

By this time the FBI had gained a good sense of its star witnesses, and the general consensus was that the players who descended on the Grant Street courthouse fell into one of two categories. "I found it very interesting to talk to the various characters and to see how they approached it," says Assistant U.S. Attorney James

Ross. "People like Lonnie Smith and Keith Hernandez—who were pretty stand-up guys—they came in, admitted what they did was wrong, and testified. Then you had other people, like Parker and Dale Berra," who, Ross notes, were very difficult to get information from even with immunity. Ross says he found this to be the most interesting facet of the proceedings and draws a parallel between those involved with the cocaine scandal and those named in baseball's new saga, that of steroid use, "where you had guys like Jason Giambi and Andy Petitte, who were willing to admit to wrongdoing, and those that weren't."

Morrison and Craig echo this sentiment. "Lonnie Smith was very forthcoming, one of the nicest guys," Morrison says, while with others, "it was like pulling teeth."

Despite Keith Hernandez's continued public denials and bouts with former union head Kenneth Moffett, the agents gave Hernandez high marks as well, calling him "a very intelligent guy" whose testimony they found compelling. They also felt that he had come to grips with his cocaine addiction. Of John Milner, Craig says, "Milner wasn't a real talkative guy, but he was honest and forthright about using drugs."

If anyone was still skeptical about Dale Berra's involvement with cocaine, those doubts were put to rest later in May when Agent Craig, while aiding another agent in searching a home on a separate drug case, came across a photo of Berra with a suspected drug dealer. "What a nitwit he was," Craig says of Berra.

Meanwhile, Shelby Greer's gesture to help the government came too late in the game. In fact, in the end Greer may have been better off keeping his mouth shut. In his May 14 interview with the FBI, Greer disclosed a bevy of detailed information, most of which concerned Pirates outfielder Dave Parker. Greer told agents how the Pirates players began distancing themselves from him around 1982, as he was "told by Dave Parker, Lee Lacy, and Dale Berra that he was 'too hot' to be around... a result of rumors that had reached the Pittsburgh Pirates management that he was involved with cocaine with the Pittsburgh Pirates players."

Greer advised the agents that he had met and sold to additional players from around the league through the years, including Dusty Baker, Enos Cabell, and Pascual Perez. He also described Parker as being known to other national league players as the "Pittsburgh contact" for cocaine.

"That's the kind of stuff that drove us nuts," Agent Craig says. "And we didn't get this [information] until after it was too late." Craig adds, "He was just a lucky bastard. He was enabling. He was flying these guys in" and setting the deals up as the players came to Pittsburgh. Craig also noted that Greer alleged that after Parker finished playing winter ball in Venezuela, he bragged about bringing coke home in his baby's carry-on bag or "stroller or something."

"The hardest one was Parker," Craig says, regarding having granted the star immunity. Ross agrees. "I'd have to say of all the witnesses, [Parker] was more involved than others."

Ross could also foresee the public's displeasure once the whole affair went public. "The immunity issue was very significant with Dave Parker, because ultimately his testimony would reveal that he was coordinating some of the purchases," Ross says. "Ballplayers would come into Pittsburgh and come to him, and he would arrange for a supplier… but early on we did not know that. In other words, it was almost like Parker was not necessarily the source, but he was assisting the source in getting [cocaine] to someone else."

So did Parker's actions constitute distribution? "That certainly did, that's why he could have been considered an unindicted co-conspirator," Ross says.

Other athletes during this period didn't fare as well as Parker. In 1983 Washington Redskins safety Tony Peters had been abruptly awoken in the middle of the night in his Dickenson College dorm room in Carlisle, Pennsylvania, during training camp. Peters, who had never missed a start in his 115 professional football games, was indicted, along with seven other men, by a federal grand jury and charged with conspiring to distribute cocaine. Peters was accused of acting as the middleman in a transaction involving $115,000 worth. He received a suspended prison term and four years probation, was fined ten thousand dollars, and was forced to complete five hundred hours of community work.

Despite the fact that no players were set to be arrested in Pittsburgh, one thing became clear to the agents as their investigation unfolded: cocaine was the first thing many of these players thought about in the morning and was at the forefront of their daily activities. While Ross was amazed to learn what was really going on in baseball, Agent Craig found it unnerving. He certainly wasn't surprised that players were using drugs, but he was shocked at the scope and extent of it. A lifelong baseball fan, he says his faith in America's national pastime was severely shaken. "I'm not sure I ever got over it—that exposure to the underbelly of professional athletes."

For a large number of players in the early 1980s, their passion for cocaine began to surpass their passion for the game. It was all about hooking up for the present moment or setting things up for later. As for the games, it was merely about getting by.

"I started losing interest in things. I didn't care about the game. The majority of the time we were in a hurry to get the game over with and do it all over again," Lonnie Smith told the *New York Times*. He also spoke of the pregame discussions he had with his adversaries. "We would have conversations sometimes," he said, "trying to find out who had connections, who could get something. It was usually during practice before a game, loosening up, running sprints, talking to guys."

Tim Raines was one of several players who, exhausted from the late nights of partying, began using inning breaks as an opportunity to catch a nap in the dugout. It seemed as if America's heroes were spending more time chasing drugs than they were fly balls.

=

As LOCAL reporters continued to work their stories and players continued to deny any implication of wrongdoing, the buzz surrounding the grand jury investigation in Pittsburgh began to spread nationally. By May the word was definitely out as programs from *NBC Nightly News* to ABC's *Nightline* began to broadcast stories discussing the drug probe in Pittsburgh. A May piece in the *New York Daily News* in particular sent shockwaves around the country and left journalists itching for answers. The story contended that "one published report... indicated a source had said indictments could include 'the biggest name in Pittsburgh sports.'" The published report cited was baseball writer Chris Mortensen's April 28 story in the *Atlanta Journal-Constitution*. Later Mortensen spoke about how the grand jury investigation had become a hot topic among baseball writers.

"All the writers are pumping each other for information, practically every night now. But it's funny, none of the players or team officials anywhere have had much to say about it, even privately," Mortensen told the *Post-Gazette*'s Carl Remensky.

Mortensen spoke of being "paranoid" about missing something concerning the drug probe. "Atlanta is one of the few National League clubs which hasn't had a player testify.... I just worry that every time the team has a day off, one of them is going to sneak off and show up in front of a grand jury in Pittsburgh," he said.

The speculation did not stop with Pittsburgh either, as reports were surfacing that Pittsburgh was just the first leg of the investigation, with future probes being discussed in Atlanta and St. Louis, among other places. With such news spreading fast, Commissioner Peter Ueberroth was feeling the heat. A list published in *Sports Illustrated* in 1984 showed that sixteen major-leaguers had been convicted or treated for the use of hard drugs since 1980, while three additional players had publically acknowledged use by the first quarter of 1985. Not to mention that court papers from the Kansas City scandal also reportedly revealed an additional thirty-five major league players as cocaine users. Drug use by players was seen as becoming out of control. Ueberroth could not stand by idly.

On May 7, 1985, Ueberroth jumped into the fray with pointed statements meant to show he had a handle on the situation. The commissioner announced that random drug urinalysis tests would be administered to all baseball personnel. Everybody—owners, batboys, secretaries, as well as all minor league players—would be tested. There was only one exception. The major league players themselves were to be excluded for now. There was the small problem of the Players Association and the collective bargaining agreement that would need to be dealt with first if something were to be accomplished on that front. Ueberroth hoped that public sentiment would persuade the players to submit to tests voluntarily or get the union to soften its stance against mandatory testing.

Twenty-four hours later Ueberroth ratcheted things up even further when he let out the dreaded *g*-word: gambling. Fearing that illegal drug use could potentially cause more problems for the sport than even the 1919 Chicago Black Sox scandal had, Ueberroth said, "The [commissioner's] office was created as a result of people being paid in relation to gambling. I think the potential of drugs causing a problem is far more severe because you have a dependency problem and the reaction to drugs—the inability to judge correctly." Such a scenario had recently come to pass in basketball at Tulane University, where, as the Associated Press reported, "Investigators said players were supplied with drugs and money in return for shaving points."

Ueberroth summed things up. "Testing just seems to be the way to go," he said. "There's been far too many drug stories involving baseball in the past years and certainly in the past two or three weeks. We know there is a problem. We're going to eliminate it. That's the message." In a separate interview in the *New York Times*, he added, "The integrity of the game is everything. We've got to eliminate illegal substances from the game, substances which can be used to control people, such as apparently happened at Tulane."

"The Commissioner Gets Tough" was the headline almost a week later in *Sports Illustrated*, after Ueberroth brought a Loyola Marymount University commencement crowd to its feet following another fiery speech. "Somebody has to say 'enough is enough' against drugs," Ueberroth announced. "Baseball's going to accomplish this. It's a little tiny segment of society. We're going to remove drugs and be an example."

As might be expected, the outburst from Ueberroth did not sit well with the union or its acting executive director, Donald Fehr. Unhappy that the union was not consulted before public proclamations were made about drug testing, Fehr dismissed Ueber-roth's speech as grandstanding. Fehr felt that the league's current arrangement, which provided for voluntary testing, was working satisfactorily. Fehr also expressed concerns regarding the invasion of the players' privacy through testing. Considering the timing of the commissioner's statements, whether they constituted grandstanding or not, they were certainly calculated.

Also in the *Sports Illustrated* article, Keith Hernandez was once again named as a witness at the grand jury proceedings in Pittsburgh. This was followed by yet another round of denials. Hernandez's agent, Jack Childers, said in a phone interview with the magazine, "You're talking about ancient history as far as he's involved. That's way in the past." But after playing a tape recording of the interview for Hernandez, Childers said that the first baseman became upset and denied "any involvement in cocaine, ever."

There was only one thing that could contradict Hernandez's and the other players' public avowals of innocence, and that was whatever news would soon come out of Pittsburgh. Speculation ran rampant. A lot of players, including New York Yankee and American League Player Representative Don Baylor, felt the news would be damning. "I don't know any names, but it's going to come down pretty hard on players. They actually have proof." Or, as Ueberroth told the *Today* show, "I think it's going to be bad. There will be things that will be damaging to the game."

The answer to the question everyone was asking was coming. The federal government had what they needed. Grand jury testimony had come to a close in Pittsburgh, and indictments were expected on the thirtieth of May.

12

Busted

THERE'S A MAN GOIN' 'ROUND TAKIN' NAMES.
AND HE DECIDES WHO TO FREE AND WHO TO BLAME.
EVERYBODY WON'T BE TREATED ALL THE SAME.
THERE'LL BE A GOLDEN LADDER REACHING DOWN.
    —JOHNNY CASH, FROM "WHEN THE MAN COMES TO TOWN"

IN LATE May, Dale Shiffman awoke early one morning and sprinted toward the bathroom. Blood was streaming from his nose, a result of consuming a large amount of cocaine hours earlier. He had also drunk the majority of a bottle of scotch. Shiffman looked in the mirror and couldn't believe what he saw. The blood continued to gush, with Shiffman catching it in his hands and dropping it into the sink. He looked up pleadingly and shook his fist in defiance. "God, if you're up there, do something in my life!" he demanded. Shiffman had grown sick of the party.

On the evening of Thursday, May 30, at 5:30 P.M., seven indictments were handed down by a federal grand jury and sealed by U.S. Magistrate Robert C. Mitchell. The names of the seven men would be made public only after the men were in custody. A short time later, a Philadelphia lawyer representing the Philadelphia chef Curtis Strong announced that he had been contacted by U. S. Attorney J. Alan Johnson with word that his client should surrender to FBI agents in Philadelphia. Strong's was the first name officially linked to the major league drug investigation.

Shiffman had just finished playing a doubleheader for the High Rollers. Following the games, he contemplated driving home to take a shower and change clothes, then he thought better of it. The mere idea of going home made his stomach churn with dread. He read the papers like everybody else. In fact, Shiffman had recently called childhood friend and attorney Gary Ogg to voice his concerns. Ogg reassured Shiffman, telling him not to worry. "No way the FBI is going after you nickel-and-dimers," Ogg said. "They're going after big-time coke dealers, the big fish."

Shiffman was less sure. He thought back to what Rod Scurry had confessed almost half a year earlier—that he and the other players had given Shiffman up. The only thing left now was for the authorities to finally show their hand. Shiffman decided to keep his uniform on and go out as he was, in search of the quickest bottle of scotch. That night he crashed, along with a small group of friends, at a friend's place in Bethel Park, just around the corner from his house.

At six-thirty the next morning, May 31, Shiffman was awoken by the sound of a ringing telephone. Finally someone picked it up. It was the mother of one of the friends assembled in the house, who told her son she had seen the FBI at the door of Shiffman's house. What happened next was a blur. Somehow clued in to Shiffman's whereabouts, the FBI raided the home within moments of the concerned mother's phone call. Girls were screaming, guns were drawn, and just like that it was all over. Shiffman was in the custody of six FBI agents.

Shiffman was then escorted to his own house for the agents to conduct a search. Inside Shiffman's home, agents confiscated a few bags with cocaine residue; pieces of paper with names, initials, notations, and phone numbers that investigators believed were records of his cocaine business; and a bindle—a piece of drug paraphernalia. They also found a book entitled *The Complete Guide to the Street Drug Game.*

In a classic example of "be careful what you wish for," Shiffman's prayers from nights earlier had been answered. His days of abusing drugs would quickly be coming to an end. On the way downtown to FBI headquarters on Grant Street, with Shiffman handcuffed in the back seat, the agents made another stop to pick up a suspect from a separate case. "Hey, man," the suspect remarked, "did you hear about the guy they got with 111 counts?" Shiffman could only smile. He was that man.

The indictment against thirty-three-year-old Dale Shiffman was so large it was bound with rubber bands. Included among the charges were eighty-seven counts matching each of the eighty-seven days the Pirates were in Pittsburgh during the 1983 baseball season. According to a study done by the *New York Times*, of the 165 total counts covered in the indictments against the seven men, "dates of 133 counts match dates on which the Pirates were home during the seasons from 1980 through 1984." A total of 80 percent of the counts could be linked to major league baseball.

Unlike Shiffman, Kevin Connolly had been looking forward to this moment. For months now he had felt like he was living in limbo, wondering what was taking so long. He knew what awaited him and just wanted to get the inevitable over with. The quicker he went to prison, he reasoned, the quicker he could get out of prison and put this whole saga behind him. When the indictments came down, with two counts against Connolly, he quickly surrendered at FBI offices inside the federal building. Interestingly, he would look back at his time working with the FBI and call it "a blast." It helped that the bulk of their work together took place inside bars and taverns, and Connolly rarely had to pay for the drinks.

Robert McCue's mother found out about her son's involvement in the investigation when she was greeted at her door by four FBI agents at eight o'clock on the morning of the arrests. "I didn't know a thing. I was stunned, totally stunned," she told the *Pittsburgh Press*. "They went through my whole house." Mrs. McCue noted that her son had recently moved out. "My son had lived with me, but I didn't know a thing about him. I knew nothing of his goings-on. I didn't know his friends.... It was as if he was a boarder in my house."

By the end of the day all seven men were in custody, with Greer on ten counts; Balzer, two counts; McCue, thirteen counts; and Strong, sixteen counts; all joining Connolly in surrendering, while Jeffrey Mosco, twelve counts, was arrested at his home. Suddenly Connolly understood why there had been such a delay with his arrest. His lawyer informed him that the FBI was trying to group everyone together for the baseball case, which amused Connolly. He accepted that he was indeed in the wrong and guilty of selling illegal drugs. He just felt it was odd, with all of the cocaine he had been buying and selling, that he was being arrested as part of this major league baseball case, considering that very little of his trade had been to members of the Pittsburgh Pirates. Connolly believed that the feds had waited on his arrest in order to make their case look more substantial and "ring-like" for the sake of the public.

"It looked better the more people they brought in," says Connolly, who knew all the men arrested except for Strong. "Look, they included Tommy Balzer, who didn't even like those two [Berra and Scurry] or know them that well. Mosco knew them, but he wasn't selling much, he was more like a friend.... He wasn't no coke dealer."

On June 1, the headline in the *Pittsburgh Post-Gazette* gave the defense attorneys hired to represent these men all the ammunition they would need moving forward: "Seven 'Fans' Arrested on Cocaine Charges."

As information rolled in regarding those indicted, the media created an image of the seven men that was quite different from what many had expected following months of publicity and nationwide speculation. For starters, two heating repairmen and a couple guys who still lived with their mothers didn't exactly scream "big time." Anyone who had been expecting players to be arrested was sure to have been disappointed.

In a harbinger of things to come, Curtis Strong's attorney, Adam O. Renfroe Jr., wasted little time in taking his client's case to the press. Before the indictments were even unsealed, in fact, Renfroe could be heard telling the media, "Players who are making $800,000, a million a year, are saying a guy who makes a couple hundred bucks a week is a big drug dealer—a guy who doesn't even have a car.... Mr. Strong is a pawn in this."

Strong, who had no prior criminal record, had catered the Philadelphia Phillies' first five home contests of the 1985 season before being dismissed for what Phillies publicist Larry Shenk called excessive prices. Strong had reportedly been hired by the team on the recommendation of pitcher Al Holland.

Upon learning of the indictments, *Pittsburgh Post-Gazette* assistant city editor Fritz Huysman's initial reaction was, "Geez, that's it?" *Post-Gazette* reporter Jan Ackerman's response was similar, as she remembered looking at the other journalists covering the case in bewilderment. Everyone had been anticipating such big things, yet it appeared as if the men with the money were being spared. The "big" baseball scandal, in the words of Ackerman, was being pinned on "these schmucks from the South Hills for selling bags of coke." The seven were also described by various outlets as "wannabes," "groupies," and "starstruck."

Considering that these events were taking place during the height of Reagan's War on Drugs campaign, Ackerman saw the arrests as nothing more than an opportunity for the government to show that it was tough on drugs. In her experience, she explained, it is often decided at the beginning of a case who will and will not be indicted. Prosecutors don't let the facts lead to indictments; rather, it is *who* they decide to indict that leads to the gathering of the necessary evidence. Dan Donovan of the *Pittsburgh Press* also pointed toward the War on Drugs theme. "They got seven fans who shared coke with players. No one would remember the names Shiffman, Strong, et cetera, in ten years except the prosecutors who used them to get the point across about being tough on drugs," Donovan says.

For his part, Agent Wells Morrison says simply, "We had no friends in this case; we followed the evidence."

DALE SHIFFMAN called May 31 "the worst day" of his life. He paused before adding, "Until the next day." That's when his attorney informed him that his friend Kevin Koch was the one who had given him up. While Shiffman may have subconsciously been looking forward to a forced end to his partying days, once in prison such thoughts had trouble surfacing through his anger. "I was livid," he later recalled to a Pittsburgh newscaster. He never imagined Koch could turn against him. The whole situation had him baffled. He had thought of himself as just one of the guys; why was he getting the short end of the stick?

During an interview with reporters, Shiffman's attorney, Gary Ogg, called Shiffman a scapegoat and said, "Someone has to take the brunt of this, and unfortunately he's the one." Ogg then claimed the players testified under oath in an attempt to "save their careers and their lives."

"I wasn't doing anything a whole lot different than [the players]," Shiffman said. "But why were they given the chance to have full immunity, to walk, and then continue to play?"

To Shiffman, the whole thing stunk. "Here's Rod Scurry and Dale Berra and the boys, and they're out there playing a kid's game, making millions of dollars. Here's my friend, the Pirate Parrot, going out to all these clubs, enjoying himself after he wore a wire," Shiffman told Bryant Gumbel in 2006. "And here's me, sitting in a jail cell." Shiffman, unlike the others indicted, was denied bail, partly because they feared he might seek retribution on his dear friend Koch.

Shiffman had it partially right. Rod Scurry and the boys were still making their money and enjoying the game of baseball. In fact, Scurry had been riding a particular hot streak on the mound of late. The headline in the sports section of the *Pittsburgh Press* on June 2, just after the arrests, read, "Scurry Stars in 6–3 Win." The pitcher struck out four Atlanta Braves over three scoreless innings to pick up the save. It had been Scurry's second straight outstanding relief performance.

Kevin Koch, however, was doing anything but enjoying himself. One of the first questions he had asked the agents when they initially approached him in November 1984 was whether he would be able to keep his job. "We have no say in that," they had replied. Koch knew at that point that his Parrot gig was over. After the indictments were handed down, the Pirates quickly fired him, although they did do him the favor of letting him publicly resign. The United Press International (UPI) reported, "Kevin Koch, the original Pirate Parrot who has thrilled youngsters at Pittsburgh Pirate games for seven years with his wacky antics, has resigned for personal reasons."

After an unnamed government source leaked Koch's name as a witness for the government, it didn't take long for television news crews to show up on his lawn. "My name had been so splattered all over the place. It was hard... a rough deal from there," Koch says. The moment it became public that he had worn a wire, any semblance of the life he had known was gone. "It was like... from having every friend in the world, giving box seats away... to having nobody at all. Completely nothing." Koch was vilified. He had escaped prison but quickly realized he was left with little else. "Who am I going to go to?" he asks. "All of my friends had been in that circle. Now my best friend, I had worn a wire against. Where am I going to go?"

Koch was lampooned in a *Pittsburgh Post-Gazette* editorial cartoon with the caption "Polly want a nice hit of coke?!" In the same edition of his hometown paper he was called "Stool Parrot." But nothing was worse than what he was enduring within his own mind. "I felt like Judas," he told Bryant Gumbel. "It was the most horrible thing I ever had to do in my life. If I could have done it over again... I would have told the FBI, 'Do what you're going to do to me.'"

He had turned on Shiffman, and now Pittsburgh, "the city I grew up in, the city I loved," turned on him.

—————

NEEDLESS TO say the Pittsburgh Pirates organization was at the center of the storm, but the attack on the city was no less fierce. In the words of team owner Dan Galbreath, "The other part that's very disturbing is that around the country, Pittsburgh's been mentioned so prominently and unfairly as a major area [of drug availability], and I don't think it has been involved any more than any other city. The city as well as the Pirates have taken some bad raps on it."

The scandal had taken on a life of its own. Said manager Chuck Tanner, a man known for his cheery disposition, "I've never been involved where there have been more distractions. It's been a very difficult year for everything, as if there was a black cloud hanging over us." Team captain Bill Madlock noted that the ball club was receiving more attention than any last-place team in history. He compared his team's plight to a soap opera, classifying it as "just another installment in *How the Pirates Turn.*"

With the team up for sale and suffering from poor attendance, not to mention an image problem that had some calling their stadium the National League drugstore, the Pirates responded with a flurry of odd moves. First, on May 23, they fired general manager Harding Peterson. Galbreath said the move was made in order to inject the club with "new ideas" and "fresh blood." In his place Galbreath hired the team's old GM and the man Peterson had succeeded, sixty-six-year-old Joe L. Brown. Not exactly the freshest blood.

Then, after news of the arrests made its way into the newspapers, the Pirates made the seemingly belated gesture of locking down both the home- and visiting-team clubhouses at Three Rivers Stadium and placing three security guards outside the door of each, along with signs reading NO SALESMEN, NO CHILDREN, NO FRIENDS, NO EX-PLAYERS OR VENDORS ARE ALLOWED IN THE CLUBHOUSE. This led to the obvious question, hadn't those responsible for bringing drugs into the clubhouse already been apprehended? Finally, on June 15, the Pirates tried to distract the public by hiring the legendary and hugely popular Willie Stargell, who had retired following the 1982 season, to coach first base. Teams weren't known to make midseason coaching changes at first base often.

The Pirates' troubles were not isolated to events off the field. On the playing field things were going no better for the club. In fact they were awful. Already coming off a last-place 1984 campaign, by the second week in June the team's record stood at 17-36. They were not just playing poorly; they were well on their way into the record books as one of the worst teams in Pirates history.

"We were just bad," explains pitcher Don Robinson. "The whole year was just bad." Even Kevin Koch could see it prior to his ouster. "It was unraveling," Koch says. "I can remember Rod going out one game, out of his mind, tooted up. They called him in, and he was all over the place. He had an unbelievable curveball, a good fastball, but that day, it was like, wow, to lose control like that and not even be *near* the plate." Scurry's recent streak of outstanding performances was over. Before the season's end, he would be declared AWOL by the team for missing a game, suspended for violating the terms of his aftercare program, and finally sold to the New York Yankees for the proverbial "bag of balls."

Bill Madlock summarized the state of affairs in the Steel City to the *Sporting News*, saying, "I know I'm a professional, and I'm expected to blot out all the crap and just do my job on the field. Well, that's easier said than done." He complained about the uncertainty surrounding the team's possible sale, as well as a lack of excitement both on the field and in the bleachers, and commented that his team-mates were walking around like they were "stepping on eggshells because of the [drug] situation." As Pirates catcher Tony Pena told GM Joe L. Brown upon Brown's return to the club, "Joe, our team has the worst attitude in baseball."

Team owner Dan Galbreath had heard enough complaining and took some players to the woodshed. "You know Madlock has been mouthing off a lot lately. Now maybe you can get away with that if you're doing a [good] job. But Madlock wasn't hitting, and he was sloppy fat."

Madlock was traded to the Dodgers on August 31.

The rattle of music and celebration that had once reverberated around the team was gone. Morale was low, and the clubhouse had become lifeless. "You can't be successful playing baseball unless you have fun," said Willie Stargell after his return. "The Pirates need to start having fun again."

One Pirate, who wished not to be named, offered a somewhat different view. "This ain't the Family," he said bluntly.

====

IN A thirteen-page report sent from FBI offices in Pittsburgh to the bureau director on June 14, the Pittsburgh investigation was summarized. It read in part:

USA [U.S. Attorney] Johnson has maintained that this case is not an investigation of Major League Baseball. It is an investigation of several cocaine dealers who gained access to ballplayers through various introductions and advanced their drug trade through these associations. Nonetheless, baseball has been inextricably involved throughout the course of this investigation. Players have used their status to take known dealers into the locker rooms of their teams. Players have introduced known dealers to their friends and teammates, and have facilitated the distribution of cocaine to other players. They have furthered a code of silence regarding other players known to have serious cocaine addiction and to assist these players in continuing to use cocaine. They have recommended known dealers for employment by their team. They have invited known dealers to travel with their team on road trips to sell cocaine in other Major League cities. They have invited known dealers to their homes and to homes of their friends for social occasions. Non-player team employees have furnished cocaine to young players. A player agent furnished cocaine to his client during World Series competition. A player allowed a known dealer to live in his residence during the off-season. Players allowed known dealers to use their hotel rooms while on road trips. Players bought cocaine from dealers while in groups and used the cocaine with them. Players continued to associate with dealers even after being advised that dealers were known by the team and league security offices. During investigation, players stated they had been advised in 1981 or 1982 that two subjects in this case had been identified by League Security and players notified of same. This did not stop players or dealers from continuing their cocaine trafficking in and around stadiums. When contacted for background on one of the subjects, the commissioners' security office could not provide any information on subject or memorandum pertaining to subject. This subject shortly thereafter gained employment with a team. This employment was a result of player recommendation. It was also apparent during investigation that teams and league failed [to] take aggressive action to prevent player-dealer relationships when identity of drug using players was apparent to many in and out of baseball. A dealer was confirmed to have used inside information gained from player to bet on games. It was also common for dealers to be heavy gamblers.

The document also revealed that "in addition to subjects indicted and described above, [the Pittsburgh office] has identified numerous other cocaine dealers in other cities who sold to Major League players. Pittsburgh anticipates dissemination of this information to appropriate divisions for investigation. Also, several cocaine sources of indicted traffickers have been identified and are also under investigation."

That report succinctly described what was going on behind the scenes, but so far the only thing the American public and ticket-buying fans knew was that a group of drug dealers had been busted in Pittsburgh and that some major league players were involved. This was presumably how Major League Baseball desired to keep it. One thing the players had working in their favor was the fact that MLB had a track record of keeping cases such as this quiet. Other instances of players' cocaine activities leading to law enforcement investigations had resulted in few media leaks. This had been the case in Kansas City, where guilty pleas ensured nothing was discussed in open court.

In August 1985 the *New York Times* released a four-part series, researched and written by Murray Chass and Michael Goodwin, which examined the issue of cocaine and baseball. At the conclusion of their three-month investigation, Chass and Goodwin reported that cocaine use among professional baseball players in the early 1980s was widespread, with many players even being implicated in criminal investigations. "However, the players generally have not been prosecuted," Goodwin wrote, "and in some cases law enforcement officials have taken unusual steps to protect the players' identities."

Chass and Goodwin examined the players' success at protecting their identities in legal affairs. In 1982 three members of the Yankees were involved in a Manhattan narcotics case. The names were never revealed. In 1984 Milwaukee was the site of a case against a former ice cream vendor named Anthony J. Peters, who was sentenced to twenty-two years for running a seventeen-million-dollar-per-year cocaine operation. At least ten players from the Brewers, Chicago White Sox, and Cleveland Indians were named as cocaine users during the grand jury proceedings, but thanks to an agreement between prosecutors and defense attorneys, none of these players was named in open court as a cocaine user. According to the *New York Times* piece, defense attorneys conceded to the prosecution's request to keep the names of the players out of the case, for fear that their clients might have been viewed more harshly for having sold to the players, who up until this point had reputations as American heroes. Added Ed Miller, who worked the case as an agent for the Internal Revenue Service, "Basically, the ballplayers were pretty well protected here." Among the users spared unwanted publicity during and directly after the trial were Paul Molitor, Dick Davis, and Claudell Washington.

With each of the episodes described by Chass and Goodwin, media momentum was squelched before it had any chance of picking up steam. Now, to quiet further public speculation about the players and avoid a full-blown scandal, the seven men indicted as dealers would have to plead guilty to the original charges or work out a plea bargain. If any of them decided to go to trial, there could be trouble for the league. Hopefully there wouldn't be any young, hotshot lawyers involved, looking to stir things up and make names for themselves. The platform was certainly there for the taking.

=====

ADAM O. Renfroe Jr. had a flair about him. As an assistant district attorney in Philadelphia, while his colleagues were driving "Volkswagens or junkers," Renfroe sat behind the wheel of a bright red Cadillac and wore expensive tailored suits. Never mind that he was still working his way up the legal ladder, a man needed to look the part.

Renfroe had known Curtis Strong for twenty years. They hailed from the same Philadelphia neighborhood, and Renfroe's sister and Strong had been classmates in school. A gifted athlete, Renfroe received a football scholarship to Bethune-Cookman College in Florida and played flanker as part of their Division II football program before a shoulder injury cut his playing career short. He received his bachelor's degree from Cheyney State in 1970. In 1973 he obtained a law degree from Howard University in Washington, D.C., and one year later he received a master's degree in city planning from Harvard. Upon graduation he was offered a job by then–Philadelphia mayor Frank Rizzo and went to work in the district attorney's office. Renfroe said he had chosen the legal profession in order to "make the best use" of his skills. After his stint as an assistant district attorney and trying, in his estimation, "over two thousand cases," Renfroe went into private practice in 1979 and by 1985 had established the firm Renfroe and Renfroe with his sister.

Renfroe was known for his prowess in getting drug dealers out of trouble, and his courtroom demeanor was equally well known to his Philadelphia peers. "He has a reputation for boisterous and outlandish behavior in the courtroom," said John Haggerty, deputy for communications in the Philadelphia district attorney's office. In the western part of the state, however, he was mostly unknown, although several lawyers said they had heard stories that depicted him as "wild" and "emotional" in the courtroom.

U.S. Attorney J. Alan Johnson presented a stark contrast to Renfroe. Known as a drug buster, Johnson was a no-nonsense attorney who behaved in a businesslike manner in the courtroom. "Jerry is basically a tough guy," said his predecessor, Robert Cindrich. "And he is very serious about the narcotics problem."

Johnson, forty-one years old in 1985, kept his short dark hair and moustache in perfect order, which matched his disposition. He began his legal career as an Allegheny County assistant district attorney. In 1976 he became an assistant U.S. attorney before accepting his current position in 1981. Cindrich remarked on Johnson's focus since taking the top post. "Jerry hasn't wasted time prosecuting users of narcotics, the unfortunate people who get addicted," Cindrich said. "A majority of the cases are aimed at getting to the source of the drugs."

Despite the media frenzy surrounding the indictments, Johnson refused to comment on the proceedings. The Pittsburgh media had grown accustomed to his closed lips. In fact, *Post-Gazette* reporter Jan Ackerman referred to him as "the king of no comments." Still, Johnson didn't kid himself about the nature of any potential trials resulting from the indictments and admitted that the government knew from the beginning that "none of these trials would be routine cocaine trials." He also knew the assessment of his decisions could be, and probably would be, harsh. "You always risk criticism when you try a high-profile case," Johnson later told *USA Today*. "We sought immunity for the players for a purpose—to compel somebody to testify. We didn't get any volunteers.... These guys weren't running over here volunteering to testify." Johnson said he didn't enjoy having to grant immunity to the ballplayers but pointed out that between the two, the seller or the buyer, prosecutors routinely went after the seller. He added, "This is not a job for someone with a weak stomach."

===

AGENT BOB Craig didn't want to hear about Dale Shiffman's love of the game. The fact remained, says Craig, "They were paying him for the coke." Besides, Craig adds sarcastically, "We only had one hundred and some counts against him." Agent Wells Morrison stated that the number actually could have been higher, as "individuals advised that they purchased cocaine from Mr. Shiffman on so many occasions that it was impossible for them to recall specific dates." But either way, Craig says, "the real kicker was that we had a controlled drug buy. It's hard to refute your own voice on tape, selling drugs."

That was one thing the agents and Shiffman's legal team could agree on. "My attorney told me straight, 'You've got a 111-count indictment. I can get you off 110. I can't beat the wire,'" Shiffman said. He actually did have an alibi for quite a few of the charges, which was his presence at various softball games around the region. Still, with that one painful and irrefutable transaction between Shiffman and his best friend hanging over Shiffman, his attorney attempted to work out a deal with the government. In August, Dale Shiffman pleaded guilty to 20 of the 111 counts against him. He was sentenced to twelve years at the Federal Correctional Institute (FCI) in Loretto, Pennsylvania, a low-security prison.

Also in August, Kevin Connolly and Thomas Balzer both pleaded guilty to one count of possession with intent to distribute cocaine. Balzer cried at their sentencing, as Connolly took the heat. "Tom Balzer would have never gotten involved if it hadn't been for me," Connolly said. "He's never done anything wrong." Connolly also characterized the arrest as "the best thing that happened to me. I don't know where it would have stopped. You don't stop with cocaine until something severe happens." Connolly was sentenced to three years at FCI-Loretto and Balzer to two at FCI-Allenwood in Northeastern Pennsylvania, also a low-security prison.

Agents Morrison and Craig kept busy during the summer of 1985. With the arrests made, the agents still needed to stay in contact with the government's witnesses in case any of the remaining seven opted for a trial. They traveled to baseball agent Tom Reich's office in Hollywood with Assistant U.S. Attorney James Ross in order to meet with Reich's West Coast clients involved in the case. In Pittsburgh they met with San Francisco Giants outfielder Jeffrey Leonard and instructed him to be prepared because the U.S. attorney would be asking him some tough questions. "I'm going to be ready. Chili and I have been practicing" in the outfield, Leonard assured them, alluding to going over his testimony with Chili Davis, Leonard's outfield partner for the Giants. It was unlikely the fans encircling the outfield grass could have ever suspected such a conversation was taking place between innings.

Meanwhile Jeffrey Mosco's attorney, Stanton Levenson, couldn't get over the difference between how his client and the "other accommodation purchasers," the players, were being treated in this case. Attorney Sam Reich describes an accommodation purchaser as follows. "Say player A goes to the dealer and buys drugs and then goes back and divides it among his buddies; [then player A is] an accommodation purchaser." Stanton Levenson agreed. And that was what he considered his client to be: "an accommodator."

"It seemed to me that there were no real substantial drug dealers involved," Levenson says. "My complaint about the prosecution was always that the less powerful, less wealthy guys got prosecuted, and the big guys got off. My own particular client was a bartender, a nice guy, no prior criminal history. He befriended Dale Berra, who hung out at a bar that Jeffrey worked at. They became friends. Berra had a cocaine problem. Mosco was happy to supply him with use-type quantities. Eventually he got introduced to John Milner and Scurry, and Jeffrey began getting them use-type quantities of cocaine, I think more as an accommodation and a way to become one of the guys and hang out with these semi-stars.... I thought it was disgraceful that he gets prosecuted, and Dale Berra and Rod Scurry continue on with their careers."

With this attitude guiding them, Levenson and his client decided to hold out for the time being and look toward a possible trial.

The scoreboard of the indicted was at a standstill, with three men having pleaded guilty, three men's cases unresolved and possibly headed to trial, and one man, Curtis Strong, led by his attorney, Adam Renfroe, seemingly entertaining no options *but* a jury trial. Despite pressure from all sides, including a visit from the commissioner of baseball himself, Peter Ueberroth, as well as representatives from Attorney General Edwin Meese's office, Adam Renfroe told all comers that he wasn't interested in making a deal—unless, of course, the deal included the dropping of all charges against his client. Otherwise, he declared, it was time to "put twelve in the box" and send this case to trial.

Going into September, with three tight pennant races and Pete Rose on the threshold of making history by snatching the all-time hits record away from Ty Cobb, the biggest drug trial in baseball history, *United States v. Curtis Strong*, was set to begin. J. Alan Johnson had made out his lineup, and Lonnie Smith was back in his familiar role in the lead-off position, to be followed by Keith Hernandez. These and other witnesses who would be called to testify could be forced to miss important pennant-deciding games in order to appear in Pittsburgh.

Pittsburgh Pirates mascot Kevin Koch in 1979.

Kevin Koch in costume in 1979, the inaugural year of the Pirate Parrot.

BELOW: **The Pirates' Dave Parker during game six of the 1979 World Series.** (AP mages)

Pirates pitcher Rod Scurry.

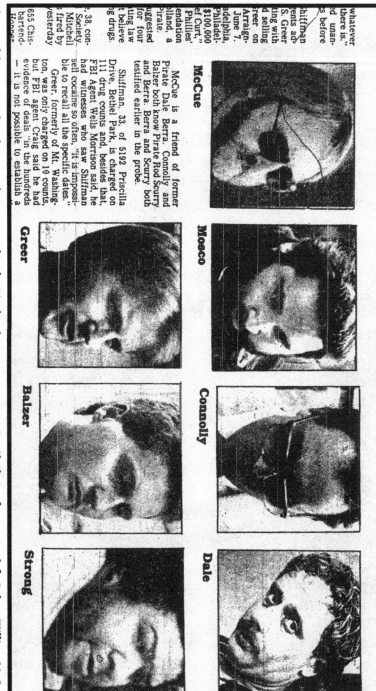

McCue

Mosco

Greer

Connolly

Balzer

Dale

Strong

whatever there is."

d unan-
s before

hiffman
ents ad-
S. Greer
ting with
d selling
reer on
Arraign-
June 7.
adelphia,
Philadel-
$100,000
er Curt," Phillies'
endation
olland, a
Pirate.
uggested
for four
to believe
ting law
ng drugs.

McCue is a friend of former Pirate Dale Berra. Connolly and Balzer both know Pirate Rod Scurry and Berra. Berra and Scurry both testified earlier in the probe.

Shiffman, 33, of 5192 Priscilla Drive, Bethel Park, is charged on 111 drug counts and, besides that, FBI Agent Wells Morrison said, he had witnesses who saw Shiffman sell cocaine so often, "it is impossible to recall all the specific dates."

Greer, formerly of Mt. Washington, was only charged on 10 counts, but FBI agent Craig said he had evidence of deals "in the hundreds — it is not possible to establish a

e, 38, con-
Society.
Mitchell
s fired by
yesterday

655 Chis-
bartend-
Hopper

Photos of the seven indicted men as they appeared in the *Pittsburgh Press* on June 1, 1985. Clockwise from upper left: Robert William McCue, Jeffrey Mosco, Kevin Connolly, Dale Shiffman, Curtis Strong, Thomas Balzer, and Shelby Greer.

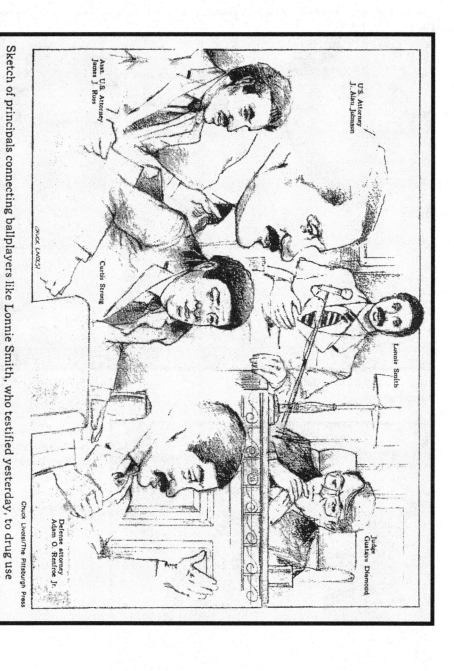

Sketch of principals connecting ballplayers like Lonnie Smith, who testified yesterday, to drug use

U.S. Attorney
J. Alan Johnson

Asst. U.S. Attorney
James J. Ross

Curtis Strong

Lonnie Smith

Defense attorney
Adam O. Renfroe Jr.

Judge
Gustave Diamond

Chuck Livolsi/The Pittsburgh Press

This sketch of the 1985 Strong trial key players ran in the _Pittsburgh Press_ on September 6.

Attorney Adam Renfroe (left) and defendant Curtis Strong outside the U.S. District Courthouse in Pittsburgh. (AP Images)

Dale Berra leaving federal court after testifying in the drug trafficking trial of former Philadelphia caterer Curtis Strong in September 1985.

(AP Images)

U.S. Attorney J. Alan Johnson.

FBI agents William "Bob" Craig (left) and Wells Morrison, pictured here in 2001 at the crash site of Flight 93 in Shanksville, Pennsylvania.

(courtesy of Bob Craig)

Left to right: Robert McCue,
Dale Shiffman, and Jeffrey
Mosco after being released from
prison in the summer of 1987.

(courtesy of Dale Shiffman)

BELOW: Kevin Koch (left) and
Dale Shiffman reunited for a
taping of HBO's *Real Sports
with Bryant Gumbel* in 2006.

(courtesy of Dale Shiffman)

13

The United States Versus Curtis Strong

I AM COVERED WITH THE BLOOD OF THE LORD.
I'M NOT TALKING; I'M CARRYING OUT HIS WILL. . . .
I AM DAVID, AND I'M GOING AGAINST GOLIATH.
—ADAM O. RENFROE JR., TALKING TO THE MEDIA
AFTER A DAY IN THE COURTROOM

THURSDAY, SEPTEMBER 5, 1985.

"That morning, I was nervous as hell," recalls James Ross. "I was thirty years old, I was a brand-spanking-new lawyer, and I was going to be opening the largest case in the country at the time. I kept thinking about what I was going to say."

Handpicked to try *United States v. Curtis Strong* alongside his boss, J. Alan Johnson, the young assistant U.S. attorney was given the task of delivering the opening statement, and he was looking for a zinger—something that would deliver a blow to the defense early and get the attention of the jury.

Ross was at his breakfast table finishing his meal when it came to him.

He strode to the brownstone federal building inspired and ready for the task at hand. But first, he would need to make his way through the gauntlet of television crews, media, fans, and other rubberneckers who had ignored the hot and humid early September temperatures and made their way to Grant Street to take in the action. Thirteen camera crews battled for position, all eager to catch the next big shot. One cameraman compared the scene to covering President Reagan's campaign. Media scofflaws who chose to ignore the NO PARKING signs posted directly in front of the courthouse were quick to learn that the newly anointed "Most Livable City in America" wasn't one to play favorites, as Pittsburgh motorcycle cops began ticketing and towing the offenders. A circus tent may as well have been erected over the whole city block.

The trial was finally set to begin. The desire for an untainted and impartial jury had led both sides to prolong the jury selection process, turning what usually took less than an afternoon into a meticulous, two-day-long affair.

The eighth-floor courtroom No. 1 was overflowing with reporters and spectators. In comparison, a normal federal criminal case might have attracted a half dozen spectators on a busy day. The proceedings would take place under the watchful eye of Judge Gustave Diamond. Considered even-keeled and calm, Diamond resembled the actor Gregory Peck, and many in the crowd began comparing him to Peck's Atticus Finch character in *To Kill a Mockingbird*. "I really haven't seen anything like this," said Diamond, a judge for seven years and a U.S. attorney before that, speaking of the packed house. He then clarified, in jest, "Oh, maybe a couple of massage parlor trials."

The affair was highly anticipated due to the expectation of not only star witnesses but also of oral combat between the two lead attorneys. The Associated Press reported the trial was "likely to feature verbal and legal sparring between the conservative Johnson and the flashy Renfroe, who clashed repeatedly in a July hearing" and also noted that Johnson "has made it evident he dislikes Renfroe's flamboyant courtroom style and the defense attorney's frequent media interviews, many of which have been critical of the U.S. attorney."

Judge Diamond intended to keep firm control of any courtroom dustups or contentious relations. "There won't be personal comments back and forth," Diamond warned. "We will not be making personal statements towards each other. You are professionals, and I expect you to act like professionals."

The judge had been forced to intercede on three separate occasions during jury selection in order to stem quarrels between Johnson and Renfroe, with one incident coming after Renfroe attempted to dismiss a potential juror for obviously being "attracted" to Johnson.

But before Johnson and Renfroe would be afforded the opportunity to further their battle, it was up to the young Ross to deliver the opening statement.

"During this case, you may hear some things about major league baseball that will distress you and upset you," Ross said. "There is one thing to keep in mind throughout: *Major league baseball is not on trial here. The defendant, Curtis Strong, is.*"

Despite his breakfast-table ephiphany, Ross didn't think the line overly spectacular. Little did he know it would become the sound bite of the trial and land Ross on *CBS Evening News* that night with Dan Rather. He may also not have realized, however, the great effect to which Strong's attorney Adam Renfroe would turn the line around.

The thirty-five-year old Renfroe spoke only two sentences before an objection was sounded from the government's side. He continued. "We will show you, ladies and gentlemen, that these heroes are nothing but criminals," he said, alluding to the government's player witnesses. "These hero-criminals actually sell and have sold drugs and still are selling the drugs to the baseball players around the league." Finally, Renfroe repeated Ross's statement, but with a twist.

"We will show you, ladies and gentlemen, that major league baseball *is* on trial," Renfroe asserted. "We will show you that not only is major league baseball on trial, but we will show you that the poor man is on trial. We will show you that the rich and the powerful can get away with anything. We will show you, ladies and gentlemen, after it is all over, that my client, Curtis Strong, is not guilty of anything but being a pitiful sports junkie who idolized ballplayers, like you or I."

Renfroe's strategy was simple. He intended to take the focus off his client and place it squarely on the dirty shoulders of the players themselves. His opening statement sounded a theme that the other defense attorneys for the Pittsburgh Seven would pick up on. Across the board, in the defendants' preliminary hearings and to the press, the same refrain was sung: these were cases of minor league dealers being played out in a major league setting.

===

LONNIE SMITH was the first baseball player to take the stand. Smith began his career with the Phillies in 1978 before moving on to the St. Louis Cardinals in 1981 and the Kansas City Royals in May 1985, four months before the start of the trial. Smith's testimony was explicit and at times poignant. Saying that cocaine made him feel "strong, brave, and invincible," Smith testified that he met Strong in 1981 through his Phillies teammate Dick Davis. He became a regular customer of Strong's and received cocaine from him wrapped in "girlie magazine papers," sometimes via the U.S. mail. He became addicted to the drug during the Cardinals' championship season of 1982. Once, in 1983, Smith recalled, "I stayed up all night using it. The next morning I was too jittery and uncontrollable to play." That was when he sought out manager Whitey Herzog and admitted he had a problem with cocaine. Smith entered a rehab center in June 1983. "It was an addiction that kept telling me that I needed it," Smith said. "I was addicted to cocaine. I was hard addicted to cocaine."

Then it was Renfroe's turn. The young attorney pounced on the witness. No holds were barred as Renfroe stormed from his seat and began to shout at, berate, and argue with Smith. Renfroe attempted to solicit as many players' names as possible from the witness. Armed with the FBI's 302 report and interview with Shelby Greer, which stated that Dave Parker had told Greer that Phillies legend Mike Schmidt used cocaine, Renfroe asked Smith about his former teammate. Johnson objected, and Judge Diamond told the jury to disregard the question because there was "no adequate basis" to bring up Schmidt's name. Renfroe plowed forward. By the end of his cross-examination, Renfroe had Smith recite the names of the Phillies who had been implicated in a 1980 amphetamine scandal—Pete Rose, Greg Luzinski, Randy Lerch, and Larry Bowa—as well as the names of two other coke users on the Phillies, Gary Matthews and Dickie Noles. Smith also said he used greenies during the 1980 season with Nino Espinosa and Bake McBride.

While repeating that he was aware of no national league players who bought or delivered drugs for profit, Smith did admit to having bought drugs for pitcher Joaquín Andújar and Keith Hernandez in the past. Andújar, the Cardinals' staff ace, was currently smoking fastballs past national league hitters to the tune of twenty victories thus far in the 1985 season. Smith further stated that Andújar would sometimes return the favor of delivering the coke, although again, without making a profit. This prompted an argument between Renfroe and Smith over the meaning and definition of "distribution." Right off the bat spectators as well as MLB officials wondered whether the actions Smith described could be interpreted as the players selling drugs, which would open up the players to possible suspensions.

By the end of the first day of testimony, Renfroe had received one threat to hold him in contempt of court, was told to stop screaming at witnesses, was forced to mercifully put an end to his over two-and-a-half-hour cross-examination of Smith after repeating the same questions, and had been admonished on so many occasions that Judge Diamond felt it only fair to remind the jury that just because a lawyer receives the judge's admonishment, it has no bearing on his opinion as to the defendant's guilt or innocence.

Johnson, meanwhile, was rebuked twice himself by Judge Diamond.

Lonnie Smith, for his part, kept his cool throughout and did his best to keep his answers direct and sometimes even humorous. In one exchange, Renfroe grilled Smith about how he knew the substance he purchased from Strong was actually cocaine.

"Who told you it was cocaine?" Renfroe asked. "Was it hearsay?"

"No," Smith said, looking at Strong. "It was his say."

After the day's session ended, Renfroe vented to the media, as would become customary during the trial. "Since May, my anger had been building over the arbitrary and capricious arrest of my client, and those emotions had to come out," he said. "There may have been a point when I turned off some people. I can only hope and pray that I did not offend anyone on the jury."

Renfroe also took a swipe at Commissioner Peter Ueberroth, telling reporters that Ueberroth knew of Andújar's drug involvement and failed to address the issue. "The commissioner is condoning this type of behavior by not doing more to those people than give them a slap on the wrist," he said.

===

BATTING SECOND for the prosecution was Mets first baseman and former Cardinal Keith Hernandez. Hernandez dropped the first true stunner of the proceedings with his declaration that in his estimation "40 percent of all major league players used cocaine in 1980." He called it "the love affair year between baseball and the drug."

Following months of denials, Hernandez finally admitted to having used cocaine and to playing in a game while under the influence of the drug. In fact he described himself as having been crazy in 1980. He told of an incident in late November of that year, when he had lost ten pounds and awoke one morning with the shakes and with his nose bleeding. "I threw a gram away, down the toilet.... It was a like a demon in me," he said of the drug.

When asked if he ever bought cocaine for other players, Hernandez responded, "Players never sell. It was there to use. It was shared.... Some would pick up some, a gram, if they had a connection. You'd give him a hundred dollars." Hernandez also painted a vivid picture of cocaine's lure. "Most of the guys who use it do it on the road after a ball game. It's white, creamy, sometimes like salt, sometimes flaky. You chop it up, make a few lines, use a straw or dollar bill, and snort it up your nose. It instantly goes into your system.... It's a feeling of being up, of being on top of the world. The word is overused, but it's a feeling of euphoria. It's an upper. When you come down, the immediate urge is to do more."

He testified to asking Lonnie Smith, his teammate in 1983 with the Cardinals, to purchase some cocaine from Strong after seeing Strong in the lobby of the Pittsburgh Hilton and Towers. When asked why he didn't simply buy it for himself, Hernandez responded, "I figured that [officials] were getting aware of the cocaine problem in major league baseball. It was pretty obvious they were. I wanted to be careful. I didn't want to be seen with Curtis. I figured they were watching him."

Following that day's proceedings Renfroe admitted to going out of his way to inconvenience the government's star witnesses. For example, he insisted on lunch recess before he had finished with Hernandez in order to force the Mets' first baseman to stay around Pittsburgh for a few more hours. "I did that on purpose. I want to make things as difficult on them as possible. They're making it difficult on my client," he told reporters.

Seven players in all were called to the stand in the ensuing days of September. Following Hernandez were Enos Cabell, Jeffrey Leonard, Dale Berra, Dave Parker, and John Milner, who had retired from the game after finishing the 1982 season. The gripping testimony that began with Smith and Hernandez continued. Or, as the *Associated Press* reported, "Here were highly paid baseball players admitting that their primary concern at times when they came to the ballpark was not to win a game, but to hide that they were high on drugs."

For the spectators of the trial, things would only get better.

Cabell spoke of his drug use increasing dramatically during the strike of 1981, which supported Sam Reich's and others' theory that that was the year when cocaine use among players became an epidemic. "That was the strike year, and we weren't playing," Cabell said. "I had nothing to do." He also seemed to play right into Renfroe's hands, assisting the attorney in establishing the poor man versus rich man theme of the trial. After discussing his yearly salary, which was between $375,000 and $450,000, Cabell declared, "I don't make that much money, if you ask me."

In their testimonies the seven players who took the stand would implicate more than twenty additional players in drug use, with the drugs of choice being not just cocaine but also amphetamines. Much of the testimony about greenies came via Dale Berra.

Renfroe: "From whom did you get amphetamines in Pittsburgh?

Berra: "From Bill Madlock."

Renfroe: "Who else, if anyone, did you get them from?"

Berra: "From Willie Stargell."

Renfroe: "Willie Stargell gave you amphetamines?"

Berra: "Yes, when he was playing for us."

Both Stargell and Madlock swiftly denied the accusation. "It's not true," said Stargell. "That's about all I can say about it."

Later Berra seemingly contradicted himself, saying, "If I asked them for [an amphetamine]... I could get one. But I didn't ask for any, and they never gave me one." He described the pills as having helped him play when he was in pain. "It makes your body feel stronger," he said.

Berra said his first meeting with Curtis Strong took place in 1982 in Dave Parker's suite at the Franklin Plaza hotel in Philadelphia, where Parker, Milner, Lee Lacy, Stargell, and several Pirates coaches were getting together. "We were going to eat some food Stargell brought us when Curtis Strong came to the door," Berra said. At which point Berra, Parker, Lacy, Milner, and Strong went into a separate room, away from Stargell and the coaches, and Berra bought a gram of cocaine.

Berra also testified to Strong's presence at Three Rivers Stadium, saying that he had seen Strong talking with Parker in the Pittsburgh clubhouse prior to a game, after which Berra said hello to Strong in the hallway. The greeting brought a warning from manager Chuck Tanner, "Don't talk to that gentleman."

When asked by reporters about Berra's testimony, Tanner responded that he had never seen or met Curtis Strong, and if he had suspected anyone might have been peddling drugs inside his team's quarters, he "would have had them taken out." He did, however, say that he had heard of "a short, fat black guy always around the hotel." A war of words and he said–she said pattern seemed to be developing between members of the one-time family. The clubhouse scene Tanner spoke of was a far cry from the setting the players described. "All the clubs follow the same rule," Tanner said. "Nobody's allowed in there, not even a brother or a father." Berra, on the other hand, testified that "the Pirates clubhouse was a pretty liberal place to be. If a player had a friend, he could come into the clubhouse."

Berra was followed on the stand by Jeffrey "Penitentiary Face" Leonard of the San Francisco Giants, who was subjected to Renfroe's grueling cross-examination. The attorney was particularly tough on the outfielder, as he continued on a course to discredit the government's witnesses. During one sequence, Leonard described the effect of cocaine as making him feel numb, to which Renfroe quickly responded, "Are you still numb in the head?"

===

By the fifth day of testimony in the trial of Curtis Strong, the man who sat in the defendant's seat had become nothing more than an afterthought. Strong had been described by the media as burly, stout, pudgy, hefty, and baby-faced, while his own attorney called him a "pitiful little jock sniffer." But besides that, Strong was barely talked about at all, certainly not by his own attorney, who was busy monopolizing the witnesses' time with lengthy cross-examinations. *USA Today* called Strong "the forgotten man at his own trial." Hours would go by without his name even being mentioned.

Wednesday, September 11, would prove to be no different for the thirty-eight-year-old chicken wing connoisseur. Former Pirates star Dave Parker was up next, attracting a standing-room-only crowd to the courthouse. Indicative of the city's priorities and focus at the time was the fact that attendance at Three Rivers Stadium the previous night had been only 3,133 for the Pirates game against the Chicago Cubs. Among the spectators in the courthouse for Parker's appearance were two members of the Cubs coaching staff, Don Zimmer and Billy Conners.

Parker described recreational cocaine use as "sort of the in-thing to do" during the Pirates World Series–winning 1979 season. "Cocaine was becoming vastly popular in society, and it was constantly available because of who I was," Parker said. Pitcher David Cone, in Roger Angell's 2001 book *A Pitcher's Story*, described the early 1980s scene similarly. "Drugs were different then. At the parties we'd be drinking and talking, having fun, and somebody would pass cocaine around on a kitchen plate. It was, 'Here, kid, you want to try some of this?' and then it would move on. Nobody made anything of it, the way they do now—it was like a picnic."

Parker explained where he would obtain the drug. "From various places," he said. "I know, after the Series, I had come in contact with a young man by the name of Greer; I got it from him, and then just other places where people would just basically give it to me."

Upon prompting from the U.S. attorney, Parker described how he had kicked his cocaine habit. "I felt like my game was more important than cocaine. I have a daughter, and that was more important than cocaine. I wanted to get married, and that was more important than cocaine. It was not a priority in my case," he said.

Parker backed up his former teammate Dale Berra's assertion that Strong was certainly a known entity to the Pirates as well as to players around the league. "Curtis was pretty well known to have cocaine… by quite a few players in the National League," Parker said. Strong was also held in such high esteem with the Pittsburgh ball club that he was invited to the Pirates' New Year's Eve party at Bill Madlock's home. Parker, like Berra, said that he was warned by his manager and other Pirates officials to keep his distance from Strong. He related a memo from the league office that was read to the team by their manager. "Chuck Tanner cautioned us about Curtis Strong, that a drug probe was going on," Parker said. He testified that the same warning was issued in regard to his acquaintance Shelby Greer. "Shelby Greer was known to be 'hot,' the way he was doing things around the ballpark," Parker said. "Shelby Greer was very well known around the Pirates organization. He was being watched by security. All the players were aware of that."

During his cross-examination, when Renfroe wasn't questioning the star on his "twenty-five-thousand-dollar Rolex watch" or "twenty-thousand-dollar diamond rings," the attorney spent the majority of Parker's time on the stand discussing his connection to Greer. Now it wasn't just the high-paid stars that were overshadowing Curtis Strong at his own trial, it was also the specter of Shelby Greer. Parker testified that he had sometimes arranged through the Pirates' traveling secretary for Shelby Greer to be on team flights. At this, Renfroe turned up the heat. "So, as a result, you were instrumental in destroying Rod Scurry's career by introducing him to Greer and cocaine, because he wasn't as strong as you?" Renfroe then asked a similar question with respect to Dale Berra, before simply making Parker the cause of all of the Pirates' woes. "As a result of your introduction of Shelby Greer, the Pirates went from the world championship to the bottom of the National League. Isn't that right, Mr. Parker?"

"That's a pretty strong statement, Mr. Renfroe," Parker responded.

"How do you carry that burden," asked Renfroe, "knowing because of you the Pirates went from the world championship to being the worst in the National League?"

"I don't carry that burden because I don't take responsibility for what adults do. Those relationships are ones that adults conduct with one another," said Parker.

As Renfroe, with voice raised, continued attacking Parker's character, the mild-mannered Judge Diamond decided he had heard enough and excused the jury before addressing Renfroe. "You are not doing your client any good, at least from my point of view, as I see it, and that form of histrionics may have some place in fiction, but it does not have any place in the courtroom," Diamond said. When Renfroe tried to reply, Diamond shook his pencil at the lawyer and shot out a terse "Do not interrupt me." Finally Johnson attempted to add his two cents, to which Diamond silenced him. "Now listen, Mr.

Johnson, I do not need any aid or assistance from the United States Attorney at this time.... I am well capable of handling it."

Diamond cautioned Renfroe that it might serve everyone's interest if he gave himself a good talking to. "I have been talking to myself since this case commenced," replied Renfroe.

Chuck Tanner was again put on the defensive following Parker's day of testimony. Reached at the stadium for his response, the manager again pleaded ignorance. "I never knew there was anyone on our ball club involved in drugs in 1983," he said. "I didn't know Strong or Greer.... The first time I saw Curtis Strong was on TV. Greer was Dave Parker's friend. I saw him one or two times in passing, and I wouldn't know him." Finally Tanner shot back, "I'm not on trial. Those guys who took cocaine are."

Parker had also backed Berra's testimony of receiving amphetamines in the Pirates' locker room. "Did I use them with the Pirates? Yes.... I got them in the clubhouse from Stargell, from Madlock," said Parker, who stressed that he was never charged for the pills. Parker described amphetamine use as common in the majors, "to combat fatigue." Madlock, meanwhile, called both Parker and Berra "liars."

The bombshell of the trial exploded the next day, Thursday, September 12, during John Milner's testimony, which drew gasps in the overcrowded courtroom. The Pirate was testifying about his use of different drugs when Renfroe began reading aloud to the court from part of the grand jury transcript in which the former outfielder described a concoction he had tried during the beginning of his career as a member of the New York Mets in 1973.

"There was this one thing called red juice," Renfroe quoted Milner as saying. "I tasted it one time during his last year, and it was really nasty. Willie had this red juice.... I guess the pharmacist made it for him. I don't know what kind of speed it was, but it kept your eyes open."

Renfroe stopped reading and looked up. "Willie who?" he asked Milner.

"Willie Mays. I went into his locker and got it," Milner responded.

"Willie Mays?" Renfroe asked, to be sure.

"The great one, yes," Milner replied.

Johnson remembers a sudden "jolt" reverberating throughout the courtroom and says he was reminded of an old movie scene where reporters would scurry out the courtroom doors to the nearest pay phone to report the news. Milner did add that he never actually *saw* Mays ingest the liquid, nor had Mays given it to him. Regardless, in the trial of this sometime-caterer, the name of one of baseball's greatest players had just surfaced in reference to drug use. Whether Curtis Strong's chances were looking good or not, Adam Renfroe had succeeded in one thing: major league baseball absolutely *was* on trial. Bruce Keidan, a columnist for the *Pittsburgh Post-Gazette*, compared Renfroe to a magician who has "managed to transform himself into the prosecuting attorney. Instead of defending Strong, he is trying major league baseball." Added Keidan, "I don't know whether Adam Renfroe can saw a lady in half or pull a rabbit out of a hat, but he is pretty good at the old magician's trick of misdirecting our attention. He is doing his damnedest to make Curtis Strong disappear.... It is quite a trick."

Keidan explained that when he covered baseball in the late 1960s, amphetamines were readily available around big league ball clubs. So much so that if a starting pitcher did not take them prior to the game, "he was regarded as something of a freak." Keidan put amphetamine use in context, saying that at the time, they were also used by a great deal of students during late-night cram sessions, truck drivers, and football players, not to mention heavy ladies who "ate them with their ice cream sundaes" in an attempt to lose weight. But nonetheless, Keidan wrote, "Renfroe, being a magician, has made us forget all that."

Mays denied the accusation. His longtime physician appeared on *CBS Evening News* with Dan Rather to say the mixture was Phenergin VC, a cough syrup used by Mays for sinus problems and colds he had been experiencing at the time.

Milner attested to also using amphetamines as a member of the Pirates, saying the pills sometimes mysteriously appeared in his locker when he arrived at the ballpark. "I don't know who dispensed them. They'd always be in my locker. Not every game. Usually games in the second half of the season when the players are worn out and a little tired," said Milner. "Everybody doesn't take them.... I just know I'd take 'em." (Kevin Connolly also spoke of this mysterious pill fairy, saying Rod Scurry used to bring his greenies home to Connolly to dole out to their lady friends, who enjoyed the pills. Scurry never asked for them, Connolly says, they would already be in his locker.)

Pressed by Renfroe to divulge the source of the greenies, Milner wouldn't bite.

Renfroe: "Who gave them to you, Mr. Milner?"

Milner: "I don't know."

Renfroe: "Did they drop out of the ceiling?"

Milner: "No."

Renfroe: "Did the fairy godmother place them there?"

Milner: "You never know."

Later on the stand, Milner described a typical day in the life. "You'd stay up all night doing coke and wouldn't get to bed until 3:00 A.M., 3:30. Your heart is pounding, and you're tired, but you can't sleep, so you don't get up until 2:00 p.m. or 3:00 p.m. There's no time to relax because it's time to go to the ballpark. So you take a few 'greenies' and some coffee to wake up. Then you have a few reds before the game."

Renfroe continued to talk about everyone except Curtis Strong. At one point, he was even able to get Milner to agree that Shelby Greer was "in fact, an associate of the Pittsburgh Pirates, wasn't he?" "Yes, he was," Milner answered. This agreement led Renfroe to begin calling Greer "an associate member of the Pittsburgh Pirates."

By this point in the trial Renfroe had become firmly entrenched under the skin of his peers. During Milner's testimony he conjured up conspiracy theories, accusing Johnson of working with Milner's attorney, Sam Reich, to keep the players out of trouble. "You are trying now to use Curtis because there was a conspiracy on the part of Mr. Reich and Mr. Johnson," accused Renfroe. Johnson slammed his fist to the courtroom table in a fiery objection.

The following morning Johnson was still seething. Before another day of testimony began, he asked to approach the bench, where he informed the judge that the prosecutors had again heard a radio interview with Adam Renfroe in which he attacked a government witness—this time Dave Parker—despite Judge Diamond's order that Renfroe was to "discontinue making statements about credibility of witnesses."

"I want to put on the record again that I think Mr. Renfroe has been totally out of control," Johnson said. "He has made a mockery of this court's order. He has made a mockery of these proceedings. His remarks yesterday about my association with Mr. Reich are just an example."

"What do you want to put on the record?" asked Judge Diamond.

"I think Mr. Renfroe should not only be admonished, but he should be sanctioned," responded Johnson. "I think Your Honor has been trying to be as even-handed as you always are, but he has pushed this court and pushed this whole proceeding into a circus, and I think, at a certain point, something has to be done, even if it is a mistrial. The government has a right to a fair trial, too, and Mr. Renfroe continuously tries this thing on the courthouse steps.... He has come in here from Philadelphia, and he has acted in this court like no other lawyer in my fourteen years of experience as a trial lawyer."

Renfroe later joked that his theatrics would undoubtedly be good for business. "My fees will go up 20 percent after this case," he said.

====

EXPECTATIONS WERE high as Curtis Strong's defense team prepared to call its first witness. Spectators anticipated at least five or six celebrities would take the stand and the spectacular show would continue rolling right along. Names floating around included Willie Mays, Willie Stargell, Joaquín Andújar, and former commissioner Bowie Kuhn. Renfroe had even named Pete Rose as a possible witness. Rose was only a week removed from breaking Ty Cobb's all-time hits mark. Such rumors once again drove courtroom attendance past the one hundred mark. However, to everyone's surprise, Renfroe called no more players to the stand, only manager Chuck Tanner and friends and family of the defendant.

Tanner was nothing if not consistent, despite allegations to the contrary. This was seemingly the reason he had been called. Renfroe was banking on the fact that Tanner would continue to stay his course, denying any knowledge of Strong being around the ball club and thus raising the question, if Strong was such a presence, how could the manager of the team not have known about him? Tanner did just that, contradicting pieces of Berra's and Parker's testimonies concerning the manager having knowledge of Strong's presence inside the Pirates' clubhouse. "I have my own office, and I rarely go into the clubhouse—maybe once or twice a year," Tanner said. "I don't have time to go in the clubhouse and see who's in there." He then testified that his office was a mere twenty to thirty steps away from the clubhouse. He acknowledged that at one time there had been a much more liberal clubhouse policy. But after players were arrested on drug charges in Kansas City, he said, clubhouse security had been ramped up at the suggestion of the commissioner's office.

As he had done previously, Tanner denied having ever seen Curtis Strong or having warned his players to stay away from Strong. He did, however, repeat that he had heard whispers of "a short, fat black guy that hangs around the hotel." Tanner testified that these rumors led him to call a hotel bar to inform Berra about an "unsavory-looking character" hanging around the hotel and to tell Berra to avoid him. Tanner said he never suspected Berra of being a drug user. "I never asked him about [drugs]," he said. However, when asked about Berra just a week earlier, Tanner had told the *Post-Gazette*, "They hid it from me pretty well. Especially Dale. I asked him several times about it. He always said, 'No way would I ever do that.' This surprises and disappoints me."

Maybe the best summation of Tanner's answers came from a fifteen-year-old student from nearby Montour High School who had taken in the trial with a friend since classes were cancelled due to a teachers' strike. After hearing Tanner's testimony, the youngster told reporters that the manager "doesn't remember a lot." He also commented that it wasn't a surprise to hear of players using drugs. "All the older players have to take drugs," the student said. "They can't move as fast as the younger players."

Assistant U.S. Attorney James Ross found Tanner's deflection of responsibility hard to swallow. "Strong and some of the others were in the Pirates' locker room on a nightly basis after these games," he recalls. "And it came out that people were warning Tanner, 'You gotta get this guy the hell out of there.' So for [Pirates management] to express shock—" Ross shakes his head. Even today, he isn't buying it.

Curtis Strong had shown little emotion during the two-week-old trial, but with the testimony of his parents, Albert and Helen, Strong finally began to crack. Speaking on behalf of their son, each parent told of how well respected Strong was within his Philadelphia community and described what a good son he was. Strong was seen dabbing the tears in his eyes. Strong's father wiped away tears of his own, saying of his son's arrest, "It hurt me in my heart." However, Renfroe quickly turned the spotlight back on himself, asking Strong's mother if her son ever wore expensive clothing or jewelry, stereotypical of a drug kingpin. "Is your son a flashy guy like me?" he asked.

The only thing remaining before the jury would adjourn to make its decision was for the two battling men in ties to give their closing arguments. Renfroe promised to deliver a show, informing the media, "You can expect a cold-blooded dogfight. I'm going to throw everything at [the jury] but the kitchen sink.... It's going to be a street fight. There's going to be a rumble in that courtroom."

Baseball's best and brightest were long gone from Pittsburgh and back to their respective cities. Curtis Strong was left behind to await his fate. Upon his return to New York City, Keith Hernandez was greeted at Shea Stadium with a hero's welcome and a standing ovation.

Prior to the attorneys' closing arguments, Judge Diamond ruled that the issue of player immunity could not be raised in closing statements. He wanted the jury to focus on the charges against Strong, and those charges only. Never mind that Renfroe made the question of why immunity was granted to the players and not to his client a central piece of his defense, such statements would no longer be allowed.

First up was J. Alan Johnson. "It has been a hard-fought case," Johnson told the jury. "But Mr. Renfroe has attempted to divert your attention in every way possible, quite artfully I might add, away from your duties in this case. He has tried to put baseball management on trial, Shelby Greer on trial, the commissioner of baseball on trial, the players' lawyers, the FBI, the United States Attorney's Office, really everyone but his client. That is what you are here for. That is what he is here for. Ladies and gentlemen, this is an age-old tactic. Don't be fooled by that tactic. Because you are going to be called upon to decide one thing: is this defendant, Curtis Strong, in this particular case, guilty of the charges in the indictment?"

Johnson pointed out that Strong's customers were a salesman's dream. "Curtis Strong knew he had the ideal clientele for a drug dealer. Young men with money, on the road with a lot of time on their hands… professional baseball players." Johnson did not try to legitimize the actions of these players, however, saying, "That doesn't mean what those players did was right. It was illegal…. The government does not stand here and tell you that these ballplayers don't have a lot to be ashamed of. They have a lot to be ashamed of in a lot of ways…. They disgraced themselves and their profession… their teams and their cities. But they were not the source of the drugs…. Look at the source," he said.

Next came Renfroe. In speaking of his client, he said, "Even if I was looking at it from outside, I would say, 'Hey, if this is the guy that is spoiling Chevrolets, hot dogs, and apple pie, and he is the one that is destroying our people, and our little kids are looking up to these heroes, this is the boy that is doing it, put him in jail, get rid of him.' But is he the one? Is he the one that is destroying the spinal cord of America? Or is it the ballplayers and the managers and the owners, with all this money, trying to cover it up and use him as a scapegoat and then washing it underneath the rug? And [after] you have got rid of [Strong] and put him in jail.... Let's go. Let's play ball. Is that America? It is the big people against the little people. It is the haves and the have-nots.... I am not trying to sensationalize this thing. Yes, I have talked a lot, and you might think I have talked too much, and my mother says, 'Yes, you talk too much, shut up.'"

Talk Renfroe did, with passion and vigor. He ranted about the lack of evidence: "Where's the dope?" He attacked the credibility of the players, and their immunity, Judge Diamond's warning notwithstanding. *What manner of men are these?* became his rallying call. "What manner of men are these? The government seeks to have you, as jurors, legalize the use of cocaine by major league ballplayers."

Renfroe then specified his wrath. "Ladies and gentlemen, Keith Hernandez refused to divulge the name of another cocaine supplier who was a major league ballplayer. He refused to do so, even though he had immunity.... Don't let him spit in your face and tell you it is raining. But he is in New York, to a standing ovation, laughing at us here in Pittsburgh.

"Jeff Leonard, the six-million-dollar man. Would he lie, up there on that stand? Ask yourself, if you received six million dollars, and you would lose it, would you lie, up there on that stand? You ask yourself that.

"Dave Parker. Holy God, Dave Parker. What manner of a man is he? Two-thousand-dollar alligator shoes on, twenty-five-thousand-dollar watches, diamond and gold on each hand.... Dave Parker, the Venezuela connection. Dave Parker, ladies and gentlemen. His cocaine man was right next to him in the plane.... If [the Pirates] had their own cocaine connection, their own man, right here in Pittsburgh, sitting with them, going all over the place with them, why would Curt have to come here to give them a little bit of cocaine? Is it believable?

"Is your sense of justice so bizarre that you would look favorably on these people?" he asked the jury.

The attorney then apologized to the jury for his sometimes disorderly and demonstrative behavior. "But the first day I came in here I was so emotional," Renfroe said, "I had a hard time separating my profession from my friendship with Curtis Strong.... Why in all of America, with all the drug dealers, why is it the same Curtis I used to hold hands with in school who is on trial here?"

Renfroe, who had requested a Bible just prior to the day's proceedings getting underway, finished his seventy-five-minute closing argument reading from the twenty-seventh Psalm. Eyes toward the heavens, Renfroe beseeched the Lord, "Deliver me not over unto the will of mine enemies. For false witnesses are risen up against me."

As America awaited the jury's decision, the shock of the trial was still settling in. It was hard to put a finger on why the whole affair had been so startling and powerful. It wasn't so much the knowledge that players were using cocaine that had shocked the public; it was the rawness with which they described their experiences. One minute they told sordid tales of bleeding and shaking, dumping drugs into toilets, hotel room debauchery, and other behaviors typical of a stone-cold addict. It was a depraved setting. At other times they were completely blasé about drug use. Enos Cabell spoke offhandedly of getting two or three hits a game while he was high. John Milner said that he always knew when pitcher J. R. Richard was using during a game, because Richard wouldn't be nearly as fast a pitcher. There was a seemingly total lack of respect among players for the sport they played, the game so many Americans wished they themselves had been blessed with the talent and opportunity to continue playing into adulthood. These men were the envy of not just young children but grown men. Through Little League almost all boys, whether geeky or brawny, had once played the game, so a rooting interest was instilled within them for baseball, more so than for any other American sport. During the trial of Curtis Strong, however, the game was described as being nothing more than an afterthought to the men who were being paid millions to play it. And as became evident through the players' testimony, no legend of the game would ever be above reproach again. The sport's seedier underside had been revealed.

Locally, the trial elicited strong reactions. Nearby college students took to skipping class to watch it. Taxi driver Joe Stachowski succinctly explained why he wouldn't be attending any Buccos games in the future. "I'll be damned if I'm gonna support any player's drug habit," he said.

Nationally, sentiment wavered. Wally Walsh of the fan group United Fan Action Network in Portland, Oregon, told *USA Today*, "Nobody likes to pay money to watch people using dope. The fans in general think everybody does it." Colorado farmer Dan Stadelman agreed. "To me, I guess they're all involved, the way it sounds." Others looked at the trial's finger-pointing sideshow as shameless and unfair to those who were unable to defend themselves. "Seems to be a lot of name dropping. I don't think it's fair," said a Columbus, Ohio, fan. The *LA Times* referred to the affair in Pittsburgh as "baseball's name dropping cocaine trial." Harvard law professor Arthur Miller contemplated issues such as the rights of the third person. "This aspect of the law troubles me mightily," Miller told *USA Today*. "I feel very deeply about the rights of third persons, but it is hard for me to see how to do it better." In cases dealing with government witnesses who are given immunity, such name dropping often occurs. The only way to avoid it would be for segments of trials to proceed in private, out of earshot of spectators. "And then the media scream," Miller said. "Unfortunately, the system doesn't work perfectly." This was no comfort to guys like Willie Mays. "Why am I going to be on trial for what he says he thinks he saw in my locker?" Mays wondered to the media following the mention of his name in John Milner's testimony. "It's a shame a man can be crucified for one statement, to play all those years and have one statement crucify me. I hope the people won't take that one statement and crucify me."

Other players supported Mays and those who weren't present at the trial to clear their names. "It's shameful," said California Angels outfielder Gary Pettis. "Former great players who can't defend themselves are having their names dragged through the mess."

J. Alan Johnson deflected blame, pointing instead to Adam Renfroe as the culprit, since the names had come out during Renfroe's cross-examinations. Renfroe wasn't having it. "I didn't bring their names out," he said. "It was these five-million-dollar ballplayers who have been criminally using cocaine for five years who brought Willie Mays's name out, Willie Stargell out." However, as attorney Sam Reich pointed out, the player-witnesses had no other choice than to answer the questions asked of them truthfully, before adding, "Their names had no business coming up at that trial. Amphetamines and red juice had nothing to do with this case."

As Curtis Strong stood outside the courthouse awaiting the verdict, he was asked by reporters for his thoughts. Strong was unsure. "I don't know," he said. "I think, but then I don't want to think.... I don't know." As far as public sentiment regarding Strong's guilt, Renfroe's attempt to stir up class warfare seemed to be resonating with the common man. Many felt that without the government having produced any hard evidence, Strong could be put away based only on the confessions of addicts with bad memories—in other words, the players. The question was, were such witnesses credible? A Pittsburgh-area school teacher and thirteen-year Pirates season ticket holder, Cynthia Colarusso, who followed the trial, told *USA Today*, "Strong should have been given immunity, and the players should have been prosecuted." Added local bar owner Bob Kotula, "Why should those people get immunity? Some businessman who gets caught, he's away in federal prison. A ballplayer, a guy sitting here, we're all the same."

Assistant U.S. Attorney James Ross can understand the public's negative perception of the proceedings but explains that, despite the size of the witnesses' pocketbooks, this really was nothing more than a standard case, and a small one at that. In the years after *United States v. Curtis Strong* Ross developed a speech that he routinely gave to the jury in drug cases, with respect to the issue of witness credibility. It went in part, "Ladies and gentleman, the government is presenting you a case of people who were dealing drugs. How else would you infiltrate a drug organization than by the people who are using [the drugs]? I'm certainly not going to go to a Catholic priest, for instance, because a dealer wouldn't act that way in front of a priest. The only time a drug dealer acts the way he does is in front of the people who are his customers. So naturally the people you have to bring in to tell the story are the people who lived it and breathed it every day."

Journalist Dan Donovan concurs with the sentiments in Ross's speech and says that during his time covering the courts he came to realize that it was standard procedure for purchasers in drug cases to be granted immunity. If defense attorneys cry injustice, it is simply because they are on the "wrong side of immunity" in a particular case.

Ross says the Strong case all came down to money. "It was hard for the public to accept because these people you were granting immunity to... they were making a million dollars a year, and they were getting a walk for something they did that tarnished baseball's image."

=====

AT 1:15 P.M. on September 20, after nine hours of deliberation spread over the course of two days, the jury reached a decision. However, prior to the reading of the verdict, Judge Diamond issued a foreboding statement directed to attorney Adam Renfroe Jr. "At the conclusion of the proceedings, regardless of what the verdict is, I have a proceeding involving you. You are to remain in the courtroom, and everybody remain in place," declared Judge Diamond. At that point J. Alan Johnson leaned over to agents Morrison and Craig and said, "Diamond's going to drop the hammer on him."

After fourteen days and much ado, the end had finally come. At 2:00 P.M. the courtroom became silent, and the court clerk read the jury's findings one count at a time. Curtis Strong was found guilty on eleven of the fourteen counts of selling cocaine to major league baseball players. Strong showed no emotion. Sentencing was set for October 21, at which time he would face up to fifteen years in prison for each of the eleven charges.

After Strong was escorted away by bailiffs, Judge Diamond set his sights on the defendant's attorney. He sentenced Renfroe to thirty days in jail for contempt of court. The judge said he would submit details of his ruling to the Pennsylvania Supreme Court for possible disciplinary action against Renfroe. According to the Associated Press, "He disciplined Renfroe because the attorney argued, in violation of an earlier ruling, that by finding Strong guilty, the jury would be condoning the government's granting of immunity to the player-witnesses."

Speaking publicly for the first time about the case, Judge Diamond explained that there were "probably seventy" items Renfroe could have been held in contempt for and said his conduct was disruptive to the dignity and authority of the court. "There is no reason why counsel should ever defy the rulings of the court," Diamond said.

Renfroe, for his part, made it clear he was not about to throw in the towel. "It's not over until the fat lady sings," he said later outside the courtroom, pointing to the likelihood of an appeal. Of his contempt charge, the attorney said, "I fought zealously and hard in a manner [Judge Diamond]'s never seen before. I at no time intended to show disrespect to the court."

Speaking with the media following the reading of the verdict, the jurors provided some interesting insights into the impassioned courtroom scene. David Irvin, a Pittsburgh truck driver, said, "It was clear Curtis Strong was dealing dope." Irvin did, however, feel that the ballplayers were equally guilty. "I think it's too bad something can't be done about them," he said. "I don't believe that Mr. Strong is the biggest pusher in Pittsburgh or Philadelphia. I think he's a small man who got caught up in it. But he broke the law." Added juror Faith Hoskinson, "I feel bad that he's going to jail. But if you do the crime, you've got to do the time."

An alternate juror, Gayle E. Silkroski, who was reached at her home following the trial, expressed a contrasting perspective. Silkroski, who watched the events from the jury box before being dismissed prior to deliberations, said she would have voted to acquit. "Without going over the testimony and the facts, you might say I would have had reasonable doubt," Silkroski said. "There's Curtis getting blamed for everything when most of the players testified they did the same thing, sell cocaine." She also found some of the players' testimony unbelievable and found it strange they could be so sure of some dates yet unsure of others. For instance, Jeffrey Leonard remembered the exact dates of cocaine purchases from Strong yet couldn't bring to mind his own wedding anniversary. Wells Morrison points out that recollections of the specific dates of cocaine purchases were indeed possible because ballplayers' lives revolve around the dates of their games, and therefore a player might clearly remember that he bought coke on the first game of a series in Pittsburgh, for example, or prior to a West Coast trip.

Juror Betty Clay, a nurse from Indiana, Pennsylvania, added some color commentary as she later described Dale Berra in the *Indiana Gazette* as "kind of cocky" and Chuck Tanner as a "nervous wreck." She pointed out, "They got [Tanner] to say he never saw Curtis Strong in the Pittsburgh clubhouse in his entire life." Clay saved her most fervent descriptions for the star of the show. "We [jurors] called it the Mr. Renfroe Show. He was so rude to us and the judge. He defied the judge time and time again. He knew he wasn't allowed to do what he did.... At times, you doubted he could be educated through high school, let alone law school. He used street talk and couldn't pronounce a lot of words." Clay added to the *Post-Gazette*, "I just never cared for his delivery. I never believed very much of what he said."

James Ross held a more favorable impression of the Philadelphia lawyer. He says that while it often may have seemed as though the opposing attorneys shared a mutual disdain for one another, the reality was quite different. Renfroe could "piss you off during the day," Ross recalls, "but at the end of the day he'd come over and make a joke" and put things at ease. "I always got along fine with him," Ross says. "Everybody has a different style. Renfroe is a grandstander; that was his style. Whether that was right or wrong, I don't know. Whether that played well in the case, I don't know. The courtroom was kind of his stage." Ross praises Renfroe's savvy. "He was one of those guys; he had—excuse the expression—big balls. He was not afraid of anybody or anything. That was his style."

Sam Reich agrees. "Renfroe had some of the most outstanding trial skills of any defense lawyer that I've ever seen in action." Reich, who also taught trial tactics at downtown Pittsburgh's University of Duquesne, calls Renfroe's strategy "classic drug defense 101," where even if an attorney can't get an acquittal, "you hurt the witness; you embarrass them. You humiliate them. You make them implicate their best friends and members of their families, and you make them regret the day they were born—certainly the day they agreed to cooperate with the government."

Despite saluting Renfroe's aplomb, Reich can't agree with his decision to take Strong's case to trial. "The trial killed him," Reich says. "The Strong case was a case that cried out for a plea bargain."

While the average person may have looked at the case and agreed with Renfroe's assertion that the prosecution lacked hard physical evidence, such omissions mattered little to a veteran counselor such as Reich, who points out that there was corroboration among witnesses about meetings taking place, not to mention hotel records. However, Reich is quick to point out that "someone saying you did something is damaging. *It counts.* Especially when you have eight to ten people saying the same thing. Testimony alone was damaging."

Reich recalls it took no longer than the first witness stepping down from the stand before he knew Strong was in trouble. "Lonnie Smith's testimony … the way he gave it, the straightforward nature, the pathetic nature of it—it absolutely killed Curtis Strong. And it was no longer possible to argue that Curtis Strong was this small-potatoes caterer who was helping his buddies." Reich points to parts of Smith's testimony in which he spoke of trying to get clean and remove drugs from his life only to have Strong contact him in the winter and ultimately send Smith coke through the mail. "That made it certain that if Strong was convicted, his sentence would be much more severe than if he pled," Reich says.

Judge Diamond hoped some good would ultimately come from the high-profile case. Following the reading of the verdict he told the media, "There are millions of baseball fans out there—of all ages. Because of the publicity, we have now brought the matter of the cocaine problem in this country to the attention of young people. Maybe they have found that their idols have feet of clay." He suggested that the trial could serve to have more effect in showcasing the dangers of drugs than any "advertising campaign ever could have done."

James Ross shares this view and says they could have prosecuted Colombian drug lords with multiple kilos of cocaine and it would never have generated the same amount of publicity nationwide. Despite the fact that this case involved relatively small quantities of drugs, says Ross, "it showed how much of society was impacted by this problem."

Before sentencing Strong on November 4, Judge Diamond took a parting shot at the players, stating they "were not virginal innocents." He also held little regard for the fans who supported them. "When those people stand up and applaud Keith Hernandez, or whoever they were applauding, then they are applauding a disreputable element of society," Diamond said. "The fact that the fans should give a standing ovation, I think is a terrible commentary on our society."

Strong was sentenced to twelve years in a low-security prison.

===

IN A separate courtroom down the hall from Judge Diamond's, another trial was going on—that of Robert "Rav" McCue, which had begun during the Strong trial, on September 16. This trial was described—as might be expected given the absence of showman Adam Renfroe—as a quiet and objective affair. "If you walked into [Judge] Cohill's courtroom, it would be hard to appreciate that there was any public interest," Reich says. "It was almost like you might fall asleep."

McCue was charged with selling cocaine on thirteen separate occasions for a total of $760. Only two players testified in the trial— John Milner and Dale Berra, both saying they purchased cocaine from McCue. Milner further attested to sharing and buying drugs from Dave Parker, but that didn't matter; while Parker got off scot-free, McCue was found guilty of seven of the thirteen charges.

At McCue's sentencing, Judge Maurice B. Cohill felt he would be remiss if he didn't share his disdain for not only the players but also the leaders of baseball. Cohill said the players "debased themselves, their families, their friends, the laws of this country, and the millions of people who look up to them." Addressing McCue, he said, "You are, in my judgment, only one of the parties who has injured his fellow man in this case.... Those who manage baseball teams, especially those who personally manage players on the field, have, through their acts of omission, made it easy for you to violate the laws and impugn the integrity of the game of baseball.... In other words the toleration of drug use among players by baseball management helped to create this market [for cocaine]. Without such tolerance, you might not be here today, and the enormous public trust granted to professional baseball by the American public might still be intact."

Reading from a two-and-a-half-page statement, Cohill used the term "managerial sloth" to describe the cause of the damage done to professional baseball and the youth of America. "Whether the managers' blindness to their players' personal and professional degeneration on the playing field and in the clubhouse is because they weren't looking or because they weren't seeing when they did is largely immaterial," Cohill said.

And so, one more person could be added to those having a hard time believing that guys like Chuck Tanner didn't know what was going on in the Pirates clubhouse. Tanner has since vehemently maintained innocence. "How can I look back with any regrets? I didn't know anything about it. What did I do wrong?... If anybody says that, that's bull," Tanner told the *Pittsburgh Post-Gazette* in 1995. Tanner commented that drug counselors had once told him the way to spot drug users was to look for guys who were late, lazy, or not wanting to work. "But the guys on my team who were supposed to be using drugs weren't like that at all," Tanner said. "They were energetic, enthusiastic. They played hurt. Heck, Dale Berra played with a broken leg."

Judge Cohill, however, counseled that if you paid enough attention, then you would surely notice drug activity. He suggested that it was time to stop making things more difficult than they were and to apply some simple common sense. "I consider my office staff to be like a second family," he said. "I hire my law clerks on the basis of their abilities. I always look for the best and the brightest law school graduates. If one of them started coming to work with a hangover or drunk or under the influence of drugs, I might not realize it at once, but if their productivity, efficiency, and mental capabilities started to fall off, I would surely know pretty fast."

He then offered his unsolicited recommendations for America's national pastime. "It may be presumptuous of me to tell owners of baseball teams how they should act or managers how they should manage, but I would feel that I have neglected my duty if I didn't say anything," Cohill said. "If the ownership and the Players Association can't agree on a satisfactory drug-detection program, the owners should at least require their managers to get some professional training in spotting these problems. Such training is available, and if anyone wants to know where, I'll tell them."

McCue was sentenced to ten years at FCI-Allenwood on October 30, 1985.

In early October Shelby Greer pleaded guilty. He was subsequently sentenced to twelve years, which he served at the Federal Correctional Institution in Danbury, Connecticut. By March 1986, with the sentencing of Jeffrey Mosco, who was the last holdout and had finally agreed to a plea bargain, all seven men indicted in May 1985 were behind bars. The judge at Mosco's sentencing criticized the U.S. Attorney's Office for granting immunity to the ballplayers and noted the defendant's less-than-glamorous lifestyle. "According to the presentence report his financial condition is as such," said Judge Donald E. Ziegler. "He lives with his mother, he is on welfare, he has no automobile. The car is in his mother's name. He has a personal loan of four or five thousand dollars, no assets, and two thousand dollars borrowed from his sister. Now is this the lifestyle of a profiteer?"

James Ross explained that often drug dealers have nothing to show for it once they are arrested because in some cases the dealers simply spend their money on more cocaine and the lifestyle they are living. Judge and prosecutor later shared this exchange after Ross argued against Mosco's request for probation.

Judge Ziegler: "Well, you granted immunity to distributors, didn't you?"

Mr. Ross: "Not to distributors, to users, Your Honor."

Judge Ziegler: "I thought you stated they distributed among themselves."

Mr. Ross: "They shared, but not for profit, Your Honor."

Judge Ziegler: "I see. But they did distribute, didn't they?"

Mr. Ross: "They shared with others; I will admit that on the record."

Judge Ziegler: "You have granted immunity to distributors, and you are urging me to make an example out of this man, aren't you? What type of an example has been set concerning these distributors of cocaine? To wit: most of them are in Florida today at large salaries in a nice warm climate pursuing an occupation that most of the people in this courtroom would be pleased to exchange. Is that the example that has been set for society?"

Remarkably, after only a year and a half on the job, Ross withstood the pressure and delivered a solid rebuttal.

"Yes, it is, Your Honor," Ross said, simply. "For this reason: without their testimony, without granting them immunity, we would not be here today, and this man would still be over at Michael J's dealing cocaine."

Mosco was sentenced to four years at the Federal Correctional Institute in Loretto, Pennsylvania, on March 7, 1986. Mosco compared his involvement in the cocaine transactions to that of the players, stating he thought he was simply doing his friends a favor. "I didn't go knocking on their doors peddling that stuff," he told the *New York Times.* "They came to me, pestering me to get the stuff. I was a bartender." The same article states that Dale Berra corroborated Mosco's description of merely acting as a middleman, passing money and product from one person to another.

Away from the courthouse, those in positions of power in the major leagues felt that with the sentencings of the seven men, baseball had ridded itself of its problems. Said Pirates GM Joe L. Brown after the trials, in October 1985, "Baseball is now on a course that will remove any threat of any widespread—or perhaps any—use of such substances in the future."

The Pirates finished the 1985 regular season with a record of 57–104, leaving them a mere 43.5 games off the pace in the National League East. Total attendance for the year sat at 735,900, the second-lowest mark in the league.

=====

FOLLOWING HIS defeat in the Curtis Strong trial, Adam Renfroe's year went from bad to worse. On February 25, 1986, he was once again arrested, this time for obstruction of justice and attempting to bribe a federal witness to change her testimony. It was at this point that Renfroe admitted to having a cocaine addiction of his own, one that spanned nearly sixteen years. At Renfroe's bribery trial, witnesses testified that Renfroe had often been "provided with prostitutes as well as cocaine from his clients."

Suddenly Curtis Strong seemed to have plenty of reasons to try for an appeal. He petitioned the court to grant him a new trial. In the transcripts of Strong's petition to vacate his sentence, new light was shed on his counsel during his 1985 baseball trial. "Within a year of the Strong trial," the petition read, "Mr. Renfroe was convicted of attempted bribery and obstruction of justice. Testimony at Mr. Renfroe's sentencing proceedings established that he had used cocaine for sixteen years, a period which included his representation of Mr. Strong."

Strong's new legal team based his appeal on two grounds of ineffective counsel, first claiming that "Mr. Renfroe's cocaine habit so impaired his mental faculties that he was ineffective." "Mentally incapacitated counsel is no counsel," the affidavit read. In addition it was argued that Renfroe had never offered Strong adequate plea options. This became apparent when Strong's new attorney, Wendell G. Freeland, explained to him that getting off with mere probation should have been considered a highly unlikely result to come from his 1985 indictment. "Mr. Strong's reaction to my statements was one of total shock," Freeland wrote. "Mr. Renfroe was ineffective because he did not attempt plea negotiations on his client's behalf.... Curtis Strong has based his petition for habeas relief primarily on grounds that he was denied effective assistance of counsel because his trial lawyer by his own admission was addicted to cocaine from the time of the filing of the indictment through the appellate process. Here, it is clear that the petitioner was ignorant of his choices and his chances to succeed at trial; he was unfamiliar with the criminal justice system and given no meaningful opportunity by his trial counsel to enter into plea discussions with the government."

Judge Diamond denied Strong's appeal, saying, "Mr. Renfroe presented a vigorous and adequate defense. He was coherent and adroit at all times."

Adam Renfroe was found guilty and sentenced to five years in federal prison and three years' probation as a result of the obstruction and bribery charges. But not before Renfroe attempted to have his sentencing delayed so he could finish his drug treatment program and "prevent a catastrophe with respect to psychological and emotional welfare."

PART IV

AFTERMATH

14

The Response

I WAS ON DRUGS EVERY TIME I TOOK THE FIELD. QUITE
FRANKLY, I HAD A CHANCE TO INJURE A LOT OF LIVES.
THANK GOD, I DIDN'T HURT ANYONE.
    —DOCK ELLIS, OWNER OF A NINETY-MILE-PER-HOUR FASTBALL

O
N AUGUST 4, 1921, Commissioner Kennesaw Mountain Landis, a former judge, handed out lifetime bans to eight men
from the Chicago White Sox who were implicated, yet never
convicted, of fixing the 1919 World Series. On the heels of the Curtis
Strong trial, some sixty-four years later, at least one lawman was
calling for the same. Joseph DiGenova, U.S. attorney in Washington,
D.C., let his beliefs be known in a speech to the Pentagon chapter
of the Federal Bar Association. Appearing in an Associated Press
report, the speech read in part, "Those overpaid, overrated, pampered, overlionized, spoiled brats who have corrupted a great game
should be thrown out of baseball." DiGenova said the players had
already received enough leniency by avoiding criminal charges. "It's
the commissioner's call. What he does will influence not just baseball, but millions of kids all over this country."

The pressure was mounting for Peter Ueberroth, the well-coifed
commissioner who just a year earlier had been named *Time* magazine's Man of the Year for his role as organizer of the ubersuccessful
1984 Los Angeles Olympics.

As was the case in the Black Sox scandal, the damage done to baseball this time around was undeniable. Drugs had sullied the game's image. Execution on the field had suffered. Some of the league's premier players admitted as much themselves in Chass and Goodwin's series of *Times* articles.

"It certainly hurt my performance," said Tim Raines of his habitual cocaine use. "I struck out a lot more; my vision was lessened. A lot of times I'd go up to the plate and the ball was right down the middle and I'd jump back, thinking it was at my head. The umpire would call it a strike, and I'd start arguing. He'd say, 'That ball was right down the middle.' When you're on drugs, you don't feel you're doing anything wrong."

"Look at my defense," Lonnie Smith said, acknowledging the consequences of his drug abuse. "It seemed like I was averaging two or three errors a game. I was getting picked off.... When I became so addicted it's like I went through the motions, and all I wanted to do was get it over with and go back and start all over again."

Smith pointed out to the *Times* that most observers didn't feel like his game was affected because he was still getting hits and maintaining a decent average. But Smith knew, he says today, how much his performance was suffering from drug use. "I didn't feel like I was hitting the ball right," he says. "I mean, I was hitting a lot of balls on the handle. I was getting a lot of duck corks over the outfield. I wasn't hitting with authority. There was a lot of jam shots, a lotta slow grounders, and luckily I was able to leg out a few, although I don't know how, because it felt like I was running with weights."

Baseball executives shared Smith's and Raines's opinions concerning the effects of drugs on the game. John McHale, president of the Montreal Expos, told the *New York Times* that he believed cocaine was the reason his team did not win its division in 1982. "I don't think there's any doubt in '82 that whole scenario cost us a chance to win," McHale said. "We felt we should have won in '82. When we all woke up to what was going on, we found there were at least eight players on our club who were into this thing. There's no question in my mind and [manager] Jim Fanning's mind...that cost us a chance to win."

Shortly after the trials St. Louis manager Whitey Herzog echoed Keith Hernandez's witness-box estimate that 40 percent of all players were using cocaine during this period, including eleven "heavy users" on his Cardinals team. Herzog detailed road trips to Montreal, where, he said, the drug was easily accessible to his players. "It got so bad," Herzog told the *New York Times*, "that when we went to Montreal, which was where they all seemed to get it, I had to have us fly in on the day of the game. That way, I knew we'd play decent for one night, even though the rest of the trip might be a lost cause."

The question now was what the league would do to remedy the situation, not to mention to ensure that such widespread drug use did not infiltrate the game in the future. Would all the evidence be enough to convince those in power not to merely punish players but to implement real policy change?

Sharing the headlines during the trials of Curtis Strong and Robert McCue was the ongoing debate between the players union and owners over the issue of drug testing. The policy in baseball at the time, which had been agreed upon in May 1984 under Commissioner Bowie Kuhn, was that of reasonable-cause testing. Under this joint agreement, owners could have a player tested if there was reasonable suspicion that the player was using drugs, primarily cocaine. Drugs such as marijuana, amphetamines, and alcohol were excluded under the agreement. In essence this agreement allowed management to test known users.

Then, a year later, in May 1985, just prior to the arrests in Pittsburgh, Peter Ueberroth made his grand announcement of mandatory testing for all Major League Baseball employees excluding major league players. A new collective bargaining agreement between the owners and the Players Association was agreed to, following a two-day strike in August 1985. This accord left the joint agreement pertaining to drugs in place. At the time there were more important things for the two sides to argue over, most prominently the issue of money. Drug policy was not even reported among the talking points in coming to a new agreement. Instead, the negotiations centered around salary arbitration, players' benefit plans (which included television revenues), a salary cap, and salary escalation.

Nonetheless, in September 1985 Ueberroth again used the spotlight of the Pittsburgh investigation as a showcase for his drug-testing platform. On the heels of news out of the Justice Department that in the future it would be taking a closer look "at requests by U. S. attorneys to grant immunity to professional athletes involved in drug trials," Ueberroth took the opportunity to join in with the immunity bashers by not only declaring that granting immunity to the seven players "probably was the wrong thing" but also hitching on to attorney Adam Renfroe's refrain and announcing that baseball was indeed "on trial." Hoping to ride the tide of public sentiment, which was in support of drug testing, Ueberroth called a news conference to announce that he had sent letters directly to every major league player asking him to voluntarily submit to drug testing. The letter was hand-delivered to each player, with instructions given for him to answer yes or no to the proposal. Cribbing from a 1921 Kennesaw Mountain Landis speech, Ueberroth summoned the strength of the game's first commissioner. "I want every player to feel I stand behind him," he said, "so long as he is on the square." Furthermore, Ueberroth told the press, "A cloud hangs over baseball. It's a cloud called drugs, and it's permeated our game.... Testing is the only way to show our public and the fans that baseball is clean."

Ueberroth went on to say that failure to eradicate drugs' presence from the game would result in "a decade in which baseball has become synonymous with drugs. We will have turned off a generation of kids and dealt a financial body blow to the game." Finally, Ueberroth laid it on the line: "This is baseball's last chance."

The commissioner suggested that testing was in the players' best interest. "The players are already guilty by association," he said. "There is cynical speculation every time a player misjudges a ball or plays below expectations. We cannot let this season conclude without positively attacking the problem."

Lonnie Smith says he agreed with Ueberroth's assertion and welcomed testing. His attitude was, "If I can't prove that I'm clean, there is always going to be accusations. If I should snap on the field during an argument, or if I get in trouble after a game, it's going to be because I was on drugs. And if I don't have something that proves I'm not doing drugs, then who's going to believe me?"

The Players Association's executive director, Donald Fehr, saw things differently. "I view today's events with a fair measure of distress and sadness," Fehr told the media. He called Ueberroth's actions of bypassing the union and attempting to negotiate directly with the players as possibly "unlawful" and "entirely inappropriate." Fehr said the plan was "a plain, old-fashioned attempt not to bargain." He further characterized the move as nothing more than a news-grab, and one that was "demonstrably unlikely to advance the ball further.... His actions have exacerbated the problem," Fehr said.

"If they have a proposal to make, make the proposal," Fehr said. "If there are specifics involved, tell us what they are. We are not refusing anything in a collective bargaining sense, but don't go directly to the players."

Days later, just as the jury announced Robert McCue's verdict, Peter Ueberroth issued a statement explaining his unusual steps and saying the move was brought on by pressure from the players themselves. Using the term "overwhelming consensus" to describe the players' desire to clean up the game, Ueberroth also noted that the players had a "clear belief that testing is a solution." After initially attempting to circumvent the union, the commissioner now said he hoped to work with the union to have a plan installed by the World Series, which was only three weeks away.

All but four teams put the testing question to a vote. The reaction within baseball to Ueberroth's union-bypass play was mixed. It angered some, and others dismissed it outright, while many seemed ready to join in the call for testing. Regardless of their stance on the issue of testing, however, nearly all players agreed that any move on the testing front would have to come through negotiations with the union.

The results of the New York Mets vote showed Mets players voting unanimously in favor of voluntary testing, as long as the Players Association worked out all the details. "I think everyone feels something's got to be done, but it's a matter that should be hammered out between the commissioner and the Players Association," said Mets pitcher Ron Darling.

Pirates players and coaches also voted in favor of a testing program. "The players want drug testing but only with our union's approval of the program. We are looking for ways of cleaning up baseball and showing the fans that baseball is a clean sport," said Pirates player representative Jim Morrison.

Tommy Herr of the St. Louis Cardinals said, "There is a growing faction of players that are tired of protecting drug users." Earlier in the year, Bobby Grich of the California Angels similarly said, "I would be proud to be a part of baseball coming to the forefront of the issue. It seems like cocaine is becoming too popular and too powerful."

Milwaukee catcher Ted Simmons expressed a different sentiment. "If my owner asks me, I will do it. But if anybody mandates that I do it, I won't. You're breaking a man's constitutional rights to privacy," Simmons said.

Down at the union office, however, the men without numbers on their backs took a much different view. The Players Association reportedly said the players were "virtually unanimous" in their opposition to Ueberroth's request for drug tests. "He got an answer from the players. The answer was that if he wishes to discuss matters of this nature, he should do it through the appropriate channels—the union," said Eugene Orza, associate general counsel for the union, to the Associated Press. Orza also downplayed testing's effectiveness, saying, "The overwhelming weight of expert medical literature is that testing is not a solution because it necessarily establishes in the minds of those being tested a potentially coercive atmosphere, and a coercive atmosphere is not conducive to eradicating whatever problem there might be."

The foundation of the commissioner's plan was to implement random, unannounced urinalysis tests three times per year starting in 1986. No punitive action would be taken against those testing positive. "Anyone with a positive test would receive immediate, continued testing and treatment" as well as "counseling and help appropriate to the individual."

Donald Fehr described the plan as incomplete. "The drug-testing proposal has never been made in a detailed-enough fashion for any responsible person to bite into it to negotiate," Fehr said on *CBS Morning News*. "It's really to sign a blank check, and that's not something that anybody is going to do."

Other baseball executives described the problem as being above the union. "Drugs are not a union problem," said Dallas Green, general manager of the Chicago Cubs. "Regardless of what the union may think, it is up to every player on this team to agree to the voluntary testing to show the entire baseball world that drugs have not taken over our game."

Public sentiment supported drug testing in baseball. The Reverend Jesse Jackson was reported by *Jet* magazine to have urged "players to go on 'the moral offensive' by voluntarily adopting a drug-testing program that they and management can live with, instead of being forced" into one. Drug testing as a whole was gaining prominence as a tool for companies across the country. Twenty-five percent of Fortune 500 companies were now, at a minimum, performing pre-employment urinalysis in 1985. Other segments of society to implement drug testing at the time were police officers, soldiers, railroad workers, teachers, and students at some institutions. Testing, however, was frequently being met by legal opposition and would, more often than not, ultimately be overturned in court proceedings.

On October 22, in the midst of World Series action between the St. Louis Cardinals and the Kansas City Royals, major league baseball owners released a statement announcing they had voted unanimously to terminate the eighteen-month joint drug agreement with the Players Association. Citing an inability to "make substantial progress in reaching a drug-testing agreement," the owners decided that the current agreement, which did not include mandatory testing, "could not work."

In response, Donald Fehr commented in the *New York Times*, "I can't say it's unexpected."

After a negotiating session on October 11, Barry Rona, chief counsel for the owners, said it was clear that the union was opposed to testing, and he "did not see any point to continuing to negotiate something I thought was unattainable." From there, the clubs decided that the present drug program was not working and that "there was no sense in keeping it for the sake of keeping it."

The joint drug agreement, which included reasonable-cause drug testing, was never really given much of a chance to prove whether or not it could have been beneficial. No players were ever disciplined under the agreement. The problem with reasonable-cause testing was that despite the owners' assertion of wanting to rid the game of drugs, a case could be made that they were only interested in doing so if it wasn't at the expense of their own players. The desire to win trumped the desire for a clean sport, not to mention the desire to make a buck. Looking purely at the business end of things, as a source inside the union at the time suggests, "The owners had money invested in players; they didn't want these players in rehab or arrested." Other teams' players, maybe, but surely not their own.

"Greed stops the owners from really going after the drug problem in the game," former executive director of the Players Association Kenneth Moffett told the *Boston Globe's* Will McDonough in a surprise 1985 reappearance for the beleaguered short-time union chief. "[Owners] still want to win, and they will overlook a player's drug problems if they think it will help them win," Moffett said.

Despite the sordid revelations unearthed during the media's two-week residency in Pittsburgh, major league baseball was seemingly moving backward with the problem, which at the time was called by psychiatrist Joseph Pursch "the number-one problem in professional sports." Pursch was the medical director of CareUnit Hospitals, where he treated numerous players for drug abuse, including Tim Raines. "It should be obvious to anyone with an IQ the size of his waistline that this thing will not go away," Pursch told *USA Today*.

Those who were in a position to make the necessary changes were mired in the blame game. Donald Fehr called the owners' tearing up of the joint drug agreement "regrettable" and blamed them for the lack of progress on the problem. "Were the owners truly interested in trying to reach a resolution on this matter, they would be willing to engage in good-faith negotiations to try and resolve that matter. They have been unwilling to do so," said Fehr in October. The director of the players union went on to say that the two sides held only one meeting during which the issue of drug testing was brought up and that management had been unable or unwilling to answer any of the union's pertinent questions, including the seemingly simple query of the name of the test management wanted to install. "There have been no further meetings," Fehr said, "although we have been ready to have those meetings."

In November the union filed an unfair labor practice claim against Ueberroth and the twenty-six club owners, accusing them of circumventing the union in an attempt to implement a drug testing program.

Ueberroth, meanwhile, without giving specifics, maintained his belief that the league would adopt a drug policy soon and continued to speak caustically on the issue to everyone except the union. He conveyed his strong beliefs on the subject at the National Press Club in November. "Baseball has a responsibility of taking on drugs as a national priority," he said.

At baseball's winter meetings in December 1985, Ueberroth said he was encouraged to learn the Players Association was formulating its own drug program. A week later, however, Donald Fehr stated that the union would continue its stance against the insertion of any mandatory drug testing programs into the players' contracts. He said that players were insulted by the "guilty until proven innocent" assumption that mandatory drug testing conveyed. He expressed that the union was amenable to working with management in creating a cooperative anti-drug campaign but that the owners were, as of yet, unwilling to collaborate on a joint drug agreement with the union. In lieu of that, Fehr announced, "We will do what we can on our own" to fight drugs.

Thus, on December 19, the union released its own plan. The program was aimed at grade-school children and included the publishing and distribution of coloring books emphasizing the dangers of drugs. The book was titled *The Pros Say It's OK to Say No to Drugs,* to which New York Yankees owner George Steinbrenner commented, "These guys must think they're dealing with the sugar plum fairy. Where's the program that will educate the ballplayers? We have players that need help, and the union is trying to make people believe that no one in it uses drugs.... Pittsburgh punched a hole in that theory."

Steinbrenner, who was one of baseball's biggest critics of the players' drug use, had recently signed troubled pitcher Rod Scurry to his Yankees' ball club. Scurry, who had agreed to be drug-tested with the Pirates following his troubles, was Steinbrenner's second player—the first being Dale Berra, upon his signing the previous season—who was agreeable to testing. "The more times I can get a player to agree to that, the tougher it will be for the players union to keep insisting that we have no testing," Steinbrenner explained. "That's the only reason I'm doing it. I think the union's fixed position on testing is perfectly idiotic."

Despite the fact that baseball's drug problem was named the "number-one sports story in 1985" by UPI, owners and union officials did not agree to a drug testing program by year's end.

=

ON FEBRUARY 28, 1986, Commissioner Ueberroth announced that, after much deliberation, he had made his rulings regarding the more than twenty players involved or implicated during the Pittsburgh drug trials. Seven players were to receive a one-year suspension— *unless* they agreed to several conditions, which included donating 10 percent of their salaries to drug prevention programs, drug testing for the duration of their careers, and one hundred hours of community service. Four more players were sanctioned with a sixty-day suspension unless they agreed to similar conditions at a lower level of fifty hours of community service and a 5 percent salary donation. Ten additional players escaped suspensions but had to agree to career-long mandatory drug testing. The seven players receiving the harshest penalties were Dave Parker, Enos Cabell, Joaquín Andújar,

Dale Berra, Keith Hernandez, Lonnie Smith, and Jeffrey Leonard. Rod Scurry fell into the third group, those forced to undergo drug testing.

Ueberroth had interviewed twenty-three players following the Pittsburgh trials before meting out his judgment. "It is painfully obvious that in the early 1980s there was significant drug use among some major league players," Ueberroth said at a news conference. "It is my belief... that while we are making headway, the problem continued even through the 1985 season.... Peer pressure to use drugs was in too many cases overwhelming. This trend must be reversed." The negotiable suspensions were Commissioner Ueberroth's first actions against drug users during his tenure.

Once again it appeared that major league baseball players were allowed to use their vast wealth to avoid true suspensions, as they essentially paid to play. Pulitzer Prize–winning journalist Michael Goodwin wrote about this in his column for the *New York Daily News* in 2008. "In effect," wrote Goodwin, "they bought their way out of any punishment. Such a miscarriage of justice has real-world consequences. When laws are not enforced equally, many young athletes grow up believing their sports skills entitle them to exemptions from society's rules."

The monetary fines, which ranged from $135,000 at the top for Keith Hernandez to Lary Sorensen's $10,000, were seen as fair trade-offs for some of the players involved. "I'm just going to do whatever he wants me to do," Enos Cabell said. "It's time for this to end." Others, such as Keith Hernandez, disagreed. "Obviously, I'm not pleased with the decision of the commissioner," Hernandez said. For guys like Lonnie Smith, the punishment seemed like piling on. Hadn't he already paid for his crimes? Smith was like millions of Americans who got caught up in the coke craze during this period. But Smith had distinguished himself by his behavior after that. Here was a man who had taken it upon himself to go to rehab, get clean, and stay clean; who resurrected his career and cooperated with the league and the law; and was now being punished for his actions from years earlier.

"My biggest hurt was after," Smith says, "when Ueberroth decided he was going to level everybody with charges. That's when I felt I was mistreated… badly. Because during the whole course I was doing what everyone asked of me, from the commissioner's office on down, only to get traded because they were afraid it was going to tarnish the club."

The prescribed course of action didn't go the way Smith was promised by his team or the union. "The agreement was that they would set up all of my community service," recalls Smith. "They set up like one hour out of one hundred. Then I found myself almost out of baseball again. So I managed to scramble during the off-season, and I managed to speak at every elementary school, every middle school, every high school, and every Rotary Club in a two-and-a-half-month period. I was able to get together almost seventy hours and sent copies to the Players Association, and they agreed not to X me out of baseball."

Ballard Smith, former San Diego Padres president, acknowledged the sometimes shoddy treatment players endured. "I don't think management has always treated employees properly," Smith said at the time.

===

THE TONE between management and the union remained confrontational in 1986. Many teams, notably the Baltimore Orioles and San Francisco Giants, continued their attempts to sidestep the union and the collective bargaining agreement by putting drug testing clauses into player contracts at their own discretion. These efforts were eventually overturned by an arbitrator, Thomas Roberts, after the players union filed a grievance. The clauses were ruled to be a violation of the basic labor agreement between the owners and players. Despite the lack of both communication between owners and the union and any movement on the issue, the media was reporting that drug testing was still on the near horizon. The *New York Times*'s George Vecsey wrote in March 1986, "The drug testing to be initiated in baseball this season will not include amphetamines."

On April 8, 1986, Ueberroth announced out of the clear blue and with a total disregard for reality, "I believe baseball is going to be the first sport to be free of drugs." He also predicted that players and owners would agree to a drug testing program at some point during the upcoming season. Ueberroth was nothing if not creative. Behind the scenes, he had no firm ground to support such statements; in fact, he had gotten absolutely nowhere with regard to a drug program. Nothing had changed since the trials in Pittsburgh besides the teams actually being on flimsier footing than they had been prior to the termination of the joint drug agreement. Undeterred, Ueberroth tried once more. According to the Mitchell report, "In April 1986, Commissioner Ueberroth again reached out to players directly, urging them to support a drug testing program and proposing that testing be implemented only for the next two seasons. The Players Association criticized Ueberroth again for contacting players directly and 'exhorting' them to support the testing plan."

Ueberroth's plan called for four urine tests per year. The drugs being tested for were cocaine, marijuana, heroin, and morphine. The plan was similar to the one the Baltimore Orioles had put into the contracts of their players.

With no leaguewide drug plan in place or policy for how to deal with future offenders, a new season of baseball began. As stated in the *New York Times*, "Beyond testing, baseball needs a drug policy that defines its discipline for drug abuse. Instead of a policy, baseball now has only whatever decrees the commissioner issues."

And so a new year began on the diamond, where essentially more questions remained than had been answered.

Then something unexpected happened. Everything on the drug front went eerily quiet. By October it was World Series time, with the Red Sox battling the Mets in a dream match-up. Hardly a word was uttered about drugs, despite the previous seasons' exposure of the issue. Ueberroth continued to urge both sides to negotiate a drug program, but the consensus among baseball insiders was that the odds of that happening weren't favorable. Once again matters of monetary significance took precedence. This time the battle was over owner collusion. The collective bargaining agreement states in part, "Players shall not act in concert with other Players and Clubs shall not act in concert with other Clubs." Following the 1985 season the free agent market for players dried up. The lack of signings was seen by many (and later proven) to be a move on the part of the owners to conspire to keep players' salaries down. Despite the fact that the commissioner had made drug testing a priority the year prior, the public fervor surrounding drugs died down, and the focus was back on the field.

For the owners, business was good. The fans were still coming and even voted Keith Hernandez into the All-Star game as a starter. Fan reaction was much different than it had been after the Black Sox scandal. As journalist and author Howard Bryant commented in his book *Juicing the Game*, "In 1921, the year following discovery of the fix, the game suffered a temporary dip in attendance that scared the pants off the owners. They believed they had a credibility problem. The bottom line was being affected." The season following the Pittsburgh drug trials, attendance throughout the majors pretty much held steady, with a slight increase of 1.5 percent. Not even the Pirates suffered at the gate in 1986, as the team actually drew 265,017 more fans for the season, up 3,215 per game. The team still had terrible attendance numbers, yet the fact was there were more fans in the seats in 1986 than 1985. The trend continued leaguewide as attendance figures rose each successive year to round out the 1980s.

As far as the union was concerned, one source familiar with the Players Association commented that its position had always been to take a reactionary stance. Silently, and without acknowledgment, both sides may have finally come to an agreement on something, which was the attitude, *Why rock the boat?* Things were fine now. The drug problem had washed away. Instead of creating policy, both sides implicitly agreed to cross their fingers and hope for the best. Barry Rona, executive director of the Players Relations Committee, the owners' labor arm, admitted as much in December 1986 when he spoke with the *New York Times* about the "confidence" and "satisfaction" with the status quo among owners and how there was little pressure on him to debate the testing issue with the union.

Donald Fehr continued to suggest that he was open to negotiating the matter, citing a letter he wrote to the commissioner on July 31 concerning the drug issue that went unanswered. While the union had no problems with the former agreement, which allowed for reasonable-cause testing, there were no signs that union officials were going to change their tune regarding mandatory random testing. The owners were equally firm. Barry Rona stated that without such testing there was little reason to have a drug program at all. The owners' position, said Rona, was that without mandatory testing a drug program is left with little else besides "nice words" such as "education" and "treatment"—two areas the owners felt they needed little help with from the union.

Shortly after taking office, Ueberroth had cited drugs as the number-one problem facing baseball. Despite this and the commissioner's words that he was going to be boringly consistent on subject of drugs, the issue quietly died. Maybe, despite reports to the contrary, testing never really stood much of a chance to begin with. Too much money was on the line concerning non-drug issues, such as players' salaries and free agency, for those involved to really take a stand against drugs. The events in Pittsburgh were simply forgotten. *Drugs? What drugs?* In the eyes of MLB officials, the worst was behind them. Murray Chass summed it up best when he wrote, "Owners tend to go with the flow. During the great outcry of 1985, they raised their voices to the public volume. Now that the volume has been turned down to the lowest decibel level, they aren't about to stir up negative attention to the game."

Some players, despite their union's position, did not shy away from speaking their minds on the drug-testing debate. Rod Scurry, for one, wasn't above telling everybody that he needed to be tested. "When I came to New York, they wanted to test me every three or four days. I said I wanted it every day. I want to do it, because it doesn't leave any loopholes where I think I might be able to get away with it, even a drink."

Scurry didn't hold high hopes for the commissioner's plan, even had it been implemented. "I don't think it will do any good," Scurry said at the time. "If there is a problem in sports, in baseball, football, or basketball, the only way to know for sure if players are doing it is the same way I'm doing it—to be tested every other day."

Major league baseball players' sentiments on drug testing put them squarely into one of two camps. Those who were clean didn't feel it was necessary for them to pee in a cup to prove their innocence. They were joined by those who did drugs but felt they had things under control. They liked to party and wanted to keep that option open to them. On the other side were those who had battled addiction or were still in the throes of drugs' lure and accepted the fact that they might have a problem; they were more inclined to desire testing. Some might even say they *needed* testing.

In time, Peter Ueberroth made one last-ditch effort to get something accomplished in regard to drugs. He called a meeting with Donald Fehr, during which he made a request that bowled the union boss over. As former union chief Marvin Miller later recounted to writer Allen Barra, "When they finally got together, Ueberroth asked Fehr if the union would agree to testing, 'even if it was just for the sake of public relations.' Don told me his jaw dropped; when he told me, mine dropped."

Sixteen more years would pass before MLB would finally adopt a significant drug policy. The change would not come of its own volition.

Ueberroth stepped down as commissioner in 1989. In his defense, the commissioner's office he inherited wasn't what it once was. The role of commissioner had devolved over the years. While he called himself the "fans' commissioner," Ueberroth's real role was more as a mouthpiece for the owners. Yet in the end, the final decisions always lay with the owners, as well as with the union, where he obviously had no say. Maybe that is why Judge Kennesaw Mountain Landis, in his interview for the job, demanded that the commissioner's office be an independent one. Landis's successor, Albert B. "Happy" Chandler, once a senator and a governor from Kentucky, colorfully described the travails of the post of commissioner of baseball in *Time* magazine as follows: "Baseball owners are the toughest set of ignoramuses anyone could ever come up against. They always have been. Refreshingly dumb fellows: greedy, shortsighted, and stupid. They created this job in 1921...after the 1919 Black Sox scandal.... But I don't expect baseball ever really wanted a commissioner at all."

=

IN THE years following the Pittsburgh drug trials, baseball's list of drug casualties continued to grow. The San Diego Padres, who went to the 1984 World Series, was another team that had been suffering a particular problem with cocaine. Pitcher LaMarr Hoyt, a Cy Young Award winner as a member of the 1983 Chicago White Sox, was signed by the Padres in 1985. Following the 1985 season, Hoyt was arrested twice within thirty days for drug possession. The Padres released him after the 1986 season, and following a fourth arrest on drug charges in 1987, Hoyt was out of baseball for good. Padres second baseman Alan Wiggins and pitcher Eric Show didn't fare as well. After both players suffered from drug abuse problems, they were released by the Padres. Both players later died of drug-related causes.

Former Padres president Ballard Smith described the atmosphere in baseball at the time. "The will just wasn't there to do anything about it," Smith told the *New York Times*. "Drugs really cost our team, but apparently they weren't big enough to where it was costing the other owners."

General managers, given few alternatives, were forced to simply trade away or release their troubled players. Lonnie Smith remembers one of his experiences changing teams. "When I got traded," Smith says, "the general manager at the time claimed, 'Well, the reason we traded you is because we knew you were on drugs.' And I said, 'Well, if you knew I was on drugs, why didn't you help me instead of just casting me off to the side like that?'"

Of course, there were exceptions. If a player was talented enough, the problem was ignored. Padres GM Kevin Towers spoke frankly on this matter, as it related to steroids, to *ESPN The Magazine*'s Buster Olney, following the 2004 death of Padres and Astros star

Ken Caminiti of a drug-induced heart attack. "I hate to be the one voice for the other twenty-nine GMs, but I'd have to imagine that all of them, at one point or other, had reason to think that a ballplayer on their ball club was probably using, based on body changes and things that happened over the winter," Towers said.

Towers said that despite knowing of Caminiti's problems, he selfishly did nothing. His remaining silent and keeping Caminiti on the field, he admitted, resulted in the Padres and Towers' own career flourishing.

The blame for baseball's inaction is abundant enough to go around. Fingers have pointed at the owners, fans, and the media, but especially at the Players Association. Given such tragedies as the deaths of Alan Wiggins and Eric Show, or the derailed careers of once sure-fire Hall of Famers like Daryl Strawberry and Dwight Gooden, how could the union's stance on drug testing be seen as helping the young players it represented?

On April 21, 1986, the new owners of the Pittsburgh Pirates—in what may be considered an early indication of the franchise's tight-fisted ways that would plague the team well into the future—filed suit against Dave Parker for breach of contract. The suit claimed that Parker's well-publicized cocaine use voided the five-year contract the slugger had signed with the team in 1979. Parker was still owed over five million dollars from the club in deferred salary. The lawsuit, which was ultimately settled out of court in 1988, was the first of its kind and may have been the perfect illustration of why the union took such a strong stand against testing and had such overt distrust of baseball management.

Throughout the history of the league, baseball's owners have ruled with an iron fist, and the relationship between owners and players has always been strained. More often than not, it was the players who felt this strain most acutely. Chicago White Sox owner Charlie Comiskey wouldn't pay his men a decent wage despite the fact that he could certainly be described as one of the richest men in town. Sox players even had to pick up the tab for laundering their uniforms; hence, the term "Black Sox" was born years prior to the scandal and allegedly refers to the grungy uniforms that resulted from the players' refusal to have them cleaned. In another example of Comiskey's penny-pinching, after pitcher Eddie Cicotti was promised a ten-thousand-dollar bonus for winning thirty games, Comiskey had him benched before he could reach the mark. "To his players, he was a cheap, stingy tyrant," Eliot Asinof wrote in *Eight Men Out.*

This was a league that had in the not-so-distant past governed its players by a reserve clause, which essentially bound a player to one team, one owner, for the life of his baseball career, unless the owner decided to trade him to another owner. It is now a well-worn adage that these were grown men getting paid handsomely to play a kids' game. But where else was a man denied the basic right to choose which company he worked for or the right to ever change that company?

Despite the better financial times enjoyed by the professional baseball player in the 1980s, the question remained, what reason did the players have to trust the owners? Especially after the owners were proven guilty of colluding to keep salaries down following the 1985, 1986, and 1987 seasons. In the minds of the players, it was not a far-fetched notion that the owners might use, or even expedite, failed drug tests to rid the league of undesirables. Said Braves pitcher Terry Forster in *USA Today,* "With all the big contracts the owners would like to get rid of, who's to say somebody won't drop a pill in somebody's urine and say the test is positive?"

Interestingly, during the pretrial rhetoric of the Pirates suit against Dave Parker, the back-and-forth between attorneys had some people thinking that MLB was headed into familiar territory. Parker's attorney Tom Reich promised that should the case reach the courtroom, it would "make the [1985 drug trials] look like a marble shoot.... It will involve the history of cocaine in baseball over the last ten years, and that history is fairly extensive."

Parker's attorneys were not going to let their client be attacked as the Pirates ownership called their former star everything from fat and mediocre to moody and paranoid. In a pretrial statement filed in District Court, the Pirates claimed Parker "has already been generously overpaid," that his "performance deteriorated in every category," that he was "consistently overweight," and finally that he was responsible for "the poisoning of the team's relationship with its fans and the sports press." But Parker's legal team pointed out that the years during which Parker was alleged in the lawsuit to have played poorly coincided with the years in which he was battling injury, a point supported by his former manager Chuck Tanner, who offered his testimony on the matter. "You're damn right I'll defend him," Tanner said. "He played hard every day. I don't know anything about cocaine, but I know he played hurt."

Parker's defense team promised to drag MLB through the gutter anew. In a twenty-two-page pretrial statement, Parker's attorney Louis Willenken said, "By 1981, it became general knowledge that many players were using cocaine to one extent or another, and the Pirates certainly knew Dave, as well as others, had used cocaine. The Pirates could have but chose not to do something at that time.... The Pirates inaction is not surprising; they had a history in the 1970s and early 1980s of knowing about but ignoring drug use and substance abuse."

The attorney then went after MLB as a whole and former commissioner Bowie Kuhn specifically. According to the statement, "a vast number of baseball players were substance abusers in one form or another. Amphetamines had been handed out in the clubhouse by team physicians." And according to the *Pittsburgh Post-Gazette*, "The statement also claims that former Baseball Commissioner Bowie Kuhn ignored cocaine use until 1981, and then merely engaged in a public relations effort, failing to impose sanctions on distinguished players who used the drug."

Had the suit not been settled, even more names would have surfaced in trial. In a sworn statement former Pirates pitcher Dock Ellis said, "The overwhelming majority of major league baseball players in both leagues were substance abusers, and the symptoms were evident and ignored by management."

15

Postgame

I WISH HE'D NEVER LEARNED TO THROW
THAT CURVEBALL.
    —BETTY SCURRY, ON HER SON ROD

I N THE early morning hours of October 29, 1992, the Washoe County Sheriff's department in Reno, Nevada, received a call describing a commotion going on outside the house of Rod Scurry. Just prior to this, Betty Scurry had received two phone calls of her own. The first one was at 12:30 A.M. from her son Rod, who was home alone with his children. The thirty-six-year old was upset and calling his mother to discuss his marital woes. Forty minutes later Betty Scurry received another call; this time it was her six-year-old grandson, Rodney Jr., calling for help. His father was outside in the yard, where once again imaginary snakes were attacking the former ballplayer. Scurry was shirtless and pleading with his neighbors to help him fight off the creatures, which he said were crawling on him and biting him.

Scurry once said that his cocaine use "made him forget about wanting to be someplace else." For Scurry, it seemed that "someplace else" was an unattainable mirage. Following his stint with the Yankees, which ended in February 1987 after he was released on the heels of a drunk driving arrest (charges were later dropped), Scurry caught on with the Seattle Mariners for the 1988 season. He pitched in thirty-nine games as a middle reliever for the Mariners before being released during the off-season on December 21, 1988. The very next day he was arrested for buying two rocks of crack cocaine at a crack house in Reno. The house had been under surveillance by undercover agents. Even at home in Nevada, Scurry battled the pressures of his life the only way he knew how—with drugs. The drug-testing Scurry was forced to submit to after the Pittsburgh drug trials may have kept him clean, but once he was out of baseball there was nothing to stop him from using. Scurry received a one-year suspended sentence on a cocaine possession charge and eighteen months of probation. In exchange, he agreed to undergo drug counseling.

In the years following his arrest, Scurry enjoyed moments of sobriety—good, clean times in his life, far away from the limelight, far away from the ballpark. He ran a car wash in Reno and took pleasure in hunting, fishing, and detailing cars. For the first time since he was a teenager, Scurry was surrounded by friends and family. What led him back into harm's way and into the arms of cocaine is unclear. There were marital problems, highlighted by the recent separation from his wife, Laura, just a week earlier. There was also talk of problems with the IRS and money owed in back taxes.

No matter what the causes may have been, all the triumphant ups and horrific downs in Scurry's life led to this final moment in the yard, fighting against snakes that only he could see.

When four deputies arrived at the scene, they tried to calm the former pitcher down. But the hallucinating Scurry became angry. A struggle ensued, and deputies forced Scurry to the ground. He was subdued with handcuffs, and his feet were bound. Scurry, his body badly scraped from the tussle, finally collapsed outside his home. He was unconscious and had stopped breathing. One of the deputies performed CPR until paramedics arrived and flew him by helicopter to a nearby hospital, but by the time they arrived there, Scurry was in a coma.

"He had a faint heartbeat and faint breathing," his sister Lisa told the Associated Press. "But the doctor said even though they were

doing CPR, that doesn't mean he was getting oxygen to the brain."
His brother Rick tearfully recounts the last moments of Rod's life.
"Doctors told us after about a week that he will never, even if he ever
came out of it—he was never going to feel—the whole family talked
about it and agreed with the recommendation. We all went down
there and took turns saying good-bye, then they pulled it."

Rod Scurry died on November 5, after being removed from life
support. He had suffered heart failure and a brain hemorrhage during
his cocaine-induced struggle with police. Washoe County Coroner
Vern McCarty told the Associated Press, "The cocaine, plus violent
behavior, plus being restrained, all contributed" to his death. Scurry
left behind a two-year-old daughter, Dallas, and a son, Rodney.

To Rick and the rest of the family, the end came as a surprise. In
the last few years, Rod had been spending time with his kids and,
as Rick says, "was for the most part clean… but obviously, there
were a few things going on in the last year which led to that night."
At the time of his brother's death Rick had been unsure what those
problems could have been; Rod hadn't told his brother about his IRS
problems. "Whatever was going on there, he kept it to himself," Rick
Scurry says.

It appeared that, just as he had always done, Rod Scurry had
looked to the only crutch he knew in dealing with pressure, and once
more he had tried to deal with his problems alone. The two brothers
had ceased sharing many of the details in their lives. "Me and him,"
Rick Scurry says, "in the later years, even though we still loved each
other, and we were close, there was a wall that we kept between us.
Those intimate conversations kind of went away."

Following his brother's death, Rick Scurry heard various stories and theories about what actually happened that night, from
drugs being the cause of death to a hold the deputies used to bind
Scurry's legs and arms (since outlawed) being a factor leading to
Rod's cardiopulmonary arrest. But such theories mean little to Rod
Scurry's younger brother. "Nothing's going to bring him back. I don't
blame—" Rick says, grasping for the right words. "It was just a ten-
year ordeal that ended badly."

=

FROM INSIDE the prison walls of the Federal Correctional Institute in Loretto, Pennsylvania, Dale Shiffman considered himself the lucky one. He figured this out many years prior to Rod Scurry's death—on his second day in prison, to be exact, June 2, 1985. Fresh from learning the news that his best friend, Kevin Koch, was the man responsible for sewing up the case against him, Shiffman heard a voice in the prison's chapel. "God spoke to me audibly," Shiffman said in 2005. And when it was time for the altar call, the new inmate made a beeline toward the front of the church, practically knocking other inmates over in the process. It was there that Shiffman asked the Lord to save him. He immediately felt relieved. "It was like a forty-ton weight had been lifted off my back.... I knew right then and there something was different, something had changed in my life," Shiffman said. He realized where his path of drug and alcohol abuse was headed. Today Shiffman feels unsure whether he would have been able to stem the tide without those prison bars to contain him. "I'd probably be dead with all the drugs and drinking," he said. Prison gave him new life.

After all the backstabbing and betrayal, first by Scurry and then by Kevin Koch, in the end, instead of hatred, it is gratitude that Shiffman feels. He served just shy of two years of his twelve-year sentence. Upon his release in 1987 a friend had a job waiting for him in the Cincinnati area, where Shiffman moved and began working full-time. He has no doubt where the credit goes for turning his life around. "God transformed my life," Shiffman told the *Post-Gazette*. Within a few short years, he went from living the life of an addict to becoming a family man. "Here I am married, a great job, and three wonderful kids."

=

KEVIN KOCH, forced out of his dream job as the Pirate Parrot, attempted to ride out tough times in Pittsburgh. He gained work as a sales representative through the Steelers' Franco Harris. However, it wasn't long before Koch, left without a friend in the world and unable to live with his transgressions, fled his hometown and sought a fresh start as far away from Pittsburgh as possible. Formerly a man with a friend and a girl on each arm and no shortage of social engagements to choose from, Koch became an anonymous face in the California town of Fremont. "Nobody knew me," Koch says. "It was like bricks off my back. But it was always on my mind."

Koch continued down a path of substance abuse for a few years after his exile as he tried earnestly to gain his bearings in life. Each day he thought about the past. "Life is so funny," Koch says, reflecting on the initial Pirate Parrot audition. "If Yamie doesn't get a hold of me that day, I'm back in the 'Burgh right now—my city. I love the 'Burgh. I'll love it till the day I die."

In 1993 Koch received word from his sister that his old friend Dale Shiffman was looking for him. Koch's initial reaction from his West Coast home was, "Why can't this all just go away?" However, his sister told him that Dale was different now, that he had changed.

On a trip to Pittsburgh to visit his family that same year, Koch met with the friend he had betrayed eight years earlier. The past he had desperately been trying to put behind him was now staring him in the face. Koch could tell right away that he was looking at a different person. "I knew Dale better than anybody," Koch says. "I could see the change." Gone was the young, hard-partying man about town, the old "Mr. Pittsburgh" who Koch described as "nonstop."

Koch was greeted by a new man. But more importantly, Koch was greeted with forgiveness. Shiffman had traveled from Cincinnati to Pittsburgh in order to relieve his friend's burden.

The two men reunited again in 2006, when they appeared together on *Real Sports with Bryant Gumbel*. Discussing his 1993 meeting with Koch, Shiffman told Gumbel, "I remember tears just running down his face, he was weeping like I've not heard anyone cry, and he just said, 'I'd give my life to undo what I did to you.'"

Koch described how his sense of guilt, while not fully abated, was lessened by Shiffman's absolution in 1993, and how he had finally felt able to move on with his life. The former class clown, whose baby face has hardened with time, once again fought back tears as he recalled, "It's just the compassion alone that he had, it gets me now."

Before parting ways the two shared their unique handshake, a salutation they had invented some thirty years ago. Despite this nod to their youth, both men agreed the past was now behind them. They were finally happy again and living in the moment.

===

KEVIN CONNOLLY had thought that, because of his cooperation with authorities, he would receive a very lenient sentence for his crime. Instead, he almost cried upon hearing he was sentenced to a two-year stint. "You better check those papers," Connolly remembers saying. "Something's wrong, man." Still, he acknowledges the sentence would have been much steeper in today's legal climate. He served just over twenty-one months at Loretto, where he played on a softball team alongside Dale Shiffman. He continues to work in the construction business and lives in Pittsburgh.

Thomas Balzer served thirteen months at the Federal Correctional Institute in Allenwood, Pennsylvania, where he played on the prison's basketball team. Balzer resides in Pittsburgh.

Curtis Strong spent all but two days short of four years in prison. Strong resides near Philadelphia.

Shelby Greer served two years and nine months. He continues to live in and work in Pittsburgh.

Jeffrey Mosco served one year of his four-year sentence. He still lives in the Pittsburgh area.

Robert William McCue passed away in 2001 after serving eleven months of his ten-year sentence.

===

ON APRIL 20, 1989, nearly four months to the day after Rod Scurry was busted in Reno, Dale Berra was arrested on possession of cocaine charges at his home in Glen Ridge, New Jersey. Berra was one of twenty-five people indicted as part of a five-county drug raid. His professional baseball career had ended the previous season in the minor leagues. He had been cut by the Yankees on July 28, 1986, before making his final appearance in a major league uniform while playing sparingly for the Houston Astros during the 1987 season. After Berra completed a three-year pretrial intervention program in 1992, the charges against him were dropped.

=====

LONNIE SMITH looks back at his involvement with cocaine and sees only missed opportunities. "I like to think if I hadn't got involved that my career might have been better than it was," he says. "Sure I was blessed to have played on some great teams, but I think I could have put up much better numbers. Not so much to be a Hall of Famer, but a lot more respected than I am now.

"A lot of people don't see me as a great player," he says. "Some see me as a person that almost ruined the game due to the fact that I went into rehab and also of the trial and some of the things I said that some people didn't like. So you know, I think if I hadn't got so involved in it... I think my career would have taken a better turn."

Smith understands that there isn't anything he could have done differently once he got clean, specifically in terms of the federal investigation. "The [FBI] had a list of who they wanted to interview, and they interviewed each one of them individually. But everyone assumed I pointed fingers at everybody."

The truth of the matter was that each of the players the FBI interviewed talked. While some did it kicking and screaming and fighting the authorities at every turn, others, like Smith, were described by the FBI and U.S. attorneys as dignified. Nevertheless, he was the first one on the stand, and he feels the stigma associated with that has followed him ever since.

Smith remains the only player in history to play on three different World Series champion teams in the same decade. He is a career .288 hitter over seventeen major league seasons. Today Smith is a family man in rural Georgia. He keeps busy as a doting father, shuttling his kids from one extracurricular activity to the next.

=

BESIDES ROD Scurry, perhaps nobody paid as high a price for his involvement in the Pittsburgh drug trials as Dave Parker. It is his name that has become synonymous with the cocaine era.

In 1985, at the age of thirty-four, Parker, with his drug use behind him, battled back from injury to put up MVP-worthy numbers, hitting .312 with thirty-four home runs and a career-high 125 RBIs. But the accolades didn't come for Parker. He was the big name in a sordid scandal, and the MVP award went instead to the Cardinals' Willie McGee.

Dave Parker's career comeback should have been the stuff of legend. To battle back from drugs, injuries, and weight issues takes tremendous effort and dedication. He resurrected his career and led teams to two more World Series and won another ring. In the music industry a return to form is greeted by applause, honor, and distinction—the "virtue of the survivor." But Parker is never looked at as a survivor. He is, instead, baseball's unforgiven man.

This status is clearly to blame for Parker's failure to gain entry into the Hall of Fame, despite the fact that, as Parker says, there "are a lot of guys that are in the Hall that had incidents during that time" with cocaine. Other drug users, players such as Paul Molitor or Ferguson Jenkins, didn't suffer in Hall of Fame purgatory like Parker. It is clearly a touchy subject for the man roundly hailed as the best player in baseball from 1975 to 1980. "I think it's a fucking joke that I'm not in the Hall of Fame," Parker plainly states.

Statistics would seem to support Parker's claim. His absence from Cooperstown seemingly cannot be a matter of numbers. Compare Parker's career numbers against 2009 Hall of Fame inductee, Boston Red Sox outfielder Jim Rice.

Parker: .290 Avg.; 2,712 hits; 339 HRs; 1,493 RBIs; 1 MVP; 2 rings; 2 batting titles; 3 Gold Gloves

Rice: .298 Avg; 2,452 hits; 382 HRs; 1,451 RBIs; 1 MVP; 0 rings; 0 batting titles; 0 Gold Gloves

When talking about home runs, Parker quickly points out that, unlike some of today's home run kings, his numbers are not inflated. "Thirty was legit; we didn't have a juiced ball. We had quality pitchers. You had two or three, maybe four good starters in every city you went to. You go into New York, and you had Seaver, Matlack, and Koosman. Those were no joke. You go into Philly, you got Reed and Carlton, and don't be thinking about Houston, where you got J. R. [Richard], Wilson, Ryan, and Scott."

Numbers used to be what baseball was all about. They were until recently the backbone of the game. And numbers, just like Parker, tell it straight. "I hit until the end. I wasn't a player who they allowed to reach his milestones, and hit .220, or .230. I won't mention names, but there were some guys in the American League that hit .237 and got a three-million-dollar raise. The good old boys network allowed these players to go ahead and achieve their milestones, but that was never open for me. I hit until the last day. I could probably go out and hit now."

When asked about his role in the Pittsburgh scandal, Parker openly admits he used cocaine. This admission in and of itself could arguably be applauded in this day of big league denials. He also points out, "I wasn't peddling nothing. All I was peddling was line drives, doubles, and home runs.... I was electrifying." Today, Parker resides in the Cincinnati area, where he owns and operates several Popeyes chicken restaurants.

———

As THE years rolled by for the Pittsburgh Pirates, the team had trouble distancing itself from the cocaine scandal. According to former Pirates' vice president Steve Greenberg, it was almost as though the trials had become an "appendage to the organization." As the man faced with the task of selling tickets for the club, Greenberg had to live and deal with this stigma on a daily basis.

"It was hard to see the light at the end of the tunnel," says Greenberg. "The tunnel was so long."

Despite the fact that the FBI's investigation was leaguewide in scope, "because it was in Pittsburgh and called the Pittsburgh drug trials," Greenberg told the *Pittsburgh Press*, "the association was more with the club than it should have been. If it had been in Houston or St. Louis, it wouldn't have been the same impact. Because it was in Pittsburgh, we lived with it twenty-four hours a day."

The Galbreath family sold the Pirates in 1985 to a group of local businesspeople. With the team reportedly losing money and failing to attract fans, there was uncertainty about whether the Pirates would stay in Pittsburgh even under the new ownership. By 1988, however, the franchise started to turn the corner, finishing second in the standings, but more important, drawing a record number of fans to Three Rivers Stadium. By 1990, the Pirates climbed up from the bottom and were back on top of the National League East standings. They also topped the two-million mark in attendance for the first time.

Déjà Vu

O N THE June 23, 1969, cover of *Sports Illustrated* is a silhouette of a man, an athlete, surrounded by six groupings of pills, one of them a cluster of anabolic steroids. The headline reads, "Drugs: A Threat to Sport." The three-part series by Bil Gilbert begins, "The pill, capsule, vial, and needle have become fixtures of the locker room as athletes increasingly turn to drugs in the hope of improving performances."

Gilbert observed that, while people in society make up their own minds about what kind of drugs they use, "the athlete, a participant in organized games, cannot be permitted this luxury." He urged sports officials to stop ignoring the problem and realize it was "high time to make some rules," warning, "drugs can kill sport." Written more than forty years ago, Gilbert's words are prophetic to say the least.

Whatever the answers, the drug problem in major league baseball should have been dealt with decades ago. The steroid era should never have been allowed to take place. The months or even years directly following the Pittsburgh trials of 1985, although late, would have nevertheless been a good time for the league to start. Drug use was out in the open, and the timing was right. As to whether or not the implementation of a mandatory drug testing program after the trials in Pittsburgh would have helped deter the use of steroids in the game, opponents often call it a matter of apples and oranges. Apologists claim even if drugs of abuse (as cocaine, heroin, and the like became termed) had been tested for, that still would not have caught the cheaters because performance-enhancing drugs were *not* being tested for and therefore would have gone undetected. True. However, this is assuming that the league would have made no necessary adjustments to its drug-testing policy, such as expanding the type of drugs tested for.

If an agreement had been reached in the 1980s, and the league was serious about keeping drugs from the game, then tweaking the testing program to include PEDs would have been much easier than starting from scratch and getting the union to agree to the basic principle of testing all over again. The biggest hurdle would have been cleared. But again, it comes down to desire. Baseball failed to act, as Lee Jenkins of the *New York Times* once pointed out, "because of reluctance by the union and because of owners unwilling to point fingers at their own players."

It would not have taken long to notice that a different drug was rising in prevalence. Steroids came onto the scene practically on the heels of the cocaine scandal. A quick scan of the sports page was all the proof anyone would have needed to see where things were headed with steroids, which had become a problem in colleges, high schools, and even junior high schools at the time. Professional football players were coming out of the steroid closet and admitting to using them. On the world stage, Olympian Ben Johnson was stripped of his gold medal because of steroids in 1988.

Or what about simply listening to baseball's own medical personnel? In an interview in 2007 Larry Starr, the former trainer for the Cincinnati Reds and Florida Marlins, said he noticed steroid clues as far back as 1984. At the winter meetings following the 1988 season, with members of the owners group and the Players Association represented, Starr and other team medical personnel tried to alert the league about the issue. "I have notes from the winter meetings," Starr told *Florida Today* in 2007. "And team physicians stood up and said, 'Look, we need to do something about this. We've got a problem here if we don't do something about it.' That was 1988."

Starr remembered one specific player who ended the 1989 season at 171 pounds. The same player reported to spring training 1990 with his weight up to 205 pounds, while his body fat had decreased.

As a member of the Oakland A's for the 1988 and 1989 seasons, Dave Parker had a firsthand look at the origins of the "Bash Brothers" of Jose Canseco and Mark McGwire. "To be right on the team with Jose, he was fairly open about it. Jose would come in the weight room once a week and lift everything in the weight room," Parker remembers. "And when he would have a verbal discrepancy with other players, the first thing they would yell was 'you steroid-shooting motherfucker'... you know, stuff like that." Baseball fans soon joined in with Canseco's teammates, as happened during a playoff series at Boston's Fenway Park in 1988 when Sox fans began shouting "Steroids! Steroids!" at Canseco.

Parker doesn't hold any illusions about whether his superiors knew what was going on. "I think baseball had to know. It's abnormal for a guy to go and get twenty-five pounds of muscle over an off-season and increase his home run average over 100 percent... over 200 percent," says Parker. "It would have been hard not to see."

Baseball had numerous opportunities to address its drug problems. However, as Parker points out, "Baseball was going through a crisis with the public, their fan base. Guys were averaging a million dollars a year, and they have a labor dispute, a strike [in 1994, which resulted in the cancellation of the World Series].... They turned the fans off, and they needed something to reinject the fans back into the industry. So what they did was they juiced the ball up, and guys juiced themselves up. And that's when you had this wonderful home run thing."

The "wonderful home run thing" Parker is referring to came in 1998 during the season-long home run derby contest between Mark McGwire and Sammy Sosa, both attempting to top Roger Maris's

longstanding and cherished home run record of sixty-one. Poor
Maris went through hell achieving his record. Now, with that mark
beaten several times since McGwire's seventy-home-run victory in
1998, Maris's record—as well as the efforts of many other sluggers of
yesterday—is rendered meaningless due to the use of performance-
enhancing drugs.

The men in charge of the Pittsburgh case never imagined things
would have come to this in the sport. J. Alan Johnson, now a defense
attorney in downtown Pittsburgh, told the *Pittsburgh Tribune Review*
in 2004 that baseball's leaders "certainly were aware of what the
problem was after the trials." He went on, "I thought they would be
a little more aggressive in how they dealt with it. From what we see
now, evidently they chose not to or just didn't."

Major League Baseball's joint drug agreement was annulled in
1985; however, according to the Mitchell Report, the foundation of
this policy endured and "served as a precedent for the 'reasonable
cause' testing that was in effect informally thereafter until the 2002
Basic Agreement added a mandatory random drug testing program
to the collective bargaining agreement." For seventeen years, the
powers that be in MLB would rely only on an "informal" drug policy—a policy that was hardly ever enforced. In the meantime, stars
like McGwire, Bonds, Clemens, and A-Rod—the faces of America's
national pastime during the past couple decades—have long ceased
being called role models. Instead they became the poster boys for
performance-enhancing drugs.

Former Assistant U.S. Attorney James Ross notices a parallel
between baseball's cocaine years and the steroid era that ensued. "It
was pretty obvious as early as '80, '81, '82, that something was going
on in baseball. People were talking about it even before, and nothing
was done. Just like when people saw Barry Bonds... hit seventy-
three home runs and saw [his and other players'] arms and heads
and so forth that were much larger than when they came into the
league, and no one said anything about it... at first people are just
like, say it ain't so, Joe," Ross says.

"Jerry [Johnson] always felt and hoped if we did this right, baseball would clean up its act," Ross continues. "I think that was the goal. This case, at that point in time, had the ability to make a statement about the dangers of drug use in our society.... Baseball never learned from its mistakes. There are so many parallels between the two investigations. Different drugs, different athletes, but the same modus operandi—let's just keep it quiet. I can't imagine that the commissioner of baseball didn't know that Bonds and McGwire were on steroids. Everyone else was saying it, but the commissioner didn't know?"

Thinking back to the Pittsburgh scandal, Ross continues, "Back then, once we learned what was going on, I can't believe the Pirates didn't know. [John Milner] was doing lines of coke in the bathroom. For baseball not to know back then that something was going on, I just find it parallel to what's happening now... twenty-five years later."

Commissioner Bud Selig stated that he did not know of the league's steroid problems until the 1998 season. "I never even heard about it," Selig said in 2005. "I ran a team, and nobody was closer to their players, and I never heard any comment from them. It wasn't until 1998 or '99 that I heard the discussion."

Former trainer Larry Starr finds such statements far-fetched and thinks that both the commissioner's office and the Players Association knew about steroid use much earlier. Starr told journalist Hal McCoy about seeing players rush out of the clubhouse to watch Mark McGwire and Sammy Sosa take batting practice, "because they all knew what they were doing and wanted to see the results."

If the players all knew, Starr argues, how could baseball's leaders deny knowing what was going on? Starr agrees with management's claim that that they couldn't *prove* steroid use without mandatory testing, but he told the *Contra Costa Times*, "Don't say there weren't any signs, suspicions, or rumors. To say that truthfully? No way. There was enough physical and statistical evidence about what was happening."

Bud Selig practiced for his role as commissioner as an owner of the Milwaukee Brewers. "Without integrity in our sport, we have nothing," Selig told his hometown *Milwaukee Sentinel* in 1985. "I believe in a level of on-the-field and off-the-field conduct." Years later he called the issue of PEDs "a matter of integrity." Integrity is a common high-minded baseball word. It seems like each commissioner has uttered the word at some point or another. Peter Ueberroth announced prior to the Pittsburgh drug trials, "The integrity of the game is everything." This repeated tough talk from the commissioners is probably the most offensive thing about the steroids era. Over and over they make proclamations and plead innocence, while in reality, players were given carte blanche for decades to abuse not only themselves but also the game's history and competitive spirit. It would be hard to find anything resembling integrity in major league baseball's handling of the drug issue.

Still, nobody accepts responsibility. Selig never knew. Fehr and the union had to defend the players' right to privacy, a right they must no longer deserve considering the union has since agreed to testing for all the same drugs discussed in 1985. Why is testing no longer such a severe threat to a person's constitutional right to privacy? Fehr recently stopped just short of accepting part of the blame, saying in 2009, "If we, if I had known or understood what the circumstances were a little better, then perhaps we would have moved a little sooner."

Again, despite being surrounded by a mountain of evidence, another leader claims not to have known. As Tom Verducci of *Sports Illustrated* wrote following Fehr's semi-apology, "Of course he knew what was going on. . . . Rick Helling, an executive board member, told Fehr as far back as 1998, and in each subsequent year, he had a huge steroid problem on his hands."

Washington Post columnist and baseball enthusiast George F. Will points directly at Fehr and his cohorts for baseball's drug problems. "The union was unquestionably the most long-lasting and biggest impediment to a timely imposition of a testing regime," Will said.

But again, blame casts such a large net. The players clearly must accept their share of the burden. Major league players debased themselves. Some ruined their careers on drugs. Certainly many players cheated the game, the fans, and the sport's history.

Yet some say players merely operated within the rules defined for them. Respected *Los Angeles Times* columnist Jim Murray sarcastically asked whether using cocaine was "a crime on the streets but not in the dugout." Concerning the steroid era, Larry Starr is quick to defend the players. "They didn't abuse the system," he said. "They used the system." Such an attitude can be traced all the way back to the days of the Black Sox scandal, when jury foreman Harry Brigham, during the grand jury proceeding investigating the game's fix, announced, "There was no one around to keep the gamblers away." One only needs to substitute the word "drugs" for "gamblers," and after ninety years the core question remains, where was the leadership? They were too busy making grandiose statements about the integrity of the sport. To once again borrow from Eliot Asinof's *Eight Men Out* to sum up the misguided nature and utter gall it takes to make such statements: "It would be difficult to admire any baseball potentate who assumed the rule of a bold and perspicacious man after so many years of equivocation."

Reflecting on the fallout from the great 1919 scandal, Asinof wrote:

Baseball was a manifestation of the greatest of America at play. It was our national game; its stars were national heroes, revered by kids and adults alike, in all classes of our society. In the public mind, the image was pure and patriotic. The game had become part of our culture, intruding on our very speech patterns: "He began life with *two strikes* on him.... I'll take a *rain check* on that lunch...."

Now, suddenly, that pride was shattered. The National Pastime was nothing more than another show of corruption. To a kid—as to many adults—it seemed terribly indicative. If

baseball was corrupt, then *anything* might be—and probably
was....

It is impossible to add up bitterness like a batting average.
How great was the layer of cynicism that settled over the nation?
How many kids developed tolerance for a lie, for a betrayal, for
corruption itself?

It's noteworthy that Asinof's words about the earliest of baseball's three biggest scandals are perfectly transferrable to each of the
others.

Acknowledgments

I WOULD LIKE to thank all the people who took the time to talk to me about this case, particularly Dale Shiffman, who got the ball rolling, as well as Kevin Koch, Kevin Connolly, Rick Scurry, Jan Ackerman, Sam Reich, Dave Parker, Lonnie Smith, and James Ross. Special thanks to Bob Craig and Wells Morrison, whom I bothered on countless occasions. Their details and insights into the investigation were instrumental in the telling of this story. Mr. Craig, it was a pleasure listening to your stories, not just concerning this case but the ones throughout your career.

Thanks to my agent, Steven Harris at CSG Literary Partner, for your work in getting this project off the ground and on the road to being published, and to Chicago Review Press and Yuval Taylor and Lisa Reardon for all of your guidance.

Linda Parker at the *Post-Gazette*, I appreciate your assistance.

Finally I would like to recognize the efforts of Abe Gray and of my clerical assistants, Hank and Emerson, and to thank my mother, Betti, for her unwavering support.

Notes

I N GENERAL, quotations presented in the past tense are from existing interviews, while quotes originating from the author's personal interviews or correspondence with the following individuals between the years 2007 and 2009 are offered in the present tense: Jan Ackerman, Randy Brandt, Craig Cacek, Kevin Connolly, William "Bob" Craig, Dan Donovan, Steve Greenberg, Shelby Greer, Al Holland, Fritz Huysman, J. Alan Johnson, James E. Kelley Jr., Kevin Koch, Stanton Levenson, Wells Morrison, John Nickoloff, Dave Parker, Sam Reich, Adam Renfroe, Don Robinson, Jim Rooker, James J. Ross, Steve Schanwald, Rick Scurry, Dale Shiffman, Lonnie Smith, and Dr. Charles Yesalis.

Prologue: Tough Talk

Somebody has to say   *Sports Illustrated* 5-20-85
Our fans deserve a game   WKYC.com
the best program of any sport   *New York Times* 12-6-88
A golden age may be defined   *Total Baseball*

1 The Parrot

It has to be someone   *The Valley Independent* 3-30-79
Shiffman sometimes playing   *Pittsburgh Post-Gazette* 6-25-85
The advertisements that played   *Pittsburgh Press* 2-11-79
several dozen unemployed actors   Associated Press 2-25-79

Man, I'm really nervous   Koch interview
Wait until opening day   Koch interview
I felt like   *The Good, the Bad, the Ugly Pittsburgh Pirates*

2 The Pirates

It is supposed   *New Yorker* 11-26-79
They looked at me   Koch interview
In the old days   *Sports Illustrated* 12-24-79
We're a blue-collar team   *Tales from 1979 Pittsburgh Pirates*
a shot and a beer   *Sports Illustrated* 12-24-79
hell with the lid   James Parton (1868)
I like the warmth   *Sports Illustrated* 12-24-79
It may not be   Rooker interview
look around and suddenly   *New Yorker* 11-26-79
Paul Waner used to wander   *The Pirates*
We can win it   *The Pirates*
age, injury, and giveaway defense   *Sports Illustrated* 4-9-79
Stargell was a man   Associated Press 4-9-01; *Sports Illustrated* 4-9-01
I'll go out to talk   *Sports Illustrated* 12-24-79
"Stargell's Stars" were considered   *Tales from 1979 Pittsburgh Pirates*
traditionally has the loudest   *Sports Illustrated* 4-9-79
knots of people shouting   *New Yorker* 11-26-79
Second baseman Phil Garner   *New Yorker* 11-26-79
Stargell walked directly   Rooker interview
We got Pancho Villa   *Sports Illustrated* 12-24-79
The cream always rises   Rooker interview
Nice going, Dude Parrot   *Pittsburgh Post-Gazette* 10-5-79
The festive mood   *New York Times* 10-6-79
An explosion was imminent   *Pittsburgh Post-Gazette* 10-6-79
It's my first World Series   United Press International 10-6-79
World Series Is Fun Again   *New York Times* 10-18-79
Come on Pops,   *Pittsburgh Post-Gazette* 10-18-79
President Carter, who assisted   *New York Times* 10-18-85
And now I'd like   *New York Times* 10-18-79
There has been a closeness   Associated Press 10-18-79
The morning box score   *Pittsburgh Post-Gazette; New York Times*
    10-18/19-79
He absolutely met   Schanwald interview
a genuine local celebrity   *Pittsburgh Post-Gazette* 10-5-79

Shaking his Parrot head   *USA TODAY* 9-3-85
It wasn't all fun   *Pittsburgh Post-Gazette* 10-5-79
If Kevin continues   *Pittsburgh Post-Gazette* 10-5-79
young, single, and taking on   *USA Today* 9-3-85

3 The Loner Meets the Star

He was a natural   *Willie Stargell: An Autobiography*
Shelby Greer had just boarded   Greer interview
It had been a long   *Sports Illustrated* 4-9-79
I learned to slide   *Sports Illustrated* 4-9-79
In 1970 Dave Parker was   *The Pirates*
The great Ali says   *Sports Illustrated* 4-9-79
In November 1979   *United States of America v. Curtis Strong*; FBI 302
     Report (interview of Shelby Greer)
As Shelby Greer settled   Greer interview
Former Montour superintendent   *Pittsburgh Press* 5-31-85
Shelby was a nice kid   *Pittsburgh Post-Gazette* 6-25-85
a tall, blond,   *Pittsburgh Post-Gazette* 5-31-85
at some of Pittsburgh's   *Pittsburgh Press* 5-31-85
Greer first tried cocaine   Greer interview
transporting back with him   FBI 302 Report (interview of Shelby Greer)
Orioles infielder Billy Smith   *New York Times* 3-3-84
Lee Lacy was even said   Craig interview
At times it seemed   *Sports Illustrated* 6-23-69
pills, salves, injections   *The Nation* 5-25-85
false feelings of power   ESPN.com 9-6-07
In most locker rooms   *Boston Globe* 1-14-05
When Ellis thought   Parker interview
Ellis would later admit   *New York Times* 8-22-85
Dock Ellis was without question   *Dallas Observer* 6-16-05
It was a Friday morning   *Dallas Observer* 6-16-05
Dave Parker asserts   Parker interview
This was a man   *United States of America v. Curtis Strong*

4 The Lefty

I love baseball   *Reno Evening Gazette* 1-3-75
He was drafted   Associated Press 11-27-92
I feel really good   *Reno Evening Gazette* 1-3-75

During a series that season   Brandt interview

In July 1977   *Reno Evening Gazette* 7-28-77

There was a lot   *Nevada State Journal* 1-7-77

In 1979, with the Pirates   *Sports Illustrated* 5-28-84

That's a lonely life   Associated Press 11-27-92

Scurry, along with teammates   Cacek interview; *Pittsburgh Press*; *United States of America v. Curtis Strong*

I remember the first time   *Sports Illustrated* 5-28-84

You see Dale,   Parker interview

In Portland, Scurry and Berra   Cacek interview; *United States of America v. Curtis Strong*

In the old days   *New York Times* 3-20-84

Cacek says he   Cacek interview

Scurry was off   Cacek interview; *Pittsburgh Post-Gazette* 3-18-80

in the Dominican League   *Pittsburgh Post-Gazette* 3-18-80

He is, at once   *Pittsburgh Post-Gazette* 3-18-80

We babied him   *Pittsburgh Press* 4-18-80

Rod Scurry has worked   *Pittsburgh Press* 4-18-80

He got to know Dale Berra   *United States of America v. Curtis Strong*; Parker interview

Curtis Strong was a former   *Pittsburgh Post-Gazette* 5-31-85

He was introduced to   *United States of America v. Curtis Strong*

Milner was first introduced   *United States of America v. Curtis Strong*

spoken with Bert Blyleven   FBI 302 Report (interview of Shelby Greer)

It gives them   *New York Times* 8-22-85

5 Big League Call-up

You always get a special kick   BaseballAlmanac.com

The butterflies have already started   *Pittsburgh Post-Gazette* 4-19-81

Growing up, Scurry   Associated Press 11-19-92

Scurry's aspirations to pitch   *Pittsburgh Press* 4-19-81, 4-20-81; *Pittsburgh Post-Gazette* 4-19-81, 4-20-81

The kid has an outstanding   *Pittsburgh Post-Gazette* 4-20-81

A poll of scouts   *When the Bucs Won It All*

Scurry Can't Sleep   *Pittsburgh Press* 4-20-81

His memorable first   *Pittsburgh Post-Gazette* 6-11-95

It was like [Scurry]   Koch interview

Soon, the circle expanded   Shiffman interview

I got to stand out there   *The Good, The Bad, and The Ugly Pittsburgh Pirates*

a real car buff   *Pittsburgh Post-Gazette* 6-25-85

hanging out with athletes   Shiffman interview

Shiffman and Koch, like so many others   Koch and Shiffman interviews

During this time,   FBI 302 Report (interview of Shelby Greer)

got to be pretty good   *Pittsburgh Press* 5-10-84

He had a hard time   Associated Press 11-27-92

If I had it   *United States of America v. Curtis Strong*

In fact, it was so common   *United States of America v. Curtis Strong*

6 The Kings of Pittsburgh

Whatever the price   *Time* 7-6-81

you sponsored each other's   *Pittsburgh Post-Gazette* 7-29-01

That night we all   Connolly interview

In Atlanta he ran into   FBI 302 Report (interview of Shelby Greer)

Scurry's career ascent   *Pittsburgh Press* 5-10-84; *Sports Illustrated* 5-28-84

He snorted a gram before   *Sports Illustrated* 5-28-84

Finally it got to   *Pittsburgh Press* 5-10-84

A year after meeting   Connolly interview

They don't have anything   *Pittsburgh Post-Gazette* 6-1-85

He was a steady worker   *Pittsburgh Post-Gazette* 5-31-85

Connolly's neighbors described   *Pittsburgh Post-Gazette* 6-1-85

It was when darkness fell   Connolly interview

The Pirates' John Milner   Sam Reich interview

Michael J's is the type   *Pittsburgh Press* 9-10-85

Milner advised Berra   *United States of America v. Curtis Strong*

The bartender at Michael J's   *United States of America v. Jeffrey Lynn Mosco*

Mosco and Berra grew close   *United States of America v. Curtis Strong*

The bar wasn't much,   *United States of America v. Robert William McCue*

The problem with groupies   *The Wrong Stuff*

Growing up, Koch   *Pittsburgh Post-Gazette* 10-5-79

Even *I* was able to 'bed'   *Real Sports with Bryant Gumbel* 9-19-06

The Parrot is a genuine   *Pittsburgh Post-Gazette* 10-5-79

I pretty much had   Koch interview

Drop-dead gorgeous   Shiffman interview

I used to roll around   *Pittsburgh Post-Gazette* 10-5-79

His many antics   *USA Today* 9-3-85

Dale's a great guy   *Pittsburgh Post-Gazette* 6-01-85
I think he   *Pittsburgh Post-Gazette* 6-25-85
a safe, nonaddicting euphoriant   "Cocaine Dependence"

7 Strung Out

Erythroxylum coca is a   *Cocaine: An Unauthorized Biography*
It's as though the need   *New York Times Magazine* 9-1-74
And if you are forward   *The Life and Work of Sigmund Freud*
During this period medical firms   "History: The American Experience
    with Stimulants"
a whole new field   *A Brief History of Cocaine*
the moderate use of   *Cocaine: An Unauthorized Biography*
Athletes... and baseball players   "History: The American Experience
    with Stimulants"
The ideal brain tonic   *Life* May 1984
anesthetic surgical procedure   *Cocaine: An Unauthorized Biography*
Spurred by stories circulating   *New York Times Magazine* 9-1-74
The bohemians, gamblers, prostitutes, burglars   *Neotropical
    Companion*
Orgasms go better   *Newsweek* 9-27-71
the original 'war' on drugs   *Hep-Cats, Narcs, and Pipe Dreams*
probably the most benign   "The Great Cocaine Myth"
In Miami the price   *Life* May 1984
something that was a fad   Parker interview
It was so prevalent in society   *Real Sports with Bryant Gumbel* 9-19-06
I have seen a lot   *New York Times* 8-19-85
Anytime there's a   *New York Times* 8-19-85
Fame, fortune, free time   "Cocaine Abuse and Sports"
You got people   Parker interview
On July 20, 1980,   *Pittsburgh Press* 7-21-80
home. Where they've watched him   *Pittsburgh Press* 7-21-80
of the forty-two talk show   *Pittsburgh Press* 2-22-81
The town has never   *Pittsburgh Press* 4-19-81
Some of the guys   Parker interview
Kevin Connolly had just   Connolly interview
Parker got Berra   *Real Sports with Bryant Gumbel* 9-19-06; *New York Times*
    8-19-85
The signs were there   *Pittsburgh Press* 9-22-85
He later told Sports Illustrated   *Sports Illustrated* 5-28-84

Scurry's teammates said nothing   Robinson interview
He was talkative one day   *Pittsburgh Press* 9-22-85
In Scurry, Kevin Connolly saw   Connolly interview
What had started out   Associated Press 11-19-92
Shiffman filled his friend   Koch interview
Scurry took off   *Sports Illustrated* 5-28-84; Associated Press 11-19-92
This time when Scurry   *Sports Illustrated* 5-28-84
Shelby Greer made   FBI 302 Report (interview of Shelby Greer)
Greer, who was later obliged   FBI 302 Report (interview of Shelby Greer);
   Greer, Shelby. "Motion to Vacate..."
for an investment   *New York Times* 12-12-78

8 A Night in L.A.

Baseball is trying to solve   *The Wrong Stuff*
the plate was jumping   *Pittsburgh Press* 4-6-84
The team traveled   Rooker, Connolly, Robinson, Morrison, and Craig
   interviews; *Sports Illustrated* 5-84; Associated Press 11-27-92
Scurry Asks for Help   *Pittsburgh Press* 4-8-84
Scurry's West Coast scandal sent   Koch and Connolly interviews
I was ashamed   *Pittsburgh Press* 5-10-84
We didn't have a prescription   "Frontline: Drug Wars: Interviews:
   Dr. Alan I. Leshner"
My husband and I   Associated Press 11-19-92
When addiction becomes a problem   Rick Scurry interview
It turned out   *Pittsburgh Post-Gazette* 5-28-85

9 The Agents

Baseball's drug culture grew   *Sports Illustrated* 9-16-1985
In March 1984, prior to   Craig, Morrison, Ross, Don Robinson
   interviews; *Pittsburgh Post-Gazette* 6-8-85, 6-11-95
On May 23, Morrison and Craig   Craig and Morrison interviews
I just got a call   Connolly interview
usually a gin and tonic   *Pittsburgh Post-Gazette* 6-25-85
James Ross was a rookie.   Ross interview
Jerry will go after   *Pittsburgh Post-Gazette* 6-1-85
When you have a   *Pittsburgh Press* 9-15-85
It wasn't like he   Ross interview
I'm not in   *Pittsburgh Press* 9-15-85

Agents Morrison and Craig continued to press   Craig and Morrison
  interviews
On November 5   Craig and Morrison interviews

10 The Wire

In early November   Shiffman interview
That Thursday evening   Koch interview
I was grasping for   *Real Sports with Bryant Gumbel* 9-19-06
Koch contacted an attorney   Koch interview

11 Grant Street

I had it in little gram bottles   *New York Times* 8-20-85
He was almost like   Ross interview
His only problem   *Pittsburgh Press* 5-13-84
An attorney for one   *Pittsburgh Press* 2-15-86
The problem is serious   *Sports Illustrated* 5-28-84
Drugs in baseball   *New York Times* 9-30-84
I am not bitter   *USA Today* 1-16-85
most persistent and difficult   *Hardball: The Education of a Baseball
  Commissioner*
the best thing   *New York Times* 3-4-85
By rehiring Miller,   *New York Times* 11-23-83
There's no doubt   *New York Times* 11-23-83, 11-24-83
Moffett cited opposition   *New York Times* 11-24-83
The joint drug and alcohol   Associated Press 9-3-83
I think that we   Associated Press 2-24-84
Drugs aren't a win-lose   *Sports Illustrated* 12-5-83
In February 1984 things   *New York Times* 2-23-84; United Press
  International 2-23-84
I've been around   *New York Times* 2-23-84
We produce the blueprint   *Sports Illustrated* 5-28-84
I think most athletes   *Sports Illustrated* 5-28-84
During his speech in Washington   *New York Times* 2-23-84
spreading trash   *New York Times* 2-24-84
the innuendos are not true   *New York Times* 2-23-84
Hernandez had the full backing   *New York Times* 2-23-84
Moffett was forced to make   *New York Times* 3-22-84
Pittsburgh Post-Gazette reporter   Ackerman interview

On January 8, 1985, Ackerman   Ackerman and Donovan interviews; *Pittsburgh Post-Gazette* 1-24-85

On January 23, 1985,   Ackerman interview; *Pittsburgh Post-Gazette* 1-23-85, 1-24-85; *Pittsburgh Press* 1-24-85

I don't even know   *Pittsburgh Post-Gazette* 1-23-85

I now confirm   *Pittsburgh Post-Gazette* 1-24-85

Pirates' GM Harding   *Pittsburgh Press* 1-25-85

Last year, a number of   *Pittsburgh Press* 1-24-85

Shelby Greer was on his   FBI 302 Report (interview of Shelby Greer); Greer, Shelby. "Motion to Vacate…".

Agents Morrison and Craig   Craig and Morrison interviews

Smith remembers the agents   Smith interview

the first words   Reich interview

Late in the evening   *New York Times* 10-19-83, 8-21-85

I suspect it was   *Hardball: The Education of a Baseball Commissioner*

the geography of the investigation   Kelley interview

By 1985 only Willie Wilson   *USA Today* 5-15-85

I definitely feel   *USA Today* 5-15-85

The events in Kansas City   Reich interview

Everybody, from the minute   ESPN.com

We knew this was   Reich interview

citing "boredom" and "peer pressure"   *Pittsburgh Press* 9-8-85

Money *is* the problem.   Associated Press 9-9-85; *Pittsburgh Press* 9-8-85

Because of his sports expertise   Donovan interview

Who? Enos?   *Pittsburgh Press* 3-21-85

They told me that   Smith interview

I guess I can   Greer interview

By this time   Craig, Morrison, and Ross interviews

What a nitwit he was   Craig interview

told by Dave Parker   FBI 302 Report (interview of Shelby Greer)

In 1983 Washington Redskins   Associated Press 8-11-83, 10-8-83

I started losing interest   *New York Times* 8-19-85

Tim Raines was one   *New York Times* 8-19-85

one published report   *Pittsburgh Post-Gazette* 5-9-85

All the writers are pumping   *Pittsburgh Post-Gazette* 5-9-85

A list published in   *Sports Illustrated* 5-28-84

court papers from the   *New York Times* 5-12-85

On May 7, 1985, Ueberroth   *USA Today* 5-8-85

The [commissioner's] office was created   *USA Today* 5-9-85

Investigators said players were supplied   Associated Press 3-30-85

Testing just seems to be   *USA Today* 5-9-85
The integrity of the game   *New York Times* 5-12-85
The Commissioner Gets Tough   *Sports Illustrated* 5-20-85
You're talking about ancient history   *Sports Illustrated* 5-20-85
the first baseman   *Sports Illustrated* 5-20-85
I don't know any names   *New York Times* 5-10-85
I think it's going   Associated Press 5-9-85, *Pittsburgh Post-Gazette* 5-9-85

12 Busted

In late May, Dale Shiffman   Shiffman interview
On the evening   *Pittsburgh Post-Gazette* 5-31-85
Shiffman had just finished   Shiffman interview
Inside Shiffman's home   *Pittsburgh Post-Gazette* 6-1-85
Hey, man,   *Pittsburgh Post-Gazette* 6-11-95
dates of 133 counts   *New York Times* 6-6-85
Robert McCue's mother   *Pittsburgh Press* 5-31-85
Suddenly Connolly understood   Connolly interview
Seven 'Fans' Arrested   *Pittsburgh Post-Gazette* 6-1-85
Players who are making   *Pittsburgh Post-Gazette* 5-31-85, 6-1-85;
    Associated Press 9-3-85
Upon learning of   Ackerman and Huysman interviews
They got seven fans   Donovan interview
We had no friends   Morrison interview
the worst day   *OnQ Magazine*
someone has to take   *Pittsburgh Press* 6-1-85
Here's Rod Scurry and   *Real Sports with Bryant Gumbel* 9-19-06
Scurry Stars in   *Pittsburgh Press* 6-1-85
Kevin Koch, however,   Koch interview
Kevin Koch, the original   United Press International 6-7-85
After an unnamed government source   Associated Press 8-9-85, Koch
    interview
Koch was lampooned in a   *Pittsburgh Post-Gazette* 8-21-85
I felt like Judas   *Real Sports with Bryant Gumbel* 9-19-06
It was the most horrible   *Oakland Tribune* 10-27-06
the city I grew up in   *Oakland Tribune* 10-27-06
The other part that's very   *Pittsburgh Post-Gazette* 6-1-85
The scandal had taken   *Pittsburgh Post-Gazette* 6-1-85; *New York Times*
    7-7-85; *Pittsburgh Press* 6-28-85
The National League drugstore   *The Pirates Reader*

First, on May 23   United Press International 5-24-85
We were just bad   Robinson interview
It was unraveling   Koch interview
I know I'm a professional   *The Sporting News* 9-9-85
Joe, our team has   *The Sporting News* 9-9-85
You know Madlock has been   *The Sporting News* 9-9-85
You can't be successful   Associated Press 7-11-85
In a thirteen-page report   U.S. Department of Justice, Federal Bureau of
    Investigation, FBIHQ file 12-9070 and Pittsburgh file 12E-PG-306-Sub B
In August 1985   *New York Times* 8-19/20/21/22-85
Adam O. Renfroe Jr.   *Pittsburgh Press* 9-17-85; *Pittsburgh Post-Gazette*
    9-9-85
Known as a drug buster   *USA Today* 5-31-85
Jerry is basically   *USA Today* 5-31-85
Jerry hasn't wasted time   *USA Today* 5-31-85
Despite the media frenzy   Ackerman interview; *USA Today* 9-16-85
none of these trials   *USA Today* 9-16-85
You always risk criticism   *USA Today* 9-16-85
Agent Bob Craig didn't want   Craig and Morrison interviews; *United
    States of America v. Dale Martin Shiffman*
My attorney told me straight   *OnQ Magazine*
Meanwhile Jeffrey Mosco's attorney,   Levenson interview

13 The United States Versus Curtis Strong

I am covered   *Pittsburgh Press* 9-14-85
That morning, I was nervous   Ross interview
Thirteen camera crews   *Pittsburgh Post-Gazette* 9-7-85
The proceedings would take place   *USA Today* 9-13-85
The affair was highly anticipated   Associated Press 9-3-85, 9-4-85
There won't be personal comments   *USA Today* 9-11-85
During this case,   *United States of America v. Curtis Strong*
Renfroe's strategy was simple   Renfroe interview
Lonnie Smith was the first   *Pittsburgh Post-Gazette* 9-6-85; Associated
    Press 9-8-85; *United States of America v. Curtis Strong*
I stayed up   *Pittsburgh Press* 9-6-85
Who told you it   *The Capital* (Annapolis, MD) 9-16-85
Since May, my anger   *Pittsburgh Post-Gazette* 9-9-85
40 percent of all   *Pittsburgh Press* 9-6-85
Players never sell   Associated Press 9-8-85

Following that day's proceedings   *Pittsburgh Post-Gazette* 9-9-85
Here were highly paid   Associated Press 9-8-85
Cabell spoke of his   Associated Press 9-7-85; *Pittsburgh Post-Gazette*
    9-10-85
In their testimonies   Associated Press 9-11-85; *USA Today* 9-11-85
Berra said his first meeting   *Pittsburgh Post-Gazette* 9-10-85
When asked by reporters   *USA Today* 9-11-85; *Pittsburgh Post-Gazette*
    9-10-85
Are you still numb   Associated Press 9-11-85
By the fifth day   *USA Today* 9-12-85; Associated Press 9-22-85; *Pittsburgh
    Press* 9-14-85
Parker described recreational cocaine use   *Pittsburgh Post-Gazette* 9-12-85;
    United States of America v. Curtis Strong
Drugs were different   *A Pitcher's Story*
From various places   *United States of America v. Curtis Strong*
Upon prompting from   *Pittsburgh Post-Gazette* 9-12-85
Parker backed up   *Pittsburgh Post-Gazette* 9-12-85; Associated Press
    9-13-85
During his cross-examination,   United Press International 9-12-85
As Renfroe, with voice raised   *United States of America v. Curtis Strong*
Diamond cautioned Renfroe   *USA Today* 9-12-85; *United States of America
    v. Curtis Strong*
I never knew   Associated Press 9-13-85
Parker had also backed Berra's testimony   Associated Press 9-13-85;
    Pittsburgh Post-Gazette 9-13-85
The bombshell of the trial   Associated Press 9-13-85; *Pittsburgh Post-
    Gazette* 9-13-85
Willie who?   *Pittsburgh Press* 9-13-85
Johnson remembers a sudden "jolt"   Johnson interview
managed to transform himself   *Pittsburgh Post-Gazette* 9-13-85
Mays denied the accusation   Associated Press 9-13-85
His longtime physician   Associated Press 9-14-85
Milner attested to also   *United States of America v. Curtis Strong*
Kevin Connolly also spoke of   Connolly interview
Milner to agree that   *United States of America v. Curtis Strong*
I want to put   *United States of America v. Curtis Strong*
My fees will go up   *USA Today* 9-13-85
Expectations were high   Associated Press 9-18/19-85
Tanner was nothing   *USA Today* 9-18/19-85; Associated Press 9-18/19-85
I have my own office   Associated Press 9-18-85

They hid it from me *Pittsburgh Press* 9-10-85
the manager "doesn't remember *USA Today* 9-18-85
Strong and some of Ross interview
Strong was seen dabbing *USA Today* 9-19-85
You can expect *USA Today* 9-19-85
Prior to the attorneys' *United States of America v. Curtis Strong*; *Pittsburgh
     Post-Gazette* 9-21-85
It has been *United States of America v. Curtis Strong*; *USA Today* 9-20-85
Curtis Strong knew Associated Press 9-20-85; *Pittsburgh Press* 9-20-85
Even if I was looking *United States of America v. Curtis Strong*
But the first day *USA Today* 9-20-85
Renfroe, who had requested *USA Today* 9-20-85
Taxi driver Joe Stachowski *The Pirates Reader*
Nobody likes to pay *USA Today* 9-6-85
To me, I guess *USA Today* 9-19-85
Seems to be a lot *USA Today* 9-12-85
This aspect of the law *USA Today* 9-19-85
Why am I going Associated Press 9-13-85
It's shameful *USA Today* 9-19-85
J. Alan Johnson deflected *USA Today* 9-19-85
I don't know *USA Today* 9-20-85
Strong should have been *USA Today* 9-12-85
Why should those people *USA Today* 9-12-85
Assistant U.S. Attorney James Ross interview
Journalist Dan Donovan concurs Donovan interview
At 1:15 P.M. *New York Times* 9-21-85
At that point Craig and Johnson interviews
After fourteen days *New York Times* 9-21-85
After Strong was escorted away Associated Press 9-22-85
probably seventy Associated Press 9-21-85
It's not over until *Pittsburgh Press* 9-21-85
I fought zealously *Pittsburgh Press* 9-21-85
It was clear Associated Press 9-21-85
I feel bad Associated Press 9-21-85
Without going over the testimony *Pittsburgh Post-Gazette* 9-20-85
kind of cocky *Indiana Gazette* 10-14-85
I just never *Pittsburgh Post-Gazette* 6-11-95
James Ross held a more Ross interview
Renfroe had some of Ross interview
There are millions of baseball United Press International 9-21-85

were not virginal innocents   Associated Press 11-5-85

If you walked into   Reich interview

McCue was charged   *Pittsburgh Post-Gazette* 9-24-85; Associated Press 9-27-85

At McCue's sentencing,   Associated Press 10-31-85; *United States of America v. Robert William McCue*

How can I look back   *Pittsburgh Post-Gazette* 6-11-95

I consider my office staff   Associated Press 10-31-85; *United States of America v. Robert William McCue*

According to the presentence   *United States of America v. Jeffrey Lynn Mosco*

I didn't go knocking   *New York Times* 3-15-85

Baseball is now   *Post-Gazette* 10-31-85

provided with prostitutes   *St. Petersburg Times* 7-5-86

Within a year   Strong, Curtis. "Motion to Vacate..."

Mr. Renfroe presented   Associated Press 8-13-87

Adam Renfroe was found guilty   *Pittsburgh Post-Gazette* 8-13-87

prevent a catastrophe   *New York Times* 7-5-86

14 The Response

I was on drugs   *USA Today* 9-18-85

Those overpaid, overrated, pampered   Associated Press 9-22-85

It certainly hurt   *New York Times* 8-20-85

Look at my defense   *New York Times* 8-20-85

I didn't feel like   Smith interview

I don't think there's any   *New York Times* 8-20-85

echoed Keith Hernandez's   *New York Times* 8-20-85, 9-28-85

On the heels of news   *Pittsburgh Press* 9-26-85

probably was the wrong thing   Associated Press 9-25-85

Ueberroth called a news conference   Associated Press 9-25-85; *New York Times* 9-25-85

a decade in which baseball   Associated Press 9-25-85

This is baseball's last chance   *Time* 10-7-85

The players are already   *New York Times* 9-25-85

If I can't prove   Smith interview

The Players Association's executive director... *representative Jim Morrison*   Associated Press 9-25/26/27-85; *New York Times* 9-25-85, 9-27-85

overwhelming consensus   Associated Press 9-28-85

There is a growing faction   Associated Press 9-8-85

I would be proud   *USA Today* 5-9-85

If my owner asks me   USA Today 9-18-85

Down at the union office   Associated Press 9-25-85, 9-26-85, 9-27-85; *New York Times* 9-26-85

The drug-testing proposal   Associated Press 9-27-85

Drugs are not   Associated Press 9-25-85

players to go on   *Jet* 6-17-85

Twenty-five percent of   *Jet* 6-10-85

On October 22, in the   Associated Press 10-23-85

make substantial progress   Associated Press 10-23-85

I can't say   *New York Times* 10-23-85

did not see any point   *New York Times* 10-23-85

The owners had money   Confidential source

Greed stops the owners   *Boston Globe* 9-12-85

the number-one problem   *USA Today* 9-12-85

Were the owners truly interested   Associated Press 10-23-85

In November the union filed   Associated Press 11-5-85

Baseball has a responsibility   United Press International 11-17-85

Ueberroth said he was   Associated Press 12-12-85

We will do what we can   Associated Press 12-20-85

The book was titled   *USA Today* 12-20-85

These guys must think   United Press International 9-19-85

number-one sports story   United Press International 12-29-85

On February 28, 1986,   United Press International 3-1-86

Ueberroth had interviewed   Associated Press 3-1-86

In effect,   *New York Daily News* 2-27-08

The monetary fines, which ranged   Associated Press 3-1-86

My biggest hurt was after   Smith interview

I don't think management   *US News & World Report* 3-17-86

The tone between management   *New York Times* 7-31-86

The drug testing   *New York Times* 3-2-86

I believe baseball   Associated Press 4-9-86

In April 1986   Mitchell report

Beyond testing, baseball needs   *New York Times* 3-2-86

Players shall not act   Associated Press 2-1-86

In 1921, the year following   *Juicing the Game*

The season following   www.baseball-reference.com

Barry Rona, executive director   *New York Times* 12-7-86

Peter Ueberroth had cited drugs   *New York Times* 3-2-86

owners tend to go   *New York Times* 12-7-86

When I came to New York,   *New York Times* 2-26-86

I don't think it will   *New York Times* 9-25-85

When they finally got together   *Salon* 6-20-02

Baseball owners are the toughest   *Time* 3-12-84

The will just wasn't there   *New York Times* 12-12-04

When I got traded   Smith interview

I hate to be the one   *ESPN The Magazine* 2-27-05

The suit claimed that   Associated Press 4-22-86

Chicago White Sox owner   *Eight Men Out*

With all the big contracts   *USA Today* 5-9-85

make the [1985 drug trials]   Associated Press 5-8-88

has already been generously overpaid   Associated Press 5-4-88

You're damn right   Associated Press 4-23-86

In a twenty-two-page   *Pittsburgh Post-Gazette* 5-21-88; Associated Press
   5-21-88

The statement also claims   *Pittsburgh Post-Gazette* 5-21-88

The overwhelming majority   Associated Press 5-21-88

15 Postgame

I wish he'd never learned   *Pittsburgh Post-Gazette* 6-11-95

In the early morning hours   Associated Press 11-19-92; *Pittsburgh Post-
Gazette* 6-11-95

Scurry once said   *Pittsburgh Post-Gazette* 3-7-85

The very next day   Associated Press 12-26-88

He had a faint heartbeat   Associated Press 11-19-92

The cocaine, plus violent behavior   Associated Press 12-16-92; *Pittsburgh
Post-Gazette* 6-11-95

From inside the prison walls   Shiffman interview; *Pittsburgh Post-Gazette*
8-14-00; *Real Sports with Bryant Gumbel* 9-19-06; *OnQ Magazine*; *The
700 Club*

Kevin Koch, forced out   Koch interview

I remember tears just   *Real Sports with Bryant Gumbel* 9-19-06

It's just the compassion alone   *Real Sports with Bryant Gumbel* 9-19-06

Kevin Connolly had thought   Connolly interview

Thomas Balzer served   *Pittsburgh Post-Gazette* 6-11-95

Dale Berra was arrested   *Pittsburgh Press* 4-21-89

After Berra completed   *New York Times* 6-18-95

Lonnie Smith looks back   Smith interview

are a lot of guys   Parker interview
I think it's a fucking joke   Parker interview
Thirty was legit.   Parker interview
According to former Pirates'   Greenberg interview; *Pittsburgh Press* 6-2-91

Epilogue: Déjà Vu

Once more, abandon   *Baseball: A Film by Ken Burns*
The pill, capsule, vial,   *Sports Illustrated* 6-23-69
because of reluctance   *New York Times* 12-12-04
I have notes from   *Florida Today* 11-27-07
To be right on   Parker interview
Sox fans began shouting   *Milwaukee Sentinel* 10-6-88
Baseball was going through   Parker interview
certainly were aware   *Pittsburgh Tribune Review* 12-19-04
It was pretty obvious   Ross interview
I never even heard   Associated Press 2-10-05
because they all knew   *Journal News* (Hamilton, Ohio) 12-14-07
Don't say there weren't   *Contra Costa Times* 3-14-05
Without integrity in our sport,   *Milwaukee Sentinel* 9-21-85
a matter of integrity   Mitchell report
The integrity of the game   *New York Times* 5-12-85, 8-22-85
If we, if I had known   *New York Times* 6-22-09; SI.com 6-23-09
The union was unquestionably   *New York Times* 6-22-09
a crime on the streets   *Hardball*
They didn't abuse the system   *Florida Today* 11-27-07
There was no one   *Eight Men Out*

Bibliography

Books

Angell, Roger. *A Pitcher's Story: Innings with David Cone*. New York: Warner Books, 2001.

Asinof, Eliot. *Eight Men Out: The Black Sox and the 1919 World Series*. New York: Owl Books, 2000.

Bryant, Howard. *Juicing the Game: Drugs, Power, and the Fight for the Soul of Major League Baseball*. New York: Viking, 2005.

Enders, Eric. *100 Years of the World Series: 1903–2004*. New York: Barnes & Noble, 2003.

Jones, Ernest. *The Life and Work of Sigmund Freud*. New York: Basic Books, Inc., 1981.

Jonnes, Jill. *Hep-Cats, Narcs, and Pipe Dreams: A History of America's Romance with Illegal Drugs*. New York: Johns Hopkins University Press, 1999.

Karch, Steven B. *A Brief History of Cocaine*. Boca Raton, FL: CRC, 1998.

Kricher, John C. *Neotropical Companion: An Introduction to the Animals, Plants, and Ecosystems of the New World Tropics*. Princeton, NJ: Princeton University Press, 1997.

Kuhn, Bowie. *Hardball: The Education of a Baseball Commissioner*. Lincoln: University of Nebraska, 1997.

Lee, Bill. *The Wrong Stuff*. New York: Three Rivers, 2006.

McCollister, John C. *Tales from the 1979 Pittsburgh Pirates: Remembering "The Fam-A-Lee"* Grand Rapids, MI: Sports, 2005.

_____. *The Good, the Bad, and the Ugly Pittsburgh Pirates: Heart-Pounding, Jaw-Dropping, and Gut-Wrenching Moments from Pittsburgh Pirates History*. New York: Triumph Books, 2008.

Peterson, Richard, ed. *The Pirates Reader*. Pittsburgh: University of Pittsburgh, 2007.

Ranier, Bill, and David Finoli. *When the Bucs Won It All: The 1979 World Champion Pittsburgh Pirates*. Boston: McFarland & Company, 2005.

Sahadi, Lou. *Pirates*. New York: Times Books, Fitzhenry & Whiteside, 1980.

Stargell, Willie, and Tom Bird. *Willie Stargell: An Autobiography*. New York: Harper & Row, 1984.

Streatfeild, Dominic. *Cocaine: An Unauthorized Biography*. New York: Picador, 2003.

Thorn, John, Pete Palmer, and Michael Gershman, eds. *Total Baseball: The Official Encyclopedia of Major League Baseball (Total Baseball, 7th ed)*. Champaign, IL: Total Sports, 2001.

Magazines

Angell, Roger. "Wilver's Way." *New Yorker*. 26 November 1979.

Callahan, Tom. "Sport: A Commissioner on Deck." *Time*. 12 March 1984.

———. "Sport: Larger and Darker By the Day." *Time*. 7 October 1985.

Creamer, Robert W., ed. "Scorecard: The Cocaine Crisis: Baseball or Sleazeball?" *Sports Illustrated*. 16 September 1985.

Crittenden, Ann, and Michael Ruby. "Cocaine: The Champagne of Drugs." *The New York Times Magazine*. 1 September 1974.

Demarest, Michael, Jonathan Beaty, Steven Holmes, and Jeff Melvoin. "Cocaine: Middle Class High." *Time*. 6 July 1981.

Fimrite, Ron. "Baseball 1979." *Sports Illustrated*. 9 April 1979.

———. "Rising from the Ashes." *Sports Illustrated*. 29 October 1979.

———. "Two Champs from the City of Champions." *Sports Illustrated*. 24 December 1979.

Gilbert, Bil. "Problems in a Turned-On World." *Sports Illustrated*. 23 June 1969.

Gomez, Linda. "America's 100 Years of Euphoria and Despair." *Life*. May 1984.

"It's the Real Thing." *Newsweek*. 27 September 1971.

Kaplan, Jim, and Ivan Maisel. "The Commissioner Gets Tough." *Sports Illustrated*. 20 May 1985.

Lipsyte, Robert. "Baseball and Drugs." *The Nation*. 25 May 1985: 613.

Maisel, Ivan. "The Stuff I Did Was Enough To Kill You." *Sports Illustrated*. 28 May 1984.

Sanoff, Alvin P. "Struggle for the Answers: Baseball's Drug Menace." *U.S. News & World Report.* 17 March 1986: 57.

Swift, E.M. "Flying into the Series." *Sports Illustrated.* 15 October 1979.

Newspapers

The *Pittsburgh Post-Gazette, Pittsburgh Press, New York Times, USA Today,* Associated Press (AP), and United Press International (UPI) were consulted on the dates surrounding the events mentioned in the book. Exact dates are cited in the endnotes.

Chass, Murray, and Michael Goodwin. "Baseball and Cocaine: A Deepening Problem." *New York Times.* 19 August 1985.

———. "Battling Drugs: Approaches Vary." *New York Times.* 22 August 1985.

———. "Cocaine Disrupts Baseball from Field to Front Office." *New York Times.* 20 August 1985.

———. "Talking Baseball, Snorting Cocaine." *New York Times.* 21 August 1985.

Deutsch, Linda. "Drugs du Jour: The Snort of Cocaine." *New York Times.* 12 December 1978.

Edes, Gordon. "Years After Exit, Miller Still Has His Say." *Boston Globe.* 14 January 2005.

Faraudo, Jeff. "Fremont Man Relayed Drugs to '80s Pirates." *Oakland Tribune.* 27 October 2006.

Finder, Chuck. "Trying Times." *Pittsburgh Post-Gazette.* 11 June 1995.

Goodwin, Michael. "Justice Comes to Major League Baseball." *New York Daily News.* 27 February 2008.

Jenkins, Lee. "A Chance for Baseball to Settle Its Drug Score." *New York Times.* 12 December 2004.

Jones, David. "Former Marlins Trainer Watches Steroids Debate with Great Interest." *Florida Today.* 27 November 2007.

Karius, Joe. "Drug Tests Could Be an Answer." *Milwaukee Sentinel.* 21 September 1985.

McAlester, Keven. "Balls Out." *Dallas Observer.* 16 June 2005.

McCoy, Hal. "Starr Says MLB Trainers Raised Steroid Problem in 1988." *Journal News* (Hamilton, OH). 14 December 2007.

Wilstein, Steve. "Scurry Family Remembers Peace Over Pain." Associated Press. 19 November 1992.

Testimony and Court Documents

Greer, Shelby. "Motion to Vacate, Set Aside, or Correct a Sentence by a Person in Federal Custody," Western District of Pennsylvania, 1988. The National Archives, Mid-Atlantic Region, 2:85 CR 125.

Strong, Curtis. "Motion to Vacate, Set Aside, or Correct a Sentence by a Person in Federal Custody," Western District of Pennsylvania, 1987. The National Archives, Mid-Atlantic Region, 2:85 CR 129.

U.S. Department of Justice, Federal Bureau of Investigation. FBI 302 Report (interview of Shelby Greer), 5/14/85.

———. FBIHQ file 12-9070 and Pittsburgh file 12E-PG-306-Sub B, obtained through the Freedom of Infomation/Privacy Acts (FOIPA) Title 5 United States Code, Section 552/552a, Subject: Robert William McCue.

United States of America v. Curtis Strong, 2:85 CR 129 (Western District of Pennsylvania 1985).

United States of America v. Dale Martin Shiffman, 2:85 CR 128 (Western District of Pennsylvania 1985).

United States of America v. Jeffrey Lynn Mosco, 2:85 CR 127 (Western District of Pennsylvania 1985).

United States of America v. Robert William McCue, 2:85 CR 126 (Western District of Pennsylvania 1985).

United States of America v. Shelby Stephen Greer, 2:85 CR 125 (Western District of Pennsylvania 1985).

United States of America v. Thomas Patrick Balzer defendant #1 and Kevin Michael Connolly defendant #2, 2:85 CR 124 (Western District of Pennsylvania 1985).

Web Sites

Baseball Almanac. http://www.baseball-almanac.com.

Barra, Allen. "Marvin Miller: Don't Trust Baseball's Drug-testing Proposal." *Salon*, 20 June 2002. http://www.salon.com/news/sports/col/barra/2002/06/20/miller/.

"Baseball Commissioner Bud Selig Responds to Mitchell Report." *WKYC*, 13 December 2007. http://www.wkyc.com/news/national/news_article.aspx?storyid=79805.

Baseball-Reference.com. http://www.baseball-reference.com.

Dawson, Will. "Dale Shiffman: When Baseball Goes Bad." *CBN*, 9-6-07. http://www.cbn.com/700club/features/amazing/Dale_Shiffman090607.aspx.

"Frontline: Drug Wars: Interviews: Dr. Alan I. Leshner." *PBS*, 2000. http://
www.pbs.org/wgbh/pages/frontline/shows/drugs/interviews/leshner
.html.

Hayes, Neil. "Ex-MLB Trainer Feels Guilty over Steroids." *NBCsports*, 24
March 2005. http://nbcsports.msnbc.com/id/7270934/.

McCoy, Hal. "Starr Says MLB Trainers Raised Steroid Problem in 1988."
JournalNews, 14 December 2007. http://www.journal-news.com/s/
content/oh/story/sports/pro/reds/2007/12/14/ddn121507starrweb.html.

Quinn, T.J. "Steroids and A Code of Silence: Baseball's Unhappy Union."
ESPN, 29 February 2008. http://sports.espn.go.com/mlb/columns/
story?columnist=quinn_tj&id=3270983.

Wadler, Gary. "Cocaine Abuse and Sports." *American College of Sports
Medicine*.
www.acsm.org/AM/Template.cfm?Section=current_
comments1&Template=/CM/ContentDisplay.cfm&ContentID=8680.

———. "Drugs and Sports: Amphetamines." *ESPN*, 9-6-07. http://espn
.go.com/special/s/drugsandsports/amphet.html.

Television/DVD

Bennett, Andrew, prod. "Under the Influence." *Real Sports with Bryant
Gumbel*. Television. HBO. 19 September 2006.

Burns, Ken, dir. *Baseball: A Film by Ken Burns: Inning 1, Our Game—1840's–
1900*. DVD. PBS Home Video, Paramount Home Entertainment, 1994.

Dawson, Will. "Dale Shiffman: When Baseball Goes Bad." *The 700 Club*.
Television. Christian Broadcasting Network, 9-6-07.

Hayes, Harold, prod. "Sports Scandal Replay." *OnQ Magazine*. Television.
PBS. WQED, Pittsburgh, PA. September 2005.

Newsletters/Reviews/Conferences

Bourne, Peter G. "The Great Cocaine Myth." *Drugs and Drug Abuse
Education Newsletter 5:5* (1974). http://www.justice.gov/dea/concern/
cocaine.html.

Gawin, M.D., Frank H., and Everett H. Ellinwood Jr., M.D. "Cocaine
Dependence." *Annual Review of Medicine*. 1989.

Musto, M.D., David F. "History: The American Experience with Stimu-
lants." The National Methamphetamine Drug Conference—ONDCP.
National Criminal Justice Reference Service. 1997. http://www.ncjrs.gov/
ondcppubs/publications/drugfact/methconf/plenary1.html.

Index